LOVE INITIATION

LEARNING THE LANGUAGE OF SOUL

JULIANNE SANTINI & JOHN MERCEDE

FEATURING: BARBRA FANG BABCOCK, KIMBERLY BARRETT,
NANCY CASEY-HUMPHREY, KELLY CONNOLLY, PATRICIA H. ELLIOTT,
DIANE MARIE GALLANT, JENNIFER KREIFELS, MELISSA LEE, TIFFANY McBRIDE,
LIZ MEITUS, REV. DR. MIMI KATE MUNROE, CHRISTINE NGUYEN,
MARION NOONE, DEBORAH OLSON, ANDREA PAQUETTE, JUDI RAIFF,
CHRISTINA SANTINI, N.S. SHAKTI, DR. TRACEY L. ULSHAFER,
JEFFREY WARREN, MARGARET WEST, ATLANTIS WOLF, CLOANNE WUNDROW

LOVE INITIATION
LEARNING THE LANGUAGE OF SOUL

JULIANNE SANTINI & JOHN MERCEDE

FEATURING: BARBRA FANG BABCOCK, KIMBERLY BARRETT, NANCY CASEY-HUMPHREY, KELLY CONNOLLY, PATRICIA H. ELLIOTT, DIANE MARIE GALLANT, JENNIFER KREIFELS, MELISSA LEE, TIFFANY MCBRIDE, LIZ MEITUS, REV. DR. MIMI KATE MUNROE, CHRISTINE NGUYEN, MARION NOONE, DEBORAH OLSON, ANDREA PAQUETTE, JUDI RAIFF, CHRISTINA SANTINI, N.S. SHAKTI, DR. TRACEY L. ULSHAFER, JEFFREY WARREN, MARGARET WEST, ATLANTIS WOLF, CLOANNE WUNDROW

Love Initiation

Learning the Language of Soul

Julianne Wudrow Santini and John Mercede

Published by Brave Healer Productions

Paperback ISBN: 978-1-961493-15-5

eBook ISBN: 978-1-961493-14-8

DEDICATION

This book is dedicated to YOU!
Thank you for choosing love, time and time again.
We're all in this together!

DISCLAIMER

This book offers health and wellness information and is designed for educational purposes only. You should not rely on this information as a substitute for, nor does it replace professional medical advice, diagnosis, or treatment. If you have any concerns or questions about your health (mental, physical, or spiritual), you should always consult a physician or other healthcare professional. Do not disregard, avoid, or delay obtaining medical or health-related advice from your healthcare professional because of something you may have read here. The use of any information provided in this book is solely at your own risk.

Developments in medical research may impact the health and wellness advice that appears here. No assurances can be given that the information contained in this book will always include the most relevant findings or developments with respect to the particular material.

Having said all that, know that the experts here have shared their tools, practices, and knowledge with you with a sincere and generous intent to assist you on your health and wellness journey. Please contact them with any questions you may have about the techniques or information they provided. They will be happy to assist you further!

ACKNOWLEDGMENTS

We are grateful for our life journey, supported and enriched by mentors and teachers from both the seen and unseen realms. Their teachings continue to enlighten us as we lead a life of love and purpose, sharing our experiences with the world.

We offer heartfelt appreciation to the authors who so bravely shared their love initiation stories. A special thank you to Laura Di Franco, publisher and CEO, the team at Brave Healer Productions, and Atlantis Wolf for their tireless efforts in bringing this book to life.

We extend our gratitude to healers, wellness practitioners, and global servers committed to fostering goodwill and peace for the well-being of all beings.

We honor our ancestors, family, and respective children, Jessica and Daniel, and Marco and Christina. We honor each other, our souls, and the path of Love.

HEART OPENING AT THE SPHINX

Illustrated by Cloanne Wundrow

THE JOURNEY

We raced to the water's edge and threw our arms open wide. It appeared like we were hugging the horizon as we released the energy of over 1200 names. Just days before, our travel companions carried sacred bundles containing the names and requested prayers through the temples and sacred sites of Egypt.

For 13 days, our group moved as a wave of love tending to the bundles. Each participant added their own flair and style to the task. Some carried it on their tummies and rubbed it like a baby bump, while others carried it confidently on their backs. The bundles moved with us as part of the larger story.

What if humanity could see initiation—and all things—through the eyes of love? Imagine what then would become possible.

This pondering played in our hearts as we walked the Initiate's Path. In response, each day offered new opportunities to surrender, soften, and become anew. You, too, are invited to experience the energy of the author's journey.

Happy travels!
Access the travel log and daily inspirations:
https://www.profoundlifewellness.com/love-egypt

THE INITIATE'S HEART
Illustrated by Barbra Fang Babcock

The Creative Process of the Initiate's Heart—A special thank you to our illustrator, Barbara Fang Babcock, for her inspired cover art. As we revealed our ideas to Barbra for the project, all she could see was a flaming heart wrapping around and caressing us. She carried this image in her heart until the painting came to life. As the painting was born, so too was the poem describing, not only her creative process, but the elements of our journey to come—the journey home!

LOVE INITIATION
THE HEART OF CREATION
By Barbra Fang Babcock

I sit and relax, waiting for inspiration
I feel the energy of my traveling companions
I feel the vibration of each hallowed stone in Egypt
I would see The Sacred Heart rising above each temple
Then burst into flames
The ashes settle around each stone, blessing the pathway forward
Only to rise again as The Sacred Heart.
More Colorful each time, more intense, more alive
An open heart, a breaking open heart, reformed for the initiate's journey.

As The Flower of Life
Connects each circle, it connects each person on the trip
The heart unifies us to ourselves and Egypt
As the paint flows from the brush,
A swirl flows with water and paint in each stroke,
The beating heart emerges in the creation
Pulsing on the canvas,
It pulls me, telling me how to orchestrate the next stroke
A symphony of color.
My tools of paints, canvas, brushes, spray bottle, stencils, fingers, straws to
move the paint, and an open pulsing heart.

https://www.barbrafangbabcock.com

WITH GRATITUDE

Thank you to our Love Initiation Energetic Supporters and Contributors from around the world!

Trudy Griswold—Angel blessings

Barbara Bertucio—Usui Reiki blessings

Dr. Diana Collins—Prayer of Jabez blessings

Karuna Joy—Sekhem All Love blessings

Andrea Klim—Astrological support

Elders Sandra and Frank Dicontie—Grandmother Moon Pipe Ceremony

Grandmother Judi Johnson and Debbie Shea Davis—Prayer Tie blessings

Stevens, Cormier, Nickerson, and Flynn-Belisle—Moon River blessings

Ahriana and Mark Platten—Ancestor and descendant blessings

Sandra Ingerman—Daily shamanic spiritual work and blessings

Susan Muchnij and Magdalena Light Circle—Magdalena blessings

Michelle McCarthy—Angelic blessings and Soul Star Clearings

Donna Mitchell Moniak—Morning alignment and living awareness

Chakaruna Jorge Delgado—Despacho Ceremony and Solar blessings

Emily Grieves and Nikis Manuel Reyes—Divine Mother and Father blessings

Alberto Hernandez—Sun and Moon Fire Ceremony

Carrie Lowe and Andre Simoneau—Ancestor and descendant blessings

Corinne Casazza and Keepers of the Flame Fraternity—VF Light decrees

Ashley Woods with the Grid of Light Project—Energetic Seed of Life

Cloanne Wundrow and Christina Santini—Ancestor and descendant blessings

Emil Shaker, Ihab Rashad, and Youssef—Door openers to the wonder of Egypt

Your love, light, and blessings carried us!

TABLE OF CONTENTS

FOREWORD

Cloanne Wundrow

A seed planted in my heart is awakening. I have returned.

It's still dark, and the morning is chilly. I'm struck by a sense of wonder. I have visited Egypt several times before, but I have never stood this close to the great Sphinx. Yet, here I am, right between its huge paws. A hush falls over our group as we're called to a moment of silence.

I close my eyes only to discover myself standing alone. My body has been washed and anointed. My long black hair is oiled and shiny. My simple, white dress graces my slender, young figure. Gold sandals adorn my feet. I feel nervous, but I know I am prepared. I am ready! The moment of initiation is here.

Slowly, my small body morphs into the huge Sphinx itself, and with the joy of awakening, I rise upward on my four massive feet. Through my immense heart of deep knowing and love, I survey my surroundings. I stand atop the Earth. From my great vantage point, I see and feel not only the vibrations of our world but also the universe. I'm awed by the magnitude of love and joy. All is connected; all is one.

Suddenly, my eyes open. It's no longer dark. I want to stay right here. I slowly pull myself away and leave with our small group of travelers. I look back, and my heart burns with the knowledge I will return. A new seed has been planted, and my heart beats with joy. I have such a very clear knowing. I will be here again with a unique and chosen group.

So now, at eighty-four, I'm not surprised that I have returned, and I'm not alone. Like the great Sphinx itself, our group, which includes my daughter, Julianne, and my granddaughter, Christina, spans generations, bridging ancestors and descendants. They come together to share personal love initiation stories. Stories that will be nurtured at the feet of the Sphinx.

Little did I realize when I stood in this very spot before that the people chosen would be planting seeds, and more surprisingly, writing a book!

We walk in the grace of the divine. Love initiations are part of our journey. The following stories nourished on the amazing trip to Egypt, planned and led by Julianne Santini and John Mercede, bring alive each author's personal experience.

Opening your heart and reading these chapters with love may awaken in you your own personal love initiation—past, present, or to come—whispered in the language of soul.

INTRODUCTION

Love Initiation: Learning the Language of Soul is a collaborative book written by a group of wellness practitioners and spiritual teachers who journeyed to sacred sites along the Initiate's Path of Egypt in 2023. Their personal stories of initiation reflect what is happening to all of humanity. It's a time of initiation on the planet, marked by war, civil unrest, and polarization in politics, health, and lifestyle.

This is not a book about the ways **to** love.

It is a book about the ways **of** love, and it's a call to action.

What if humanity could see initiation through the eyes of love?

Within these pages, you'll find individual stories of personal growth, spiritual awakening, and the resilience of our humanness in the face of difficult life situations.

What if these initiations weren't happening to us but for us?

The voices of *Love Initiation* run the gamut, presenting introspective, funny, philosophical, and gritty reflections on life and spirituality. This book speaks to the need for an inclusive approach to life while highlighting that profound changes often occur while exploring uncharted territories.

Love Initiation: Learning the Language of Soul is a book bridging awareness and intuition. It empowers you to embrace the unknown and be open to possibilities that arise from life's challenges.

Take the journey through the pages of *Love Initiation* to discover love as a powerful awakening force that leads to spiritual growth, opening a path to enlightenment.

Put on your comfy clothes and lean into this collection of stories. Let them touch your heart, inspire your spirit, and lead you on a path of love, enlightenment, and profound connection.

Your journey of love initiation awaits!

Lovingly, Julianne and John

CHAPTER 1

WAKING UP IN THE DREAM

IMAGINATION AS A SPIRITUAL PRACTICE

Julianne Santini, BSN, RN, PHN

MY LOVE INITIATION

THE MESSAGE

I imagine many years ago, my soul lovingly left me a memo on the fridge like a big, yellow Post-It Note. I'm embarrassed to admit I missed it. The great news is—it's now in plain sight in my rearview mirror.

Welcome to the unknown, from healer to patient, no longer able to jump tall buildings in a single bound. Not true, but that's how it may feel. Don't despair. Adversity makes you more fully aware of who and what you are. Sometimes, it takes a traumatic event or illness to shake you out of the way you see your existence and the world. You have everything you need. You were made for this! Remember, your experience and quality of life depend on seeing through the eyes of love. FYI: There's no turning back!

As you read this chapter, you can picture me as a cyclist, casually pointing out potholes in the road. You may see me on my 18-speed Bianchi bike with my head kissing the handlebars and riding into the sun. It has taken me a few years to realize I love every speed, every season, and every part of the journey, each navigated by my humanness and the destiny of my soul.

THE JOURNEY

"It's like I'm watching someone with cancer." My mother's words hung in the air, slipping through the gaps of awareness in my mind.

Is she talking about me? Take those words back!

It was too late. They were captured in the house and seeping into every wall. In all honesty, I felt their truth. I had the same thought, and what former oncology nurse wouldn't?

There was nowhere to escape. Every wall was a time capsule, reflecting the home my father lovingly renovated for my mother before he died of cancer.

Is my story an echo of the past? Is my illness a remnant of shared ancestry? Will I die young, too?

Up until that point, I believed anything was possible. What became increasingly obvious, however, was that my personal will did not seem to make a bit of difference with this mystery illness. I would have energy, and then I wouldn't, no matter what my thoughts or intentions were.

Imagine heading out onto the open road. You're traveling along, sun on your face and song in your heart. You have everything you could possibly need. You're enthusiastic and ready to jump into your next gig. Then, BAM! The road ends. You fall off the map. Your world is no longer round; it's flat. You're careening into the abyss as if you've ridden off the edge of a page. Your terminal freefall happens in the blink of an eye—no road, no path, no map.

What? Where am I? How did this happen? This isn't me. I'm the one who runs up pyramids with a group in tow, carrying my backpack and anyone else's. Where's my vitality? What's going on?

No one knew. My symptoms spanned multiple body systems. Initially, it was respiratory, cardiac, and circulatory, demanding ER visits at all hours. The only medication that seemed to make a difference was steroids. I was in bed for months in a foggy haze, interjected with memories of John and my son knocking on the bedroom door to check in.

Just as I was able to leave the confines of the bedroom, my immune system welcomed being the star of the show. At my worst, I was only able to eat five to ten foods without having an allergic reaction. I was on a combination of low-histamine and GERD diets. The allergist claimed I had no allergies, and yet my primary care doctor felt it mandatory to order an EpiPen. Nothing made sense.

Most days, I toggled between a vicelike pain in my muscles and gripping fatigue. The swelling in my joints made me wonder if I should cut off my rings. Inflammation was everywhere. The allopathic route and medical specialists couldn't provide definitive answers. I was getting sicker and weaker, with more systems being affected.

Desperate, I dove headfirst into naturopathic waters with the dedication of an Olympic athlete. I mastered the precision of ever-changing supplement schedules and the myriad of detox protocols for mold, fungus, parasites, and heavy metals. Name a therapy for cellular detox, and I tried it! Everything from being cooked in infrared saunas to flushed out with high doses of Vitamin C IVs.

Sleep was optional, and the brain fog was relentless. I didn't recognize my face in the mirror. *Where is the light in my eyes?* Energetically, I poured light into my cells daily. I was inspired by a long-time mentor and friend to add transfiguration to my daily practice. This work "held me up," but I wasn't improving.

Not knowing what else to do, I went back to my primary care physician.

"You have positive markers for every autoimmune test we ordered, which is impossible. I don't have anything to offer. Get yourself to a major college with advanced medical equipment and join a clinical trial."

That was it—the end of the line. I wasn't even being handed off to another specialist but left to my own devices to find an appropriate clinical trial.

It felt like the same moment from two and a half years earlier when a Peruvian shaman told me, "Your body is dead, but your spirit is in the mountains. Your body is dead, but your spirit flies with the Great Spirits of the mountains."

In both situations, I was left with no answers. Overwhelmed, I took a pause. I stopped racing. My gut was no longer functioning, but in the depth of my being, I somehow knew I had to look at this through the eyes of love.

Even with no answers, I realized I was being led through it all. Spirit was there. Dreamtime was my portal, the language of my soul, and the gateway to all love. I saw clearly with fresh eyes. I wasn't lost. I asked my soul to be my inner physician and allowed it to lead the way.

My daily practice was one of calming the nervous system, focusing on the power of my mind, and experiencing myself as light. This often led to potent periods of dreaming and "waking up" in the dream. When you're sick, it feels like nothing is possible. Your dreams begin to die. I forgot I was living in the dream, and it was time to dream anew. The discernment of each dream led to the next step and all the little ones along the way. My physical state improved, even my lab tests!

THE DREAM

A young boy at the beach was looking over a little hole. He was so intent it appeared as if he were reading the waters inside. Intrigued, I walked over.

"What do you have there?" I asked. "A sea creature or a stash of shells?"

"I'm catching a dream," he said, pointing into the hole. "Someone sent it for me."

I didn't see anything in the water but decided to play along, "How do you get it out?"

He laughed wholeheartedly, "That's what I was doing. You peer in until you see yourself in the dream. It took me a while to get the hang of it. When I started this, I was a very old man. I didn't think I was worthy of any more dreams, but I'm patient, and I practiced."

I sat down beside the boy. I couldn't resist. "How old were you?"

"Oh, very old!" he responded, emphasizing each word.

"And, who taught you?"

The boy's face softened. "The ocean," he beamed. "I like to call her The Mother of the Waters. One day, I was sitting by her crying. My head hung low, and she washed up around me. I was surprised. I didn't see the tide rolling in. The force of the wave and her love knocked me right over. She had my attention. The sound of the ocean washed away my thoughts, my doubt, and my sadness. There was just this sound, like putting my ear next to a seashell. I noticed the sound was coming from inside of me. I sat there listening as the water continued to roll in and roll out. I felt suspended, just hanging there until I was hit with another wave. A great inspiration enveloped me."

He looked at me excitedly. "The ocean holds so many dreams! She asked me to pick one, but I didn't know how. She explained, go dig a hole on the beach. Take your bucket and fill it with water until it's full enough to look in and see your reflection. Then, look upon the water, imagine the dream that's there for you, and try it on. If it's your dream, sit with it, be with it, place your hand on its reflection, and thank it. I like to scoop up the energy and place it on my heart, but I know others place it on their eyes to always be able to see."

"What if you can't find your dream?"

"Oh, that's why I'm here. Many don't recognize their dreams because they've forgotten how to dream. That's why I'm here!" he said again with a gigantic grin.

"You're a dream catcher!"

"Oh, no, I don't catch dreams; I find them. They're always free!"

I realized I was shaking my head in agreement.

How old was this little boy again? Did he ever tell me?

He continued, "Once upon a time, in a land between time and space, you asked me to meet you here. I'm a dream finder. You asked me to come back to a time when you'd begin to doubt why you're here, at a time upon the planet when there's so much fear it's hard to hear one's internal sound and when there's so much chaos, many are losing hope for future generations. You asked me to teach you what once you taught me."

The youth pointed into the hole. "I found this dream for you." My face lit up like I was given a puppy on Christmas morning. My body was buzzing from head to toe.

He ceremoniously reached in, asking, "Would you like it— the dream? May I bless you with its remembrance? I must ask. Not everyone chooses to accept their dream, to love it, and live into it."

"Yes!" I said emphatically. Every cell of my being was open to the request.

The boy scooped up some energy from the found dream and placed it on my eyes, "I bless your eyes to clearly see."

He then moved to my feet, and it felt like he was energetically washing them. "I bless your feet to move you forward."

He carefully took each hand, touching one and then the other, "I bless your hands to touch the world."

Finally, he placed his hands upon my chest, saying, "And, I bless your heart to be wide open."

Instinctively, I placed my hands on my heart and then opened my arms wide, breathing as though for the first time.

He nodded in approval. "You've got your wings!"

I realized I was waist-deep in water. Shocked and disoriented, I stood up and scrambled to get myself on shore. I turned around. The boy was gone.

Did this really happen?

I ran back into the water and accidentally tripped. Using my feet to feel beneath me, I realized I had tripped over the original hole carrying the dream. I was now sopping wet and standing in the energy of my dream in its entirety. I started to cry and laugh while the many emotions and experiences of life flooded in.

After what felt like moments and days, I noticed the fading sun and thought of the boy. I wondered who the young boy was who once was so old. I noticed a happy face drawn in the sand. This broke me wide open. It was all just too much. I felt like I couldn't hold all the goodness, the gifts, and the remembering.

I walked back to my beach towel and plopped onto that which was familiar. I calmed myself, listening to the ocean, and began to drift off. My internal sound carried me back to another time.

I loved the retreat center at Omega and Long Pond Lake. I remember the morning when everything appeared the same yet felt different. The tulle fog felt like magic hanging in the air and seemed to call me to the water's edge. I spoke to the Lady of the Lake, as I always did, but found myself doing something quite unusual. I was looking into the water and repetitively drawing a single image into the sand below—a happy face. I wondered why.

I thought of the older gentleman who was sitting by the lake. I noticed him immediately. He was wearing a brightly colored cardigan. It reminded me of my father's traditional Christmas sweater. I did my best to walk by quietly and not disturb his morning meditation. He seemed familiar but not a participant in our group. I let it go and turned my attention to the lake.

I prayed for him. I wished him every happiness. I shared with him every loving moment I had ever known, for it seemed that was what he needed. I kept praying and making happy faces in the water. I wondered if I had been heard, my heart song, my prayer, my desire for him. I didn't know.

I decided to say 'hello' as I made my way back to the cabin, but when I turned around, the chair was empty. I felt surprisingly sad he was gone. My head hung down into my hands, gentle tears flowed, and then something caught my eye. A happy face! He drew a huge, happy face in the sand. It was not there when I first walked to the lake. The only difference in our faces was a large nose that he added with the help of a red plastic cup. I laughed and laughed.

Ever so gently, my internal sound brought me back to the ocean. I imagined the boy's sun-kissed face, and I looked deeply into his eyes. I saw every face I had ever known, those whom I had taught and those who taught me, every ancestor and every descendant, and every face that was me. We were together forever in an endless embrace. Love loving all love.

THE INVITATION

Imagine your soul lovingly leaving this memo on the fridge for you.

If you can embrace the power of adversity, it will help you "wake up" to a new depth of being. You're ready. Lean in. Learn the language of your soul. Allow it to open the doorway to healing, transformation, and all love. Don't miss this opportunity, and remember, with the lens of love, anything is possible!

THE PRACTICE

Imagination is the eye of the soul.

~ Joseph Joubert

If you're feeling lost or at a crossroads, it's time to come back "online." Imagination is the key. It transcends time and dwells between the realm of pure spirit and the realm of physical manifestation. Like a cosmic telephone or interface, it bridges the divide between you and the divine and allows you to touch the soul.

Imagination is an important tool of consciousness. It can change circumstances, perceptions, or reality. It enables you to move forward and transform the old into something new. Never underestimate the reality of the imagination! Although mostly unseen, like the wind, it can be seen through the lens of love.

Your ocean of imagination awaits, and the dream finder calls! Enter the world of wonder through dreaming, journeying, meditation, contemplation, or journaling. This imaginative exercise is to awaken the dreamer, the dream, and all that is dreamt.

1. **Set your intention to enter the place of infinite possibilities—** your ocean of imagination.

2. **Play your favorite track of ocean waves.** Follow the sounds to your ocean of imagination.

3. **Use all your senses to enter fully.** The practice of sensual awareness can enrich the internal environment and move you to a sense of wholeness.

   a. Imagine what you feel. Is the sand gritty or smooth between your toes?

   b. Imagine what you see. Miles of waterfront beach or a protected rocky cove?

   c. Imagine what you smell. Fresh sea air or concession stand burgers?

   d. Imagine what you taste. Salty ocean water or sweet lemonade?

   e. Imagine what you hear. Bird calls or the sound of children playing?

4. **Meet the dream finder waiting for you and express gratitude.** If you do not see the dream finder, ask the ocean to introduce you.

5. **Ask the dream finder to gift you with the remembrance of your dream.**

   a. The dream finder may have you peer into a hole with water.

   b. Look upon the water and imagine the dream reflecting back to you.

   c. Sit with it, be with it, place your hands upon its reflection, and thank it.

   d. Try it on. Dive right in. Experience it fully. How do you feel?

   e. Scoop up the energy of the dream. Place it in your heart or on your eyes, or experience a personal remembrance blessing given to you by the dream finder.

6. **Rest with the ocean and the flow of your dream.** Feel waves of insight, inspiration, and all love.

7. **Give gratitude to the dream finder, the dream, and all that was dreamt.**

8. **Return to the ocean of imagination to embody the dream more fully.** Imagination as a practice grows strong with use and repetition. Bathe and create in its timeless moments daily.

Begin a dreaming practice that exercises your imagination, feeds your soul, and helps you come alive. By dreaming together, we enrich the collective dream. The world is waiting for you!

Visit our book resource page here:

https://www.profoundlifewellness.com/book

Julianne Santini, BSN, RN, PHN, is a brilliant transformational healer, teacher, and practitioner. With compassion as her compass, she supports individuals at life junctures and spiritual awakenings through personal sessions, group experiences, and sacred travel. Using transformational tools and energy work, she teaches ways to apply spiritual principles to daily life. She steps into the role of "dream-finder," showing people how to turn dreams into reality. She becomes their groundskeeper in Wonderland.

A certified trainer with decades of learning, she uses a combination of angelic and violet flame modalities, esoteric healing science, energy psychology, and meditation. She reflects a rich tapestry of mentors from the Philippines and India, an initiation from the Dalai Lama, and wisdom from indigenous elders throughout the Americas. Julianne graduated from the FSS curriculum and Sandra Ingerman's Shamanic Teacher Training. She is a founding member of the Society for Shamanic Practice.

Julianne's work of assisting others began as an oncology nurse in California, where she recognized mind, body, and spirit as integral parts of healing. Her diverse career includes nursing instructor, wellness center owner, urgent care center manager, and energy practitioner—all while balancing the responsibilities of being a mother of two children.

Julianne continues to teach people about their energy bodies, energy cycles, and how to navigate spiritual wake-up calls and everyday life. She continues to live her passion in Naples, Florida, as co-founder of Profound Life Wellness with John Mercede. When not working, Julianne enjoys family visits, holiday baking, cycling on her Bianchi, kayaking through the Everglades, and even firewalking!

If you need help turning your dreams into reality, Julianne will be your biggest cheerleader!

Website: www.ProfoundLifeWellness.com

Facebook: https://www.Facebook.com/JulianneWundrowSantini

Email: Julianne@ProfoundLifeWellness.com

CHAPTER 2

THE TOUCH OF LOVE

HOW TO MASTER YOUR STATE OF BEING FOR ANY LIFE SITUATION

John Mercede

MY LOVE INITIATION

I'm shivering under a pile of blankets, soaking wet with sweat, slipping in and out of consciousness, writhing in pain. It's well over one hundred degrees Fahrenheit here in Haridwar, India, at the 2011 Kumbh Mela. What began yesterday as a spiritual celebration of sight and sound has turned into a cyclone of noise that engulfs everything: people talking in languages I don't understand and music so loud it pummels me.

As the waves of foreign melody, unrecognizable lyrics, and sounds thrash me, my mind becomes entrained to the steady pulse of a man's voice chanting a single two-syllable sound, "Swa-hah." My body slows down to match the pulse of this sound, which is both unrecognizable and familiar. Every five seconds: "Swaha. Swaha. Swaha."

I stop shivering and find myself peaceful and calm amid the noise and activity. I have the experience of sitting in a cave silently chanting *Swaha*. I see all things as one. I know I'm here lying on my cot, sweating, and I know I'm chanting silently in a cave.

I hear the familiar voice of a friend. His voice is far away and in my ear at the same time, "John, you don't look so good; I'm going to go get one of the monks."

I briefly open my eyes, and the words register in my thoughts, as does the concerned look in his eyes. I acknowledge him just as a wave of nausea overcomes me, causing me to gasp.

A flash of light floods my brain, and I have the sensation of being launched from a catapult. I'm falling upward, experiencing every pulse of life at the speed of light and noticing the perfection of each pulse. Guided by light and accepting everything that is occurring and that ever occurred, I enter into emptiness. Time stands still. I lose consciousness.

Moments or hours may have passed. I have no reference to time as I wake up and become aware of my surroundings. The sounds that felt like thrashing earlier are nourishing me now. The rhythm and timing of Swaha continue as if it's my heartbeat. A monk with long white hair and a beard to the middle of his chest is alongside my cot, talking with me.

Monk: John, what's the matter with you?

Me: I don't know. I'm sick.

Monk: You're not sick. Your personality may be. But you? You are fine.

Me: No, it's, it's bad. I think I'm going to die.

Monk: Good, then die! You are with the Guru.

The monk walks away, and his words echo in my head. Prepared to die, I drift off into sleep and dream of the events that led me to be here in India, this place of love and devotion and the largest spiritual festival on the planet.

The needs of my body wake me from a deep sleep.

Well, I made it through the night. I'm not dead yet.

I walk quickly toward the toilets, stopping at the table which serves as the infirmary. I pick up a blister pack of Imodium, and I chew several as I walk, washing them down with a warm bottle of water I grabbed from the table.

I hope I'm in time to be in front of the gurus this morning.

I use a bucket of water to shower my body and run to the shared tent, quickly change into fresh clothes, and head to the area within the temporary ashram to be with the gurus.

The gurus are joyful and playful, and yet their devotion is palpable. They devote their lives to prayer, service, and love. Both gurus are sharing with the group, and one is asking questions of those who have gathered. The love that emanates from them causes my mind to go quiet and my heart to open. I feel like I'm right where I need to be, and at the same time, I'm asking myself, *what am I doing here?* As if my thoughts were heard, I hear my name being called, "John, tell me something."

Without hesitation, words awkwardly stumble out of my mouth, "Err, um, I don't even know why I'm here." Guru Ji pauses and looks into me. It's just a moment, yet it seems like she sees my whole life before replying, "It's too late for that—you're already here!"

Laughter erupts in the group, yet her eyes remain fixed upon me with a silent invitation to be still and stay present. I feel a wave move into me, which expands my awareness. It feels like I am shown the infinite nature of love.

Thoughts and questions stream and scream through my mind.

Why am I here? What is this feeling? What is love? Did my soul bring me here to remember?

I've spent the last 12 years rigorously studying, working, training, teaching, and practicing energy methods and meditation. I'm acknowledged as an expert teacher in meditation and spiritual subjects and a master-level practitioner of the martial art Aikido. *Does any of this mean anything?*

The voice of my mentor and teacher, DP, rings in my mind. As students, he'd continually remind us, "It is easy to be powerful; it's difficult to be powerful and good." He taught us that alignment to *goodwill* and to the *way of peace* is paramount. He often shared that life would provide us with opportunities to do good in the face of adversity—and in those situations, regardless of what is happening, seek only goodwill, seek only peace.

I'm in the middle of facing those opportunities DP talked about. I'm weathering a storm created by the death of my father, leaving my engineering career, and an accident that left me hobbled with disabling physical pain, along with emotional and mental distress. It's painful to move, it's painful to work, it's painful to play; I'm not able to practice Aikido. All of my previous points of identity have lost their relevance.

Ruminating on why I came to India, I notice that within the construct of spiritual practices and spiritual service, I know the infinite possibilities offered by love. Yet, in my humanness, I can only see a distillation of love show up as a moment in an embrace, a song, a movie, or a book. Now, I'm in India, surrounded by devotion and the substance of love. Here, the sounds of mantras and devotional music are both rocking me to my core and rocking me to sleep.

Did I mention the music is unceasing at the Kumbh Mela? Imagine hundreds of ashrams, hundreds of thousands of people, and countless amplified speakers playing devotional music twenty-four hours a day, every day. My body is still quite sick, and I've come to rely on Imodium and Swaha to get me through the days and nights. It's surprising I can even sleep with all the sound. Even more surprising was waking up one night to the sounds of a monk running outside our tent, ringing a bell and shouting an invitation to come and be with the gurus as they prepare the puja offering.

Being sick is not an excuse when my soul is calling! I pull myself out of bed and run after the monk through the maze of tents. My breathing is taxed, and I feel the thumping of footsteps right on my heels, coercing me to go faster. I enter into a small tent, about 15x15 feet, and see the two gurus, several pundits, and one or two monks. Somehow, I'm one of the first shishya to arrive, and I'm directed to stand directly behind Maharaj Ji. He sits cross-legged on the ground, guiding others to put a single nut or a single flower petal in a particular place. As I stand behind this nearly one-hundred-year-old man, I'm flooded with wisdom, love, and illumination that can only come from a lifetime of devotion to the divine. It's miraculous that I ended up right next to this being. I am so grateful.

Looking at the puja, I'm captivated by the beauty of it, like a piece of fine art. I wonder how long it took to create and how long they had been sitting here. It must have been hours. Maharaj Ji, who is right in front of me, says a few words and then begins to stand up. It did not feel appropriate to touch him, and being mindful of the space needed for him to stand, I pushed slightly backward into the crowd to make room for him. Rising from the ground, he looks at me with no affect, and yet his eyes sparkle as if they are diamonds. Perhaps his leg fell asleep, perhaps he lost his balance momentarily, or perhaps what happened next has no explanation.

He wobbles a little, and from a place of pure reaction, I extend the back of my hand and my forearm to provide a cushion of energy for him to lean into—something learned and practiced for years in Aikido. Immediately, it feels like he touches my arm. It is not a physical touch; it's more like an impulse. Next, I experience a sound in my ears that vibrates in my throat and then spreads to my head. From my head, it moves down my spine and into all my bones and tendons. With my body vibrating fully, light floods my head.

Where a moment before I saw his eyes sparkling like diamonds, all I can see now is brilliant light, his form barely recognizable with the intensity. I enter into a blissful state of illuminated awareness where everything is brilliant with light. I stand motionless, perhaps unable to move, and I watch with gratitude as Maharaj Ji walks away.

I remained in this expanded state of enlightened awareness and bliss for three days. My soul was continually revealing life to me in new ways and showing the infinite way of love. I would be leaving India the following day, and I decided to walk about the ashram.

As I walk, I see Maharaj Ji coming towards me on the path. He's about 20 feet away when I see him, and I feel immense gratitude and respect welling up inside of me. During my time here, I've learned it's customary to pranam (bow) in front of the guru. Overflowing with gratitude and wanting to convey respect, I kneel down and lower my head to pranam.

The moment my head touches the ground, I find myself surrounded by a cocoon of silence. Within this cocoon, the personality is hushed, along with its desire to be acknowledged as special. I enter into stillness and experience a profound acceptance. The energy of acceptance takes me through all existence, revealing the path of Soul. I see all of the life situations a person must endure and how each and every situation supports the evolution of the soul and the person. This experience of acceptance transforms into an unshakable knowing within me; every person is accepted—and has always been accepted.

With my head still on the ground and tears streaming down my cheeks, I feel someone behind me lifting me up. Wondering who's come near and why I'm being lifted from the ground, I turn to see who's there. To my surprise, no one is there. *What? How?* As I collect my thoughts, confusion gives way to wonder.

I look across the courtyard to see Maharaj Ji holding his hands open, palms facing towards me, sending blessings. He is literally lifting me up with love. Words cannot fully describe what occurred during that moment or every moment since then. What became clear is that love is reciprocal and infinite, and when one maintains a love-based state, love holds open the door to enlightenment.

To learn the language of Soul, spend time in silence, listening. Your ability to hear and discern will grow proportional to your ability to sustain a love-based state of being. When in a love-based state, it is easy to connect with the light of your soul. Love is the way.

THE PRACTICE

Here is an exercise you can use to move into any love-based state of being you have personally experienced at some time in your life. This is an exercise of recall, not imagination—this is important.

The practice is based on the fact that the brain, and consequently the body, cannot tell the difference between a real experience and a vividly recalled experience. I've added energy science to a method I learned as a racquetball athlete. On the court, it helped move me from a destructive state of being to an advantageous one—in effect, a way to get into the zone between points.

With practice, you'll be able to shift your state quickly (about one minute). Practice the steps and the complete exercise a few times to "get it." Follow with dedicated practice, and you will have full access to what is possible. Build on your successes by starting with the example outlined here before moving on to your own situation.

You will be recalling the details of an experience to bring sensory information into your brain and body. It does not matter what type of activity brought the experience to you—you're bringing back sensations to entrain your brain and body to a state of being that can be used anywhere.

For example, when I recall the details of a time when I won a Formula car race on the last turn of the last lap, I have access to sensations and feelings of calm and focused precision, clarity, and certainty. I can use that energy in a board meeting, working on a project, or playing tennis. It's energy that's available for me anytime and anywhere.

This practice will help you change from any fear-based state to any love-based state you've experienced. Suggested beginner times indicated.

1. Identify the fear-based state you're ready to leave behind. Naming what is there is always the first step. Regular awareness practice will be helpful. (TEN SECONDS)

   • When experiencing a fear-based state, you will feel contracted. (Examples: judgmental, critical, incapable, resentful, frustrated, sad, jealous)

   • When experiencing a love-based state, you will feel expanded. (Examples: joyful, happy, peaceful, compassionate, confident, enthusiastic, triumphant)

   • For this practice, use "incapable" as the fear-based contracted state.

2. Identify the love-based state you're ready to go towards. Declaring where you are going is the necessary second step. (TEN SECONDS)

   • For this practice, use "triumphant" as the love-based expanded state.

3. Become present with your body. (TEN SECONDS)

   • Stand or sit in a chair with both feet on the floor.

   • Keep your eyes open, ideally.

   • Feel free to close your eyes the first few times you do this practice.

   • Smile and take a breath, then settle into a gentle rhythm of breathing.

4. Bring your attention to the love-based state of triumphant. (TEN SECONDS)

   • Remember a time when you were triumphant. This will be a specific and actual moment. Perhaps you won a game or a contest, or you accomplished a goal, received a diploma, job, a grant, or a bonus.

5. Become aware of your body, feelings, and thoughts. Use the prompts below and move through all of your senses. (30 - 90 SECONDS)

- Recall body sensations, body positions, and posture. How are you moving? What is your posture or activity? How does your body feel? Is it hot, cold, or sweaty; are you smiling, laughing, or crying; are your clothes wet, dry, tight, or loose? Remember.

- Recall the images and colors you saw. In your mind's eye, look all around. What do you see? Are you indoors or outdoors; is it sunny or cloudy; who do you see around you; notice your hands and your feet; who or what is next to you? Remember.

- Recall the words and sounds you heard. You are there now. What do you hear? Listen. Is there an announcement, people talking, cars, machines, or music? Are you talking to others, yourself? Are others talking to you? Do you hear friends, relatives, or competitors? Remember.

- Recall what you smelled. Slow down your thoughts, flare your nostrils, and sniff. Be curious: what is that subtle fragrance? Do you smell flowers, mowed grass, air freshener, perfume, gasoline, or alcohol? Is there food cooking, the smell of the ocean? Remember.

- Recall the taste in your mouth. Is your mouth dry or moist? Do you taste sweet, salty, or stale? Lick your lips. Remember.

- Recall feelings, thoughts, and inner experiences. What feelings do you notice? Are you joyful, enthusiastic, calm, or relieved? Do you feel elated, unstoppable, confident, excited? Remember.

- Revisit all of the senses to fully remember the energies and memories. In one word, how do you feel?

6. Use your breath to embody this love-based state of triumphant. (1 minute)

- Breathe in and out gently and fully throughout these steps.

- Feel, sense, and imagine the experience and energy of "triumphant" moving through every cell of your body and aura.

- Simultaneously, become aware of (i) a point between your eyebrows, (ii) your navel, and (iii) the base of your spine. (three breaths)

- Simultaneously, become aware of (i) the center of your chest, the base of your throat, and the top of your head. (three breaths)

- Become aware of your whole body, thoughts, and feelings. Complete by exhaling sharply out your nose and clenching your fists. (three breaths).
- Silently declare "triumphant" on each exhale.

ALWAYS CHOOSE LOVE

It's been said time and time again: if you want to see love in the world, be loving. Love is infinite, reciprocal, and inclusive by nature. Know, without a doubt, that your soul will always respond in accordance with the *way of love,* and bring you to situations that support your evolution and your embodiment of love.

Love holds open the door to enlightenment.

Visit our book resource page here:

https://www.profoundlifewellness.com/book

John Mercede is a Master of healing and coaching and an expert guide for conscious living. Through their business, Profound Life Wellness, he and his partner Julianne Santini help people navigate living, working, and relating in multiple realms of reality while working through energetic crises or difficult life situations.

John grew up with a love for machines and an innate knowledge of how things work. He learned that hard work has its rewards and brought a strong work ethic and an eye for perfection into every part of his life. John is a master craftsman and fabricator who loves to build just about anything. He's a self-declared car nut who's raced Formula cars and restored three British sports cars.

Despite a demanding work history that included roles as a fabricator, designer, inventor, and engineering VP, John earned a degree in Mechanical Engineering while juggling full-time work. Later, he ventured into entrepreneurship, undertaking extensive house renovation projects. Simultaneously, he excelled in athletics, racing bicycles, becoming a sponsored racquetball player, and earning a black belt in martial arts.

A sports injury sparked his journey into energy healing, culminating in over 15 years of dedicated study and practice. During that time, he received direct transmissions and training from masters in the Philippines and India, as well as an initiation from the Dalai Lama. He also studied classic methods of transformation of consciousness, breathwork, and psychosynthesis.

Each with over 20 years of experience, John Mercede and Julianne Santini offer profound transformations. They emphasize that life is more than the passage of time; it's a catalog of experiences. John's teachings bridge ancient wisdom and contemporary life, guiding you toward joy and fulfillment. Connect with him for a personal session, a group experience, or travel to a sacred site.

Connect with John:

Website: https://www.profoundlifewellness.com

Email: john@profoundlifewellness.com

CHAPTER 3

HIJA, ABUELA, MADRE MIA

IF YOU'RE ALIVE, SO IS YOUR FAMILY

Emily Atlantis Wolf

Love is anterior to life, posterior to death,
initial of creation, and the exponent of breath.

~ Emily Dickinson

MY LOVE INITIATION

"And then Betsy said, 'We've got butter up the wahzoo!'" I said to Rose as she sat across from me in the candlelight of our half-booth at Shaw's Crab House on Hubbard Street in Chicago.

Rose laughed. She's got a full-body laugh that sends her shoulders back in her chair and lifts her head. This time she let out a big "Ha!" before riding the waves of laughter.

"This as she's getting gas station fried chicken at a pseudo-cafe walkup called Raise The Roost at an Indiana rest stop." I'm laughing with Rose, "And she asks me if I want anything."

"I don't even see that as food. It's as far from pasture-raised, heritage hens carried to the slaughterhouse on a pillow and wrapped in organic cellophane before being driven in climate-controlled overnight-express trucks to Whole Foods as you can get. I can't build heart cells with that. No way!"

Through her giggles, she says, "That's great, Mom."

"Of course it comes with mashed potatoes and biscuits. Biscuits need butter. Hence, the wahzoo."

We're both chuckling as the waitress arrives at our table.

"Welcome to Shaw's. My name is Katy, and I'll be taking care of you. Can I get you both something to drink besides water?"

We both stick with water, ice for her and no ice for me, then put in our usual order: garlic salmon sushi rolls, halibut with asparagus, haddock with carrots, and truffle mashed potatoes—all to share.

"Great," says Katy. "I'll bring out the waters and send some dinner rolls over."

"But I can't be too hard on Betsy. She is the reason I get to see you before my trip to Egypt," I said.

"Yeah, I hear you," says Rose. "Where are you staying?"

"Right across from the Sears Tower on the South Franklin side. We're sharing a room. Her niece's wedding is tomorrow afternoon, so me and you can do a grocery run to Heinen's in the morning. I told Betsy I'd be back by 1 p.m. They have trolleys to take us to St. Patrick's. Oh, and we're not leaving Sunday until noon. So you and I can get Goddess and The Baker Sunday with Fiona before I drive back."

"Sounds good," she says.

I slow down and look into Rose's 19-year-old face, radiant and open. She carries a timeless, natural beauty and doesn't wear makeup. I'm silent after a long exhale as I gaze into the emancipated features of her cleared complexion, as if seeing her for the first time in a long time. It's been two weeks since she went back to college. My baby and my only girl. After only two weeks, the new acne medication and skin routine are working for her. The battle won. My victory is being able to look at her whole face—not just her eyes—without feeling guilty that I hadn't solved that problem, along with the never-ending task list of other unsolved problems as a single mother of three.

I used to have four. They're starting to leave the nest.

Her face is petite and heart-shaped, like my mother's. Her brow is wide and crowned by long, fine hazelnut hair that falls down her back like a capelet, like her great-great-grandmother. Her nose is refined, sculpted alabaster, and I've never been able to say who gave it to her. Her cheekbones are wide and high like me, like my mother, her mother, and her mother. Her lips are tapered, and her smile is steady.

I wish my mom was here to see her.

Rose is my daughter, mi hija, or mijita.
Amy is my mother, mi madre.
Cecilia is my grandmother, mi abuela.
Eulalia is my great-grandmother, mi bisabuela.

Earlier that day, on the six-hour drive to Chicago from Cleveland, my client Betsy was trying to make conversation because she likes to talk. I deflect conversations back to people. I prefer to be reflective. She asked an innocent question, "Were you and your mom close?"

Close. Just the word makes me quiet and tearful. As the question is heard, I imagine a salty sea of tears washing over me and carrying me back to holding her hand and watching her copper-colored eyes look over my shoulder into the lands of death as she let go of her last breath. That was 14 years ago. After she died, I had to learn how to live without half of my heart, half of my bones, and half of my blood. We used to say we were one soul in two bodies.

Then I remember she came to me last year during a meditation. We were walking on a path in a dense forest on a sunny afternoon, arms around each other's waist. She was on my right. We were both angels.

"I miss you so, so much," I said as I looked at her.

She smiled, looking forward, still walking. She hip-checked me, bumping me with her left hip but staying joined, and said, "This lifetime is just a blink. Besides, we're not usually apart from each other."

I said to Betsy as I looked forward, tearful, still driving, "We were intertwined."

After a pause and a swallow, I followed up with, "How about you and your mom?" It worked. She talked for almost 45 minutes before I pulled into a rest stop on the turnpike.

At Shaw's, our garlic salmon rolls arrive at the table. I watch Rose use chopsticks to place a portion on her plate and then move each of the ginger shavings to my plate. Her fingers are long and lean. Her nails are round and white. Her hand movements are measured and slow, with a graceful flow.

My grandmother was the first to notice Rose's refined gestures as a baby and called her Sangre Azul. Blue Blood.

I wish Gram was here to see her.

I was 39 when my mother died. My mom was 59. My daughter was six.
My grandmother was nine when her mother died. And 82 when her daughter died.
I was 45 when my grandmother died. She was 88. My daughter was 11.

My grandmother, Cecilia, grew up in Brownsville, Texas, in a house with no floor. The house had walls and a roof and was built in the backyard of a relative. There was no glass in the windows. The curtains were held up by string the butcher used to wrap around the paper when they bought a holiday roast. The girls all slept in one bed. The boys slept outside in hammocks. They paid the neighbor across the alley 25 cents per month to draw water from their pump. When enough money was saved, her dad paid a man with a donkey to pull the house to their own purchased bit of land.

My grandmother was raised by her sisters and her father's sister, Aunt Mary, Titi Maria. Titi was the town healer, the curandera. The inside walls of her tiny house, set on cement blocks, were covered from floor to ceiling with prayer cards for everyone who died. She prayed over them for a good death and safe journey to spirit. Her birthday was Oct 31.

Titi's warning to my grandmother, the youngest girl in the family of six surviving children, was, "Never marry a man with green eyes. It's the devil." Titi married Pete Brown of the Brownsville family and might have been the first woman to be allowed to divorce. I think Pete was afraid of her. They had no children of their own.

My grandmother, Cecilia, had dark brown eyes, almost black, and thick, wavy hair cut short and combed up and away from her forehead. She was tall and elegant and often wore blue jeans and a white shirt tied at the waist when she wasn't in her Catholic school uniform. Nothing about her was typical.

My grandfather, Rosendo, had curly, black hair that he combed into waves and green eyes. (Most Hispanic men have thick, straight, bristly black hair and brown eyes.) He was also tall and held himself like a king. He was an only child, raised over the border in Matamoros, Mexico by his mother and two aunts after his father died. He was 17 when he enlisted in the army during World War II. He landed at Utah beach, fought, got shot, recovered, marched into Berlin, and came back to Brownsville to marry my grandmother. They looked like movie stars.

At Shaw's, our waitress returns. "Hi, ladies. Everybody okay?"

I reply, "Everything is wonderful. Thank you."

"Are you both from here or visiting?"

I reply, "I'm visiting, but I used to live here for four years. Up in Evanston."

Rose adds, "I go to school here."

"What school?"

Rose says, "SAIC. School of the Art Institute of Chicago. I'm studying to be a professor of Art History."

"Oh, that's a hard school to get into. Good for you! Well, let me get you some boxes. I'll be right back."

> My grandmother left high school, earning her GED and then a license in Cosmetology.
>
> My mother was the first person to graduate from high school in her family. A woman! She graduated Salutatorian from Holy Redeemer. She was also the first person to graduate from college. She graduated with honors from Marygrove College for Women. She married before her junior year, had me, graduated with a degree in Early Childhood Education, and had my brother three months later. She believed two kids were enough for anyone.
>
> I graduated with dual degrees in Civil Engineering and English. I minored in Environmental Engineering.

At Shaw's, the waitress returns. We order black coffee and our favorite three-layer chocolate cake to share. I saved all month to come to Chicago and eat here with Rose. Food is where I spend my money. Dinner with my Rosie means everything to me.

My great-grandmother, Eulalia, was raised in Mexico by a wealthy family who owned a grocery store. Food was important to them, too. She was petite and quiet with long, thick waves of hair that she kept in a bun, as was the custom of the times. She was a favorite child, expected to marry well. She fell in love with a ranch hand, a cowboy named Sam. They said there was a light in her eyes when she looked at him. They were always smiling at each other. Her family did not approve. They threatened to disown her if she married him. She had a choice between living a life of wealth and ease or leaving her family, their money, her home, her friends, and her country. She chose love.

> Eulalia married and left Mexico to move to Brownsville, Texas. She never returned.
>
> Cecilia married and left Brownsville to move to Detroit, Michigan, because my grandfather wanted to get away from Texas and create his own life. He got a job at General Motors.
>
> Amy married and left Detroit to move to Cleveland, Ohio, where my dad got a job.
>
> I left Cleveland to live in Baltimore and Chicago before returning to Cleveland because I married and wanted to be close to my mother before starting a family.

Sitting at Shaw's and eating cake, I look into Rose's face. Her eyes are dazzling, with copper, green, and brown flecks. Such light in them! I look down at my plate.

I wish I could have seen my great-grandmother.

I hear a woman's voice in my head: *You are seeing me.*

I look again at Rose, gazing at my daughter's face with hushed, measureless love. Her features soften. I begin to feel like I'm looking into a column of adjustable lenses. In that moment, my eyes begin to see all the faces of the women who lived before her, reflecting back at me. They are all smiling at me, all shining their light through the sparkling flecks in her eyes. They see me.

They are alive because she is alive. I have carried these women through me and given them to her. They have carried their mothers and grandmothers. I could stay looking and see the infinite line of ancestors. They are alive in my laughter, my stories, and the light that shines between us when we look into each other's eyes. We are the living love that endures the centuries. We never die.

My silent heartache is that I'm looking at the end of our story, the last of our line—a zenith. My daughter likes ladies, not gentlemen. She has no plans for children. I might be the one telling our stories to leave in the world after we both pass away. Ah, but Rose, what a triumph of feminine sovereignty! She is a blaze of white light in a dark world. Maybe she's the best and last. Immaculate conception? A mother can hope.

"So I was looking up bee hives," says Rose, breaking my reverie. "After I saw a vintage honey container. The classic, cone-shaped one."

She turns her phone to show me images she's found.

"They used to be made like baskets. Upside down. That's why you see that shape."

"Amazing!" I say, looking at the black and white photos. Every day is a school day with Rose.

"And they still used smoke to move the bees out of the hive to get the honey."

"Even the queen?" I ask.

"She's not a sea captain."

"Ha! Well, we should leave now," I say through giggles. "Neither of us will say anything funnier than that."

Our laughter discharges, rippling and boundless. We're laughing together, sending the light between us in all directions, oblivious to the eyes in the room. We are alive—wild and free.

Borrowed bodies perish,
Returning their sum and substance
To Mother Earth.

Egos expire
In one, closing exhale.

But Love is immortal light,
Ferried by every corporeal being,
Unwearied by lifetimes of living,
Indestructible.

THE PRACTICE

What is your family's love initiation? What stories do you carry for them? This practice is an invitation to gather your ancestors and bring a relative to your fire.

PART ONE - GATHERING

Find a notebook and begin writing about a branch of your family that is an easy connection. For me, I feel power and love through the female line of my mother's side of the family. I love other family members, but this line feels alive in me. Write about a line of family members or one person who feels connected to you. Living or dead. Dead is easier.

For each family member, write down answers to questions, such as

- Where did they grow up? In what circumstances?
- What did they value? What did they love to do with their time?
- Did they get married? Why or why not?
  Was that important to them?
- What were their dreams and hopes?
- What did they look like?

Look at yourself and write down patterns you see in yourself that you see in your relatives. For me, I noticed that I come from witty, intelligent women who are highly educated given the chance to pursue academics. And we all speak the love language of food. And we are willing to relocate and leave everything for love. I also noticed that we have powerful healers like my Titi Maria and myself who carry the ancient ways of connecting to spirits. Seeing your patterns helps you understand yourself and what illuminates your life's path.

PART TWO - FIRE CEREMONY

1. Pick a deceased relative and find a place where you can build an outdoor fire.

2. Bring your journal with what you know about the relative.

3. Bring tinder, kindling, and large sections of hardwood to build a fire from scratch. No lighter fluid or starter logs, please.

4. Bring offerings to add to the flames, such as sage, sweet grass, tobacco, and incense. Imagine what your relative would like. Pretend you're asking them, and they reply.

5. Bring a drum or rattle if you have one. Drum or rattle to your heartbeat, sending your love into the flames. You can also hum while putting both hands on your heart, sending your love into the flames.

6. When the fire is hot, and the offerings have been made, tear out the page in your journal and crumple it into a ball before throwing it into the middle of the flames. Add more offerings. Say the name of your relative, over and over, either out loud or to yourself, until you can feel a presence, hear a faint voice, or see them in your mind. Wait for it.

7. When you sense them, greet them with love and gratitude.

8. Tell their story to them. Ask them to fill in the details. Ask what story they want you to remember. Ask them to help you remember them and their stories.

9. Use your journal to write their story again. Write it as if you were writing it for them as a gift. Share their story with family, friends, and social media. Anywhere that feels good to you.

10. Reflect on their influence over your life story as you enjoy the meditation of gazing into the flames. Stay until you want to leave. Make final offerings. Thank all your family for guiding you to this moment. Ask them to continue supporting you. They are alive in you.

This ceremony can be done anytime, but when the veil between the physical world and spirit world is thin, you'll have more potent results. Consider doing this at full moons, equinoxes, solstices, and Nov 2, Dia de los Muertos.

If I'm gone, call me to your fire. Say my name and put a handful of tobacco, raw cacao, and a ceremonial amount of rose petals on the flames. Drum in time to your heartbeat. I'll be there.

This chapter is dedicated with love to:
Maria Eulalia Tamayo Rodriguez
Maria Cecilia Rodriguez Leal
Amy Elizabeth Leal Koch
Rose Eulalia Hellesen

Emily Atlantis Wolf is a professional healer and guide. (That means she gets paid to invent ways to heal people.) She climbed corporate ladders in civil engineering and financial investment services until 2009, when her mom died. She pivoted into healing arts, training to become a Licensed Medical Massage Therapist, Usui Reiki Master, Seneca Wolf Clan Shaman, and Master Breathwork Facilitator, among other certifications.

Since 2010, she has helped over 3,000 clients confront and care for their physical and metaphysical pain. And she's still going. From chronic muscle tightness to trauma and unexpressed emotions, Atlantis combines practical and intuitive modalities. Part of her secret is connecting to spiritual realms using breathwork, drumming, fire ceremonies, and the guidance of galactic dragons.

She offers group calls (free), writing courses, breathwork events, and retreats. Offering experiences to group gatherings is her joy. She would love to talk to you about bringing a healing ceremony to your women's retreat or corporate wellness event.

Sign up for Atlantis's email list to receive a free video that leads you through releasing one piece of stuck energy with drumming and fire.

Contact Emily Atlantis

Web: https://www.atlantiswolf.com/

Email: SanoTotum@gmail.com

CHAPTER 4

INNER WISDOM

vs

INNER CRITIC

LEARNING TO LISTEN TO YOUR SOUL'S VOICE

N.S. Shakti

MY LOVE INITIATION

Triumphant, I stood alone in the dark room.

Shadows jumped on the walls cast by a dim lamp aided by a couple of scattered candlesticks. *I finally won the war of the decade! I have my room! All mine!*

Laughing out loud with uncontrollable joy, I turn up the stereo, "It's My Life" blasts out, and I start to dance with the shadows.

Jumping on the bed, hands in the air, bouncing! I somersault off and run around the room, touching the walls, trying to catch the shadows with my fingers. I pause to trace the handsome faces smiling seductively at me from each prized poster.

A shiver passes down my spine, and I smile. *No siblings allowed.*

My space.

To.

Do.

Whatever.

I Want.

15-50

I sit at my desk late at night, typing this on my laptop. Subdued light from the cream silk-shaded lamp on my left illuminates my immediate space, and a luscious margarita-island-scented candle on the right fills my senses.

Peter Gabriel's "Passion" is playing softly in the background. I see my old friends flickering over cards and letters of appreciation on the pinboard.

Once in a while, I turn my head to the dark room behind me, sparkles twinkling, catching my eye.

A crystal here, a statuette there.

So many memories.

My heartbeat slows, and I'm smiling, thinking of you, my reader, feeling into my words, visualizing.

Surreal.

My husband is sleeping peacefully downstairs in his room.

And I am in mine.

What a joy and privilege to have my very own space through love and not war.

In that dark room of my childhood, I became enlightened.

I have magic powers!

Too much, too soon.

My older cousin's best friend was the most popular, good-looking guy at school. He was a grown-up 17-year-old, and I was nonexistent on his radar.

But last week at a birthday party, he came to pick up his kid sister.

I was sitting on a chair near the doorway. I noticed him right away, and my heart skipped a beat. I looked at him straight in the eyes; his eyes widened a little, and he smiled his crooked heartbreaker smile at me.

At me!

I deliberately turn my head towards my friend and let my long, luscious hair fall like a curtain between us.

I pretended to engage her in conversation, all the time watching him through my hair, my heart beating so hard, I could feel it in my ears.

He looks back at me a few times; then he has to go.

I let him.

He fell in love with me in that moment, and I knew it! I was the luckiest girl alive; my first love loves me back!

At school, I instantly became popular with senior girls, all wanting to be my friends.

"What's kissing like?"

"Aren't you scared you will get pregnant?"

"How do you French kiss? What is that?"

"Why don't you come to mine for a sleepover?"

"Are you free to come to my party next weekend?"

I was cast as the lead actress for the school's annual play!

I was acing my grades!

I was on top of the world.

I don't have to do anything! I just have to wish hard enough, and it happens!

I am powerful! I am God's special child.

While outside in the world, everything is bright, sweet, and epic, the shadows fill my room at night, asking me questions:

Who are you?

Why were you born into this family?

Why did you choose this life?

Do you know there is a purpose to your life?

Do you know there is a very important lesson your soul came here to learn?

Do you know what that is?

What happens when you learn this lesson? Will you die as soon as you learn it?

What are you going to do with your magic powers?

Will they last forever? Or do you think there is a number of times you can use them, like the genie with the three wishes?

What if you use them in the wrong way, and something happens to an innocent person?

And on and on. Night after night.

Valiantly, I attempt to answer the questions, sometimes.

Like every teenage girl, I have a diary, and in my naïveté, I write some answers as if they were a quiz at school. At times, I sit and just contemplate the questions and formulate some great thoughts.

But these are universal questions, direct from Source; I have no reference or clue, so I go on trying. Eventually, some of my answers began to scare me.

For the most part, I'm not enjoying this experience. It's gone on for months, and I have no one I can discuss this with, nor any answers coming from any other source save myself.

Eventually, I come up with two important points that over-ride all else:

1. I might hurt someone with my powers. *What if someone is nasty to me, and I think bad things for them, and they get warts or turn into a frog?*

2. I have to learn one really important lesson in this lifetime. *What happens when I learn it? What if that's the purpose of my life? Will I die then?*

Too much, too soon.

My conclusions were way off base, and therefore, so were my decisions about what to do with them.

I wanted to live my life. Enjoy it all—the full human experience. I didn't need this power, responsibility, or unforeseen consequences. So, if I could delay the process of finding my purpose, of learning this all-important lesson, I wouldn't die! Good plan!

One night, I stopped dancing with the shadows and declared out loud, "I don't want this anymore!"

I sat on the floor, ramrod straight, and in my mind's eye, I saw a treasure chest. I opened it and placed my magic powers and all the questions I had been grappling with inside, turned the key, and threw it away.

15-50

As I reminisce upon these experiences my younger self went through, I'm amazed. *The irony of the treasure chest!* Even at that tender age, intuitively, I knew I was locking away something precious.

The tools I was divinely gifted with are stuff that Master teachers commonly use today in 2023!

- Somatic exercises
- Self-talk
- Manifestation
- Meditation
- Downloading
- Journalling
- Visualization

I did a disservice to my purpose in my innocence and due to the lack of guidance. To this date, I thought I had a rough life and have done so much healing work around it.

It's only today—as I write these words—that it occurs to me that my life turned on its head *because* I denied my gifts!

Woah!

By locking them away, I lost the protection of my authenticity, my knowingness. I blasted myself wide open to other people's opinions, beliefs, and values.

Above all, I made space for conditioning to take place within my psyche, although it was divinely designed not to be.

Soon after the treasure chest incident, my mother fell sick and then died. My dad's narcissism was fully unleashed without her being around as a buffer, and I became a victim of psychological abuse.

Writing about how that impacted me is what made me an international bestselling author in *Wealth Codes: Sacred Strategies for Abundance.* Chapter 11: "The Beauty of the End Game - Finding Abundance Through Accepting Death." Get the book here https://www.amazon.com/Wealth-Codes-Sacred-Strategies-Abundance-ebook/dp/B0BBB4XVBP/

Standing up and being brave enough to share my words and my authentic self with the world is what brought about my first full-bodied shift.

It was like a reward from the Universe for working on myself, healing, and embarking on my journey of self-awareness over the past decade.

Locking away my gifts made them rusty and dusty. I was covered in the gunk of conditioning and had to work hard to remove all of that!

I desperately hoped my teachers would look at me and know that I knew what they spoke of directly from Source.

I fervently wished my friends, family, and colleagues would want to know about and experience the treasure chest of wonders I held in my heart.

Sometimes, the reality of this came to pass. I'd whip out the magic powers and get whatever I desired then. But because they were caged, it was a one-at-a-time kind of deal.

I amassed a wall full of certificates, seeking a point when I could fling open the chest because I was "qualified enough," "mature enough," or "experienced enough."

This was all conditioning. But also, until I was ready to realize and accept that the stuff in the treasure chest was all me and not separate, this recognition/validation eluded me.

After my shift, I set about polishing my gifts to restore them to their former glory. It's been challenging but so much fun!

During my time in this high vibrational state, I attracted a tribe of women on similar journeys who saw me for who I was, and it was their celebration of my willingness to be vulnerable and show up authentically that truly set me free.

I wrote about that experience and the challenges I faced in my next international bestselling book, *Mindset Mastery: Awareness, Meditation, Mindfulness, And Manifestation for the Spiritual Warrior.* Chapter 3: "Here We Go Again, The Practice of Radical Acceptance." Get the book here https://www.amazon.com/Mindset-Mastery-Meditation-Mindfulness-Manifestation-ebook/dp/B0BSR9J8HN

In May of 2023, I wrote a children's story as an apology to my siblings in *Brave Kids: Short Stories to Inspire Future World Changers.* Chapter 6: "Courage Blooms - Baby's Arrival Brings a Lesson in Love and Change." Get the book here https://www.amazon.com/Brave-Kids-Stories-Inspire-World-Changers-ebook/dp/B0C41V1CVB/ and with it, N.S. Shakti was born.

Words have incredible power, and this name has held me in the highest vibration, making it so that I have no option but to step into the full glory of all my powers.

$$\infty$$

On the 12th of September 2023, I experienced this powerful download, which expressed as the following poem: *Downloading:*

Twirling, swirling, free-falling
Rises up through my body
Making its way to my tongue

Brain on fire – supersonic
Is it bile? Feels so bitter
Every gland on the spongy surface

Secreting
Coincidence that it's a play on "secret"?
I taste life. Truth.

My tongue is my conscience.
My barometer to the world around me.
I taste injustice, frustration, wrong.

Misunderstood. It works as a paralytic.
Paralyzed, I am unable to speak my truth.
The truth of the message I came here to unveil.

I have no past lives in human form
I last was on earth as an amphibian, reptilian, prehistoric.
Tasting life on my tongue.

When the download finished, I found myself in the Garden of Eden and spun down the rabbit hole of good vs. evil. I spent considerable time trying to decipher how I felt about this revelation.

I intuited that it's not the snake that humans fear; it's the poison within themselves that they sense and fear. If I had appeared in front of Eve, it was not as Satan; it was simply to offer her a choice.

In Egypt, two weeks later, divinely imparted messages showed me how thoroughly snakes were enmeshed into the divine narrative from the very beginning. In engravings, in legends, and in prophecy.

At Philae, I felt the cobbled stones familiar under my belly. I heard Isis say, "Welcome home, my beloved." The tip of my tongue tingled, and I tasted my history and future at the same time.

I was transported so high up in the ether I could feel Shakti, the divine feminine energy, the activator of Gods and men; the revered serpent and I were one and the same.

I experienced this energy as timeless and eternal. It was so profound that returning to the mortal realm, to the matters of men and mice, seemed so insignificant that it has proved to be quite a task.

If you've been fascinated by my story or it has resonated with you, you're likely a Projector like me in Human Design. The understanding and practice of which have been instrumental in my journey of learning to listen to my soul's voice.

THE PRACTICE

The challenge of being incarnated in the human form is that we are made to forget the before and after. The game is to remember and revert to the Divine whilst in the 3D earthly plane of duality.

What keeps us trapped in this amnesic state is the bus-i-ness of everyday life: school, college, 9-5 jobs, running the rat race, keeping up with the Joneses, duty & obligations, material aspirations, and so on.

Our psyche is conditioned by the voices of authority recorded from childhood, which stay in our subconscious minds and play on a loop at the back of our minds. These voices of authority make up our beliefs and values. They tell us the musts, do's and don'ts, shoulds, etc., and are the internal mechanism by which the conditioning is held in place.

These voices can be those of our parents, grandparents, teachers, siblings, or anyone who was in a position to tell us what to do when we were young. The next bunch of voices are our own that we recorded as a reaction to something someone said or did that made us feel a certain way and, therefore, infer a conclusion.

On a subconscious level, we begin testing out these beliefs, and when they're proven right over and over, they become patterns. And this becomes a set track for the rest of our lives, up until we begin to do inner work and healing on our self-awareness journey.

STEP 1

All roads lead to Rome, and this is particularly true of the healing world. All modalities have the same goal, and there is something for everyone out there. The key is to start anywhere as an opportunity presents itself to you to experience something outside of the system.

- Yoga
- Meditation
- Mindfulness
- Tarot reading
- Therapy
- Reiki
- Chanting
- Crystal healing
- Breathwork
- Somatic healing
- Workshops
- Masterclasses

The list is wide and varied. Essentially, the process of de-conditioning is un-layering, healing, and re-discovering the "real you"—the person you were designed to be, here for a purpose, on Earth at this point in time.

STEP 2

Upon embarking on the self-awareness journey, the next step is to go a little deeper and focus on self-discovery and integrating what you've learned about yourself during the Step 1 phase.

This is when hypnotherapy and other psychotherapeutic techniques are extremely helpful. You should aim to un-layer deep-seated traumatic episodes that have impacted how you feel and think about yourself. Let go (decondition) and start to re-program the belief system that is no longer serving you.

STEP 3

At this stage, Human Design is a fantastic tool since, by now, you would've discovered enough about yourself to have proof that you're unique and the world so far has failed you by not honoring this.

You get to know your energy blueprint and how you're designed. The key to each of us being as unique as snowflakes and thumbprints is reflected in your reading.

This is just the beginning, yet it is so liberating to learn about your type, strategy, and authority, three simple things, yet everything about yourself starts to make complete sense, probably for the first time ever!

Now for my favorite part! No one can "teach" you your design! Because it's specific to you, only you can begin to try and understand it and how it works for you. The only way to use your reading is dynamically, by running your own Human Design Experiment.

Although there are workshops, classes, seminars, and experts out there, ultimately, you have to make it work for yourself. This is empowerment.

STEP 4

Now, you're well on your way to transitioning from self-awareness to self-actualization. At this stage, you should be fully equipped and able to differentiate between the voices that don't belong to you (inner critic) and your own (soul's) voice.

It's imperative that you surround yourself with a community made up of people who are on or around this stage of their journeys. These are your champions and cheerleaders. Being on a similar frequency, their presence will help you expand and level up. Also, prevents you from feeling "crazy," LOL.

STEP 5

Find yourself a mentor. This relationship has been contracted on a soul level and typically just waits for the right time to reveal itself. This depends on when we reach the appropriate turning point on our healing journey to be fully receptive to the transformative magic this relationship will bring into our lives.

Be careful whilst you're searching for your mentor. I look around me and see that there are so many self-proclaimed gurus and spiritual leaders. Be aware, choose carefully, and use your heart, not your mind. Listen to your soul's true voice.

I am a 70s child highly sensitized to the outcomes that come from blind faith, cult culture, and radical ways of sharing knowledge and purpose. I'll remind you again that you're unique and need not follow a herd to feel you belong.

I'm a Projector—20% of the population, designed to observe and guide. In the spirit of my Egyptian adventure, I'm an activator; I see and tell, and I hold both the ankh and the offering of choice upon my forked tongue.

I also have Heyoka healing energy, which means I'm a disruptor and go against the typical narrative or usual way of doing things to shake things up and yield fantastic results since I'm always intuitively fresh!

If your soul resonates with my words, please do reach out.

Born in the UK as **Natasha Sharma,** she is a qualified Bsc. Hons, Clinical Hypnotherapist, Bestselling International Author, Speaker, Mentor, and Hypnobirthing Instructor DipHB (KGH, UK) based out of Mumbai, India.

She adopted the nom de plume of N.S. Shakti in 2023, which has been a significant milestone in her journey from self-awareness to self-actualization.

Her passion is Money and Manifestation and its relationship to self-worth. She does this with wisdom, divinely blessed insights, sensitivity, love, and, above all, joy.

Her mission is to have conversations about death, thereby normalizing them.

In Human Design, she is a 3/5 Mental Projector, created to be a vehicle of wisdom, a guide for the people who need her, who are ready for her, who recognize her, and who invite her into their lives simply for the words she has to share and the questions she will inevitably ask. For she perceives.

Natasha means resurrection. Her spirit animal and avatar is the snake holding divine, ancient, powerful feminine energy. She embodies the healing powers of the self, of birth, death, shedding, and rebirth—of transformation, self-realization, radical acceptance, and choice.

Effortlessly traversing the conscious and subconscious realms for her own growth and that of the people she works with. Nothing gives her more power than the gratitude she experiences through being present to the transformation of others.

Boldly embodying Shakti and stepping into that raw power—of the life force, kundalini energy, and the ability to see and activate is her divine gift and purpose in the 3D world.

To start (or accelerate) your Human Design journey, transform your money story, and amp up your self-worth, follow her on Instagram and communicate with her on DM (direct message) to figure out the best way she can add value to your life.

https://www.instagram.com/nsshakti.author/

https://www.linktr.ee/natashasharma.shakti

Website: https://www.nsshakti.com

CHAPTER 5

THE QUEST FOR TRUTH AND UNITY

IMAGINING A NEW REALITY

Rev. Dr. Mimi Kate Munroe

MY LOVE INITIATION

I am fourteen, walking down the street in Jackson Heights, Queens, when I become light and am inexplicably catapulted into an unimagined awakening. Everything is glowing, not just the beautiful things like flowers, shrubs, and trees, but the buildings, cement, and even the dog poop. There is a tapestry of light interconnecting everything. I'm filled with a feeling of love, and I instantly know that this Light is God.

I grew up in an atheist household. There was no room for God or anything spiritual, and I lacked the language to convey my experience.

Carried by invisible wings, I fly home to my atheist father and burst out,

"Dad, Dad, I know what God is!"

"What?"

"God is Love,"

"You're full of shit," he says.

Despite his unsupportive response and lack of curiosity, my life was forever changed by that profound moment. Over the years, I grappled with it, ran away from it, and ultimately returned to its guiding light. This transformative moment marked my initiation into the world of the Divine.

A few years before this, I sat at the dining room table eating dinner with my mother and a boy I had a crush on. My mother invited him over, knowing full well that I was a mess of romantic confusion. She made us lobster and French fries.

The boy asks, "Why is there a Lebanese stamp on my placemat?

My mother replies, "I'm Lebanese and wanted to give you a gift from my culture."

The boy is Jewish, and he pushes himself violently back from the table, asking, "Are you trying to poison me?"

This is my first personal awareness of racial or religious discrimination.

Last Sunday, I listened as the congregation and my fellow choir members recited The Nicene Creed.

"We believe in one God, the Father, the Almighty," they intone.

I experience a significant disconnect. These words do not reflect God as the Light I experienced. I struggle, not only with the concept of God but also with organized religion. As I listen to these words, which are recited every week in churches around the world, I wonder: "Would God approve of this? Are we adhering to the fundamental principles of our faiths?"

Since the dawn of civilization, religion has played a major role in helping people make sense of life's most profound experiences and significant moments. It has been a container for stories, like the journey of the dead in ancient Egypt, the promise of eternal life in Christianity through Christ's resurrection, and Hinduism's teaching of reincarnation and enlightenment.

Religion has been a source of comfort and inspiration, culminating in great works of art and music. It has helped humanity experience awe, grandeur, and the beauty and mystery of the universe.

Nonetheless, despite these remarkable contributions, I recoil at the idea of organized religion. I cannot, in good conscience, identify as Christian. I love the community and appreciate the act of communion, but feel a strong discomfort with much of the liturgy.

Looking back through history, we're confronted with a sobering and contradictory reality. Despite professing to uphold Jesus' teachings, the Church has often acted at odds with His core message. The Christian Church, as we know it, was established over 400 years after the crucifixion of Jesus. A group of men assembled, casting their votes to determine which gospels would be included in the Bible, which many take as literal truth.

It has come to light that some of the gospels discovered in the last 200 years likely were closer to the original teachings of Jesus than those that were included. Complicating this, the oldest gospel chosen to be included in the Bible was written at least four decades after Jesus' death, leaving room for a great deal of distortion over the intervening years.

Much of the Christian liturgy is founded on the writings of Saul/Paul, who lived and wrote in closer proximity to the time of Jesus but never had a physical encounter with him. Saul persecuted early Christians until he underwent a radical conversion. He was blinded by a light and heard a voice ask him, "Saul, why do you persecute me?" His experience bears an intriguing resemblance to my experience with light as a teenager.

My mystical experience taught me that anyone and everyone can have an encounter with the Divine. I don't know why it happened to me or why mystics throughout history have experienced the profound presence of God. What I do know is that sharing my experience through words falls far short of the profundity of the experience. Even as I struggled to put the experience into words when it occurred, any description I might offer now is equally limited and fails to convey the magnificence of the experience itself.

Human history is full of occasions where individuals, organizations, and institutions have wrought havoc and cruelty in the name of religion. Time bears witness to the horrors committed under the banner of faith: the Spanish Inquisition's burning of heretics at the stake, the brutal persecution of women who practiced herbal medicine, the blood-soaked Crusades waged against Islam and the current climate of fear surrounding it, and the ongoing persecution of the Jewish people. The Native Americans were nearly decimated by the advancing settlers, who disrupted their worship practices. Countless wars, past and present, are waged in the name of religious righteousness.

Recently, war has broken out again in the Middle East. There was a brutal attack on Israel, killing civilians, and Israel is retaliating. While I cannot condone the initial attack, it's clear that thousands of years of war and violence have not solved the problems carried forward from previous generations but, instead, perpetuate more hatred and destruction. I watch the world polarize over these events and feel a familiar despair.

Contemplating the horrors of man's inhumanity to man, I ask: What would God say?

During my college years, my choir traveled the state performing concerts. In one town, we attended a local church service. The priest was offering communion, and when I asked a fellow choir member what was happening, she said, "They're giving communion. You can't receive it because you haven't been baptized."

My initial response to this statement was to ask myself, "Why would I want to participate? Would Jesus himself have denied sharing bread with me due to lack of baptism?"

I didn't think so.

Locating the divine light of my experience in any religion has been elusive. Though all faiths have God/Light as their essence, it's often obscured by conditions and restrictions, especially in the more conservative branches. Phrases like, "If you don't believe as we do, you will go to Hell" or, "We must unite the world under our faith and convert or eliminate those who do not believe as we do," reflect a human construct of spirituality, not the Divine itself.

The core teachings most faiths share are:

- Love God.
- Love others.
- Be kind.
- Be honest.
- Do not take what isn't yours.
- Allow others to live in peace.

Yet, we seem to have lost this essence, nurturing a climate of competition over whose God is stronger, better, or mightier and embroiling ourselves in a ceaseless struggle for theological supremacy.

I am called to ask, what if we refocused our faith on love? Love is a universal language that transcends boundaries. It's a healing balm for humanity's wounds and an antidote to the divisiveness we perpetuate. Why not redirect our interpretation and living of religious teachings toward the love that underpins all faiths?

Shifting our perspective can build a brighter, more harmonious world. Imagine the transformation if we were to direct the power of these texts to bring about love, understanding, compassion, and empathy!

However, the fundamental issue that underscores our divisions is not religion; it's power. Humans have always lusted for power—power over resources, territory, and people. All wars, all coups, and all chaos are rooted in the human quest for dominance, and religion is often used to fire people up.

Our world is now more connected than ever before, thanks to the rapid advance of communication technologies. Events happening elsewhere in the world that shape the lives of people we've never met are seen in real-time. We're a global community in the truest sense, bound by the same shared challenges and aspirations. Yet, our tendency to view the world through the lens of 'us versus them' still lingers. We categorize people by race, religion, nationality, etc., forgetting that, at our core, we're all part of the same human family.

I've worked in the world of scientific research for many years. Although science and religion are seen by many as divergent practices and mutually exclusive, each providing its own explanation for the mysteries of existence, the two need not be in opposition. Both science and religion, in their purest forms, seek to understand the universe and our place in it.

Science seeks to offer an understanding of the physical world and the laws that govern it, striving to answer the "why," "how," and "what" questions about the universe, peeling back the layers of reality to reveal the intricate workings of the cosmos.

Religion delves into the metaphysical aspects, exploring the purpose, meaning, and ethics that guide our lives, seeking to address the "why," "who," and "what" questions. It explores the moral and philosophical dimensions of existence.

There is a common thread that unites these seemingly divergent paths—the quest for truth.

In essence, they complement one another. And they are merging through quantum physics, where the two fields are beginning to overlap.

Albert Einstein said, "Science without religion is lame, religion without science is blind."

Imagine the profound insights that could be gained were we to allow science and religion to work together! The mysteries of the universe could be better understood through a combined lens. We could deepen our understanding of the cosmos, God, and our nature. We could, perhaps, turn from rigid beliefs to wonder.

Sai Maa Lakshmi Devi, a spiritual luminary, posed a simple yet profound question that resonated with me: "There are two energies in this world: love and fear. Which do you choose to serve?"

A dishearteningly large segment of humanity, it seems, serves fear. We allow politicians and religious leaders to fan the flames of division and discord, driving wedges between us and dividing us. This mentality obscures our shared humanity. It prompts us to affix labels and to judge one another based on the egoic fear that difference is a bad thing. It would be so much more meaningful to learn about others and respect these differences. We must remind ourselves that beneath these superficial distinctions, we're all related, members of a single human family.

The journey for many of us is a quest for light, love, and a sense of the divine. My personal experience of radiant light opened my eyes to the interconnectedness of all things and the notion that love is the ultimate manifestation of the Divine. The experience drew me into spiritual exploration and eventually to the choir loft of an Episcopal church, where I grapple with the religious liturgy, traditions, and history and question whether the teachings of love, unity, and compassion are being upheld by any of the churches and religious faiths in the world. I wonder if we allow our indoctrination into specific teachings to blind us to the more universal principles that all faiths can guide us toward when we explore and honor our differences.

The essence of the world's major religions often centers on these principles, but throughout history, religious teachings have been distorted for the pursuit of power. The conflicts and violence perpetrated in the name of religion have overshadowed and damaged the core messages of love, compassion, and understanding.

Let us not give up worship, rituals, or even religion. These can continue to lift us up and bring us out of our self-centeredness. We need the awe, music, art, and wonder that faith inspires. Plus, just as each one of us is a unique expression of the divine, we each have our own path to and relationship with the divine. Let us instead drop the "rightness/wrongness" of our or others' paths and make room for them all, worshiping in the ways that lift up the whole of humanity and coming together to share in awe and wonder.

The difficult role of the ego is to protect us, which often leads to misinterpretation and manipulation of spiritual and other beliefs for power and control. We need each other to step across differences into a conversation about how to live the best human life possible together, guided by and perhaps combining the underlying principles of all religions. Maybe the concept of 'God out there' has outworn its usefulness. Certainly, something brought everything into being. Perhaps this source is continually creating itself through us, as us. What happens if we take back responsibility and step into spiritual maturity, working together in love so that we forgive ourselves and each other instead of waiting for some outside, unseen, all-powerful source to do it for us or to us?

Who or whatever created everything also created the duality within us. Any trait any human has lies potentially within all of us, and we must choose which ones to cultivate, turning our attention to healing our stories that do not serve the highest good. The saying, "As within, so without," applies in that we see outside of ourselves what is within. When we heal within, we bring healing out to others.

We imprison ourselves in emotions because no one taught us how to be whole. We are born as love, and then events happen that overshadow us with layers that obscure this. As we peel away the layers of hurt, we may find that not only do we feel love, we are love.

A priest I know stood up every week and said, "Everyone is invited to receive communion because no one should ever remember a time when they weren't welcomed at God's table."

May all find love and welcome everywhere.

THE PRACTICE

Imagine there's no heaven…

~ John Lennon

Let's contemplate John Lennon's song, "Imagine," released in 1971:

(Click here for lyrics: https://rb.gy/0j9cw7)

(Click here to watch the official music video on YouTube. https://rb.gy/vm02in)

What is Heaven? Humans have long held the belief that there's a God above who judges us. We have limited our choices because we believe that this all-seeing, all-knowing God, usually patriarchal, is judging us as sinners. We live in fear that our innermost thoughts and our actions that are not aligned with the highest good are being seen, and God will send us to a place called Hell.

- Close your eyes and call in God as you view God.
- Gradually, focus on the things in your life that are not in alignment with the way you would like to behave towards yourself and others.
- Where do you not live fully in integrity with yourself?
- Who is the judge—you or God?
- Imagine that there's nowhere to go after death, neither a Heaven nor a Hell. Does this frighten you? Embrace the fear if it's present. Invite in the mystery and allow yourself just for a moment not to know.
- Using the breath, invite in Divine Love. Imagine each breath bringing in love in the form of golden light.
- Allow this light to hold you regardless of how you see yourself. Recognize that you're doing the best you know how to do with the tools you have.

- See if you can see yourself as a citizen of the world.
- Consider that if all humanity pulls together, there are plenty of resources and, where we think they are scarce, plenty of resourcefulness in our combined intelligence and the intelligence of the Divine to create whatever we need to support all beings on this planet.
- Which concepts would you want to die for? Are these things that are true for you, or things you've been taught are important? Would you send your children to die for them?
- Ask yourself, "Would I rather be righteous or kind?"
- Allow yourself to dream into true world peace, true world harmony. This doesn't mean there will never be disagreements or strife, but that we could view these moments as opportunities to deepen our peace and understanding, rather than allowing them to divide us further. How does this feel?
- Can you imagine the freedom of owning nothing?
- Dare to be the dreamer!

Mimi Kate Munroe is an ordained interfaith minister with a Doctorate in Ministry. Though her prior work has focused on women's health and pediatric emergency medicine research, she recently decided to devote herself full-time to ministry, including spiritual coaching, spiritual interfaith services, energy healing, and teaching mindfulness and meditation. Mimi is a Certified Intuitive Healer and a Magdalena Healing Practitioner, who uses her deep intuition and love to help people open to love. She is also an accomplished, classically trained singer.

Along with partner Patrick O'Flynn, she performs in the Pop/Folk/Rock duo, 'Patrick & Mimi.'

Mimi has led workshops in mindfulness, meditation, and singing. She is strangely not uncomfortable with death and has served as a doula for the end of life, sitting with the dying and their families in times of transition. She is currently co-creating two business partnerships, one on legacy and one on women's issues.

Mimi is the mother of two beautiful adult children, Alexander and Arianna.

If her partner would let her, she'd have a houseful of cats but contents herself with her two girls, Aurora and Cliocatra. She lives in Aurora, Colorado.

For more information, please explore my website:

www.songoflifeandsoul.com

CHAPTER 6

SLOWING AND SHINING

TOOLS TO BREAK OPEN THE TRUE YOU

Liz Meitus

MY LOVE INITIATION

It's in the presence of whispered truths that we can find the story of our purpose and allow us to complete a life fully resolved. So, it's a process, not a moment, that has been my greatest love initiation so far.

"What's your chapter about?" Julianne asked.

"Well, I'm working on it." I exhaled, "I have so many 10 o'clock breaking news stories to choose from, but I think I realized that I don't have as much attachment to those stories anymore and that I don't want anyone to feel like they have to experience my level of pain or trauma to reach healing and growth."

Julianne nodded with an understanding; that same nod was mimicked by anyone else who asked me the same question over the following weeks. I also don't want anyone to think they need the time and means to climb Machu Picchu or lay in the King's sarcophagus in the Great Pyramid to reach those heights.

Circling this story for a landing going on months, I thought it was one story and then another. With so many to pick from, my initiation Rolodex was at the ready. My initiations were always rooted in love, but many were love *and* something else, mostly love *and grief*.

From realizing the depth of my love when I held my twin boys as their bellies ballooned with each brave breath, dangling a carrot of hope before their unscheduled and premature goodbyes, to white-knuckled pain from relinquishing more than a handful of friends to the heavens too soon, to a miracle pregnancy on birth control after years of fertility assistance, that all could have been enough for one life and one incredible chapter. But along the way, I also earned badges that included pages of drug-inked scribbles and memoryless years: Teen rape, wife to ex-wife, feeling extra single as a mom struggling to keep my fetal-positioned-anxiety tween focused on her life ahead, long working hours requiring a toothbrush at the office. I sometimes donned "crazy" as a momentary prefix to a few of my titles throughout those initiations.

As it unfolded, the real story is more about the seemingly mundane moments between the big stuff that gives way to a spiritual pavement whose maps can only be charted by you. While the waves of any type of initiation don't stop, my footing has changed over time, and what used to be the subtle and quiet interludes between the loud crashing currents are what add up to be the more profound collective of my growth and potentially yours.

This process is half-inspired by my relationship with my boyfriend and half-informed by becoming my mirror. To be clear, it's not about the guy, and it never was about any guy before.

Love has always been the foundation of anything worthwhile in my life. While I've consistently been an instant-oatmeal-just-add-water kind of gal when it came to romance, I've bent or extended boundaries to make relationships work. On the other hand, I could teach a master class on how to easily detach when a situation is half-baked and waiting for it to rise from the yeast of time was taking too long.

During 2020, amidst my daughter Kaya's mounting anxiety and me distracting myself with 30 first dates (maybe not 30 exactly, but a lot for a pandemic), my tiny household of two found ourselves strolling sidewalks regularly. One handsome neighbor directly walked up to my daughter and me on the street on a sunny April day and introduced himself. Sure, I noticed we had an instant comfort, but I honestly thought he was gay, so I didn't think much about it.

Only a few months passed before he started showing up at our door again and again. When I gently asked, he couldn't articulate why he was showing up, but he continued to drop off Starbucks on tough kid mornings and seemed to keep an eye out for us. When Kaya and I both realized his humor entertained us, and he kindly took on household chores, he was even easier to have around, especially when he tackled things I only hoped a man was around to do, like putting together the trampoline. He became part of our bubble without much effort. We included him in our small pandemic gatherings, and soon, we celebrated 11 combined holidays and birthdays. When asked if he liked me more than a friend, his body shook to mutter, "Uh, no, you're not my type." Nonetheless, he earned casual invites to drive-through Pumpkin and Christmas light shows and eventually was asked by Kaya to join us in Mexico in 2021.

"Kaya, a forty-eight-year-old man is not going to come to Mexico with us," I delivered sternly.

I was wrong and then felt suddenly gut-conflicted when I heard his cheery reply to her ask, "I'd love to go!" It thrust me into imagining our shared bathroom and how the three of us look like a family.

Maybe it was the magic of tequila and ceremonial amounts of guacamole, as we weren't each other's type, and yet here we are still—we ignited a relationship in Mexico that's still unfolding.

The thing was, he didn't want a relationship; he was completely terrified of commitment and wholly consumed with maintaining his freedom. But for the first time, I didn't need him to be anything other than who he was, and he made me laugh, which is the exact medicine almost any single working mother needs.

We always had fun and laughed; I felt like I was on vacation, even on a Tuesday night unloading the dishwasher together. When it got to more serious topics, he silently slipped away, and his texts momentarily became void of kissy faces. His pace of the relationship was slower than slow, and all the normal markers I (and many of my friends) mentally set at three or six months of when someone normally said "I love you" or met each other's friends were simply not on the same track of anything remotely familiar to my past. I could've left and thought about it many times, but there was nothing wrong, per se.

But this man who pushed me time and again into a place of discovery, not having any conscious intention to do so, ended up giving me the gift of time and space to think about who I am that I didn't know I needed.

Sometimes, he wanted to walk away because he didn't want to be a part of any story, including mine. I presumed he didn't know how to be part of the kneading of the mother dough of love. *I've done this too many times. I'm not going to save him; I'm not going to save the relationship.* However, I kept leaning in because I knew my lesson wasn't over, and he made me feel safe in myself, which was more than I felt with a man in a while. However, beyond feeling safe, he kept me in wonderment. I couldn't figure him out, and for a psychic, not having all the answers is welcome and sort of fun! That and I felt able to be the weirdest, unedited version of myself around him, and that made me pause to reconfigure what love may be all together. Or maybe how loving myself harder ended up being the very thing that allowed him to love me better.

For inspiration, I recently interviewed him on how we got here, and he paused, staring off into space, and thoughtfully said, "You allowed me to do my thing and gave me my breathing room without holding it against me."

The slowness of us birthed a slowness in me, which brought forth a beauty and gift that didn't get any fanfare until now and has felt more meaningful than any ten o'clock breaking news story.

And for the first time in a long time, there was a new reason to daydream. It wasn't about what he was or was not doing right, but more the pause to find out who I was or was not in the present time—not the woman I was 20 years ago in a marriage pre-kids. *Could I possibly be in love with myself first?* There was certainly a pull I didn't expect, but I didn't realize at first that it was a pull to myself. Not him. The quiet part of me had never really been opened like a fine wine before or, rather, had been given the time to open. I just needed time to breathe. Time had burned out a lot of the previous knowingness inside, and here I was, getting space to figure out what I needed to live out a life of resolution and purpose.

It was in these long spaces between his time away at softball games and the time I spent not being overly consumed with our next step that helped. In our commitment to be home base for each other, I ended up bearing more opportunities to hear my higher self and absorb messages both distant and faint.

Then I heard something a handful of times in the quiet moments of the slow growth of an unexpected relationship: *Find a way to show new generations how to complete their pain and not pass it on to the next generation.*

Teach them to not to put it on anyone to resolve their stuff; be what they came to be and do, and become more to progress humanity and innovation.

Over the last year, I broke some of my random rules and started digging into a concept I taught years ago in one of my weekend spiritual workshops. Back then, it was about breaking rules. But this revived version came after I sleuthed together a message I both heard and felt from generations returned to dust.

There are many ways to magic and myriad ways to become yourself, and slowing down to not do anything is exactly one good way to get to magic.

Not only had I been working with outdated relationship information, but I had also been working with a set of rules that weren't exactly mine. It became clear that every time I started breaking societal rules, whether of motherhood, how to manage people at work, how I should engage in romantic relationships, or what I should have accomplished at a certain age, it chipped something away that wasn't mine to carry forward and I became more of me.

Taking it a step further, I felt more real every time I pushed the edges of a taboo. I don't mean breaking criminal rules, but these things we tag as a rule or taboo for no real reason other than it was either handed to us or we created to have some semblance of order and control. And the more practice I got, the more I relinquished the need to fix others or the past, and the more I relinquished a need to mold my partnership into anything that was or wasn't natural.

Some of you need examples. Here's what I mean about breaking rules or taboos that aren't criminal: Grow your bangs out despite being once told a long time ago that your forehead needed to be covered. Say no to joining the family for holidays if it causes a level of anxiety every year. Try wearing heels while working virtually at home; break your rule of only wearing slippers in the house. Be loud when you're supposed to whisper—what's the worst that can happen?!

As a psychic traveling in Egypt, I felt deeply that, at a distant time in our human history, we were far more balanced, and this idea of completion was commonplace. There were messages all around—both engraved and lingering in the scent of antiquity—about how life was fully completed versus what I see as having gone off track the last dozen generations. We've been slowed down by recent generations passing along all the unresolved pain, grief, and conversations to the next generation to solve, but with no malintent; they just didn't know another way. We simply can't heal the past effectively with the set of spiritual tools most of us have to work with. Some of us spend our entire lives trying to solve a problem that was never ours.

By intentionally relinquishing, or at least evaluating rules and taboos that may hinder self-innovation, you can take off the weight of anything passed down to you and become you in a new way that can help give you the space to resolve this life's lessons, pave the way for a new generation of minds unburdened by obsolete constraints. You can directly contribute to a future of creativity and propel society into uncharted territories, which feels pretty good, doesn't it? It's time to complete our cycles.

Yes, I'm saying it's time to be a little naughty with pure intent and in the nicest of ways while still growing your spiritual practice and becoming more of you.

And as for my boyfriend, because I know some of you are wondering, we're a story still being written, but I assure you, we're growing through renewal and being gentle with each other in the process. The gift of slowing down to ponder your needs in the present time may just be the thing that propels you into a new color of love.

THE PRACTICE

You are a rich tapestry of emotions and ideas, and this practice can help you realize the depth of your being and bring about your unique glow. Breaking unnecessary rules and taboos helps foster innovation in you, whatever that means to you. Read below and make it work for you. There is no wrong way to do this, and there are a hundred ways to do this differently. Explore for yourself!

1. Meditative self-reflection.

- Begin sitting in a position with your feet on the ground. Take several deep breaths and find your way to being here right now. Sometimes, I pull upon the principles of Reiki to get me here:
  - Just for today, I will not worry.
  - Just for today, I will not be angry.
  - Just for today, I will do my work honestly.

○ Just for today, I will give thanks for my many blessings.

○ Just for today, I will be kind to every living thing.

- Imagine the edge of your aura bubble and simply expand, double or quadruple in size; just give yourself more room to breathe.

- There are many ways to ground yourself. You can imagine sitting in a tree trunk connected deep into the Earth or surrounding yourself in an earthy color. You can also just imagine your inhale reaching down to your toes. Hear the space in your room and notice the little sounds from the walls or the weather outside.

- Take another deep breath or two.

- You can choose to write at first or simply close your eyes to bubble up the tiniest of rules given to you at birth or the taboos you've imposed on yourself. It's not necessary to identify their origin to release the energy from them. Just knowing these rules is the first step. Some rules may be stifling your creativity, affecting your adventures in love, or limiting progress in the tiniest ways. You can question their relevance in the context of your rapidly changing world.

- While I haven't necessarily done this in a formalized way, some of you may feel more comfortable if you define your values and priorities and how your current taboos align or conflict with these values.

2. Get breakin' and validate your actions with incremental change.

- Rather than attempting to eliminate all rules and taboos at once, try breaking just one or two at first. Sit in that energy for days or weeks and see how you feel. You may notice a little unconscious backlash from others and decide if it's harmful or just uncomfortable momentarily. Small, manageable changes are often more sustainable and allow for smoother growth.

- Just like companies building new products, you can think of your tomorrow-self like a new product. Experimentation and risk-taking are essential for your innovation.

3. Celebrate!

- Recognize that breaking unnecessary boundaries, rules, and taboos is a positive and empowering journey. Small victories deserve recognition and besides, just being you deserves a party.

The goal is not to abandon all boundaries or norms but to release those that unnecessarily limit personal growth and well-being. Strive for a balance that aligns with your authentic self and promotes what you feel is positive and fulfilling. See?! You're already shining brighter!

Straddling the duality of spiritual and corporate environments, **Liz Meitus** has been a clairvoyant soul digger as well as an award-winning marketing and advertising leader for nearly 25 years. Liz roams within to illuminate your (or your business's) authentic potential and to guide your growth. She has learned that there is a surprising amount of overlap between helping individuals in a psychic reading and helping corporate brands seek to find the right magnetism to attract their customers. Liz is passionate about connecting people (and brands) to the core of their being and shines a light on what is possible and how to bring aspirations into reach. Liz has held many titles, some of which include clairvoyant psychic, Reverend, Reiki Master, Creative Director, SVP of Corporate Communications, painter, and mother. When she's not being self-amused, you'll find her traveling to be inspired by other cultures, art, and architecture or frying up tostones in her kitchen while listening to her collection of Grateful Dead vinyl. She seeks any opportunity to be paddleboarding with her daughter, even on rough waters. Raised in St. Louis, Liz attended college at both the University of Wisconsin-Madison and the University of Kansas, graduating with a B.F.A. in Visual Communications.

For business-related inquiries, find Liz at linkedin.com/in/liz-meitus

For personal exploration, visit http://www.roamtravelwithin.com

CHAPTER 7

BEYOND THE WORDS

FACING INTIMACY

Christine Q. Nguyen, L. Ac, MSOM

MY LOVE INITIATION

I stood there staring at all of them, feeling frozen inside. I was in total awe, disgust, confusion, and admiration all at the same time. As an adult, I've been fascinated with what has felt like an unraveling mystery of how to cultivate meaningful connection, deep listening, and intimacy.

I was in a ballroom of 100 dirty hippies, some rolling on the ground in raucous laughter, some slithering around with eyes wide in fascination with everything their gaze fell upon.

How could they all be so expressive, free, and uninhibited?

Some of the women were scantily clad, with half of their butts hanging out. Many of the men with long hair sported unwashed man-buns. Some folks smelled strongly of armpit BO and cheap sandalwood oil.

Ugh. What on earth did I sign up for? How did I get here? I want to go home.

"Explore the world as if you are an alien having your first sensory experience here in this room, on this planet. Everything is new and foreign to you. How would you be?" the facilitator directed.

WTF kind of seminar is this? These people are WEIRD.

I clearly was above them. No way in Hell I was going to participate in this ridiculous exercise, yet somehow, I felt very alone. I felt fear in the pit of my gut, chained from letting myself go to be in the flow of whatever it was everyone else around me was so tapped into.

Do I let go of my own construed ideas of what professional, normal, and respectable looked like?

If I was really honest with myself, deep down, I wanted to be free and expressive in the way they all could so easily access.

Why do I feel so vulnerable right now? OMG. What's wrong with me?

Up to this point in my life, I was a self-proclaimed seminar junkie. This was not my first rodeo, yet this experience was wholly and completely new to me. I felt so alone, small, and pulled back. I was acutely aware that I was protecting myself, unable to connect with anyone. I felt like a 1000-watt spotlight was on me, painfully singling me out from the rest of the crowd, accentuating the handicap of my inability to play and skip around wildly as others did with abandon.

We have an entire hour left of this, and what am I supposed to do? Just sit here?

I awkwardly sat on the ground by myself in the middle of the crowd, hoping no one would see me and also hoping someone would engage with me so I could shake the unbearable sense of tightness in my gut, chest, and throat. Tears began to well up in my eyes, and it took all of my strength and pride to maintain some semblance of composure. I felt emotional and scared, and I didn't know why.

Among the crowd of alien explorers, a long-haired man with dark curls very slowly crawled on all fours in my direction. He slowly took in the room around him, present and deliberate. There was an air of otherworldliness that was palpable in his way of engaging his senses, his body, his breath, and the space around him. It was clear he was allowing himself to be fully in the experience of the exercise we were assigned. With an air of exotic unknowingness and awe, his eyes and all of his senses were in a captivated awareness of me, curious and open. Unexpectedly and inexplicably, I felt comfort in this connection. For the first time that night, I took a deep breath of relief into the prison and constriction of my chest and being.

Lying on his side like a relaxed, curious animal, in a gradual examination of his surroundings, his eyes eventually wandered to look into mine. I immediately felt a sort of genuine and open presence in his gaze. It probably was only seconds that we sat looking at each other, but it felt like an eternity had passed.

I felt my nervousness dissipate. There was something about the way he connected with me, something in that moment that softened me. He slowly and gently reached out to my hand in an invitation for me to grasp it. It was as if he was so present in the moment that there was an impulse moving him to reach toward me. And it seemed to be a similar impulse prompting me to cautiously clasp his hand.

In that space of silence and presence between us, his eyes gently holding me, he softly muttered, "Safety."

Unexpectedly, the pressure of tears I was holding back for the last hour released from my eyes and streamed unceasingly down my face. Amidst the loud laughter and chaos of everyone else in the room, I sat there, connecting with him in the vacuum of silence that only existed between us. He gave language to the complex universe of experience I had inside of me. One word. It was the one word that was the key that opened the lock to the constriction of my body, dissolved my rigid thoughts and judgments, and allowed my fear to melt away.

"Connection," he whispered.

More tears streamed down my face. With a deep breath, I closed my eyes and silently let go of what seemed like an old, deep grief felt throughout my whole body that I was unaware of until that very moment. None of it made any logical sense, and it didn't need to. We sat connected in that silence, in a moment of what felt sacred.

"Care," he said, still holding my hand, still with animal-like wonder, with tenderness and kindness in his eyes.

By this time, my tears had stopped. I felt a softening, ease, and a deep sense of gratitude that expanded like a warm light in my body and the space between us. His words, spontaneous, completely in tune with the moment, gently sprang forth from nothingness and freed my being from a lifetime of confinement.

That night, I drove home reflecting on the power of what happened in that connection; those three seemingly magical words spoken in those brief instances changed my life. Safety. Connection. Care. But it wasn't about the words. It was about him being so palpably present, so tuned into the silence and the space between us, that there was a spontaneous manifestation and creation of language that gave life and expression to a moment. I've never felt so much heartful abundance, grace, and gratitude in my life. There were no words that could capture the experience I was having inside. I just knew that if I had died right then and there, I'd feel content and completely fulfilled. What I experienced was a gift of true intimacy, healing, and being seen at the deepest level of my being. That was the level of presence and connection I wanted to gift to those around me.

THE PRACTICE

Exploring emotional intimacy is my passion. It's been my practice for most of my adult life. As in the story illustrated above, the key to unlocking connection isn't necessarily about saying the right words. It's about feeling and being in a continuous dance with the aliveness of the moment that allows us access to intimacy. It's about the presence and consciousness we bring that makes the difference.

The universe is infinitely expanding. We, being part of that universe, are our own universes unto ourselves. That's seven billion unique individual universes in existence on the planet. Each of us, as people, is infinitely expanding and evolving. Our lives are rich with color and dimension, with distinctive experiences, truths, and perspectives no one else could ever truly know. Knowing this is the premise of the practice below that will help cultivate intimacy with knowing yourself and knowing others.

How can we be present and quiet enough inside that we can tune in and listen to what's in the space or universe of ourselves, the universe of the other, and the shared mutual space between us? With this awareness, there is a shared common space where truth can be expressed and where unpredictable co-creativity, connection, and intimacy can happen.

WHAT'S IT LIKE TO BE YOU?

The practice below is adapted from more extensive methods I've learned over the years. It's akin to mindfulness meditation and done with another person—a relational meditation rather than an individual meditation. The intention of this exercise is for each person to deliberately slow down to notice their experience and connect to what arises from within. A revealing in-the-moment of each person's experience creates a potential for discovery, vulnerability, deepening of connection, and expansion of self with others in an intimate, real way. Here's how to do it:

1. Choose one other person to do this exercise with you. Sit facing each other a few feet away. Choose one person to be the listener and one to be the receiver.

   Listener: Your job is to be on a journey of discovery about what it's like to be the receiver.

   Receiver: Your job is to simply be yourself.

2. **Both of you:** Connect to your inner experience. Close your eyes and take a few deep breaths. Notice what arises and be open and curious about what shows up. You might have thoughts, feelings, emotions, or bodily sensations. Compassionately, allow those experiences to be present as you witness them. Perhaps you notice resisting having particular thoughts or feelings. Notice that and allow the experience of resistance to be there too.

3. After one to two minutes of connecting to yourself, slowly and gently open your eyes. Maintain your connection to your inner world and your breath. Let your eyes connect with your partner's. Notice what arises in your experience as you look at them. What thoughts, feelings, sensations, or emotions are present?

   Be aware that your partner has their own universe. Become present to a shared, felt sense of awareness of the shared space between you. Let your awareness move slowly. Listen and feel for the silence within you and around you. Be aware of what it is like to be in the space with the other person, to be connecting with them.

4. **Listener:** Start the dialogue. Verbalize what stands out most in your awareness of yourself or the other. It might be as simple as "I feel calm in your presence."

   You may then ask the receiver, "How was that for you to hear?" or "What comes up for you when I say that?"

   Hold a spacious presence for the receiver to respond.

5. **Receiver:** Maintain inner awareness. Observe what arises within and verbalize what's going on for you. You might say, "I feel a tightness in my gut when I hear you say that."

Listener: You may inquire to access a deeper experience of the receiver by asking something like, "What does tightness feel like to you?"

6. **Receiver:** This is your opportunity to tune in and express a more nuanced experience of "tightness."

   Listener: Be present to how that lands for you and reveal what it's like for you to hear the receiver express that.

   Go back and forth in this way. Remember to go slow, maybe one statement at a time. Let there be space for you each to notice what arises in the space of yourselves, each other, and between you.

   Expressing what you feel in the space between you might look like, "It seems heavy in the space between us."

7. Continue this exchange until you feel complete or want to stop. You may switch the roles of listener and receiver to do this exercise again.

   As you become more practiced, you will notice there will be more of a natural flow between you in this exercise.

Here are some things you can try and ways of being you can be aware of while practicing:

- Listen from the heart center of your body. Imagine letting that energy flow in a balanced and equal way through your head, heart, and lower abdomen. Notice how that shifts the connection with the other person or how the space between you feels. Oftentimes, it will help a person who is stuck in their head to connect more easily from their heart.

- Maintain awareness of the breath, feelings, and sensations of the body. Let your body be an instrument to inform you of what you're feeling and sensing as you let yourself be impacted by the other. If needed, place your hand on that area of your body to further bring presence to what you are feeling.
  Example:
  Place your hand on your chest where you're feeling sadness.

- Be ever curious about what arises in you, the other, and in the space between you. Assume nothing about who they are in the moment or what they've expressed. Many of us have been trained to come from a place of thinking or projecting our knowing of what an experience is like. We don't want stock answers or blanket statements here. We want to honor individual experiences and connect to what's alive in the moment.

Example: Instead of assuming smiling is from happiness, with genuine curiosity, you can ask, "What is your smiling about?" You may get an answer that surprises you, or they may open a door to an experience they're not aware of.

- Own your own experience. Make "I" statements.

  Example: "That's annoying" feels different than "I feel annoyed."

- What is your intention for communicating? Share this to create context. Context and intention are powerful and can change everything.

  Example: Intention to connect, to vent, to understand or to be seen/heard, etc.

- Welcome everything that comes into your experience. Slow down, and allow yourself to be with what has arisen within you. Let the observer part of yourself be aware of how something has impacted you. If you need a minute to feel, ask for it.

  Example: "I'd like to take a moment to give space to what you just expressed."
  Are thoughts, feelings, sensations, complexity of emotions, memories, or intuition here? How is it for you that these things are here?

- **Listener:** What's the other person's "How" or their way of being or expressing?

  Examples:
  Posture, tone of voice, pace of movement or speech, etc.
  What experience do you have when observing their body language? Do they seem at ease? Fidgety? Playful? Unmindful?

- **Listener:** What stands out the most? Many experiences may arise simultaneously about what someone says or how they are being. Try choosing the experience that stands out and express that to your partner.

- Is there a desire present? Check in to see if you want something, or perhaps ask the other if they are wanting something right now. It could be specific or general. It could be something like, "Hearing that, I want success for you" or "I notice I am feeling anxious and want more distance between us."

- Reveal and express vulnerably your inner world with the intention to connect. Notice what it feels like to withhold vs express an experience you are having. How does it impact the space, flow, and connection?

  Expressing uncomfortable feelings can be vulnerable, but ask yourself, is there anything truly to protect? That could be the raw and real stuff that opens the door to unexpected intimacy, creativity, and unscripted outcomes that are in service of growth, love, and expansion.

- **Listener:** Don't try to be perfect. The idea is to get what it's like to be the receiver or to get their world. You'll get better at this with time. Not every practice session is going to be profound or amazing. It doesn't mean something is wrong.

- **Listener:** Make guesses about what the receiver might be going through. Do you have a story about how they've come to be how they are? What must they value or care about? Be open to being wrong about your guesses (which is another way of assuming nothing).

- Maintain your humility and dignity. Stay connected to and honor your sense of self and boundaries. Express your needs and wants.

  Mastering connection, communication, and intimacy is a life-long journey. It's a practice that I'm on a continual path of learning and growing. I hope that some of these tools add to the experiences you have discovered on your own journey and will help you find deeper meaning, love, and fulfillment in your connection to others and with yourself.

Christine Nguyen, integrative healer, teacher, and coach, has been in private practice since 1999.

She is the owner of Transformational Healing Arts, where the main focus of her work is to facilitate and guide her clients to deepen inner awareness and integrate the different aspects of self to access well-being and healing. She employs her own unique style of intuitive acupuncture and Chinese medicine and integrates other alternative therapies such as Craniosacral Therapy, Visceral Manipulation, NeuroEmotional Technique (NET), massage therapy, Integrated Energy Technique (IET), shamanic healing, and other energy healing modalities into her sessions.

Christine has taught seminars in Nonviolent Communication (NVC) and intensively studied and practiced Circling Authentic Relating and Relational Leadership. She is ever-delving into various esoteric studies and is passionate about studying and implementing the work of Larry Byram at Higher Alignment to help herself and others cultivate healthy and meaningful relationships on personal, interpersonal, and transpersonal levels.

Christine has 13 years of experience in Chinese kung fu and Japanese martial arts, many years of Crossfit, and participated in road cycling tours. Today, Christine has retired from pushing her body to extremes and enjoys exploring nutrition and tinkering in the kitchen from time to time. She is a first-generation Vietnamese-American, is proudly identified as part of the LGBTQ+ community, and is originally from Albuquerque, New Mexico. She currently resides in the Denver, Colorado area.

You can reach her at:

Website: www.HealingArtsColorado.com

Email: HealingArtsColorado@gmail.com

CHAPTER 8

FEAR BUSTING DISCERNMENT

A UNIQUE AND EASY PORTAL TO EMPOWERMENT

Patricia H. Elliott, LCSW

MY LOVE INITIATION

FEAR BUSTING BY OPENING YOUR HEART

For all of us, one or two defining moments of our childhood shape who we are as adults. Sometimes, these moments, which seem trivial on the outside but create patterns deep within, develop blueprints that dictate how we will respond to given situations as we grow older. However, the blueprint is often a defense mechanism created by a child's mind. It's imperative that we discover these patterns and seek to rectify them.

We must use our hearts to reshape the blueprint, responding with a powerful healing love instead of a protective barrier that no longer serves us.

When I was seven years old, I had one such experience that was life-changing and shaped my response to angry (or even irritated) men for many years to come. I was running into the house, and as I opened the screen door, I allowed it to slam behind me; my dad, standing there, suddenly rounded on me. He snatched me up as I was running, lifted me from under my arms, and pulled me into his face, shouting, "Young lady!" He held me so close that the heat from his breath and the stink of the beer he drank the night before washed over me in a nauseating cloud. I saw his jaw working, the muscles in his face tight and contorted, twisting into something I didn't recognize. He was enraged that I allowed the door to slam behind me.

I came to understand that anything could be a punishable offense; my stomach froze, my legs felt limp and useless, my throat tightened as if choked, and my body was awash with the needling sensation of panic. I wanted to run, but my father held me firmly. My face was filled with terror, and this look of terror somehow registered with my father as he continued to look at me. His face changed slowly, and the corners of his mouth turned upward. As he tried to hide his laughter, a snicker arose, and I saw something ghoulish in his face. He looked away to compose himself and then returned to his angry indignation. This happened so many times that I lost track. Each time, he pulled me into his face, saying, "Young lady!" Unable to maintain the rage I witnessed before, he turned his face away in an attempt to hide his laughter. After several repetitions of this behavior, he finally put me down without a word and left me standing there by myself as he went back to what he was doing. I remained rooted to the spot. *I wondered if he would find me, return to his lecture, and punish me. I tried to work out what I had done that made him so enraged with me because it made no sense to my seven-year-old mind. My mind worked hard to process this strange behavior; my inability to understand what had just happened kept that icy ball in the pit of my stomach.*

Every footstep, creak of the floor, a door opening and closing, the sound of his voice, every time he entered a room or I walked in to find him there, pinned me down with a heavy weight throughout my body. A queasiness rolled through my belly, my skin alight in a painful fire, and a voice deep in my mind kept whispering, *run!* Though I couldn't get my legs to work. I remained in this state of hyper-vigilance, flight or fight coursing through my veins until he left for work that evening.

My father's initial reaction of anger and no subsequent explanation or resolution created a reaction of fear whenever I was around angry men. Therefore, a pattern of avoidance and fear was born that day. This pattern continued throughout my life, causing my heart to shut down and to avoid any man with a semblance of anger, which developed into a lack of assertiveness in myself. A pattern of fear was cemented into my body, and I reacted in avoidance and with a shutdown heart whenever confronted with anyone angry. This started a pattern of withdrawal that continued until I had an experience in the late 1980s.

At this point, I started my pursuit of a spiritual path. I learned to meditate, and I listened to different spiritual teachers daily. So, on this day in the 1980s, I was driving with my young child in my bright red Astro van, listening to my current favorite spiritual teacher. He was relating a story about the power of love and the power of the heart to heal. Unbeknownst to me, I was about to have a breakthrough revelation that would heal my wounded heart and change my paradigm and survival conclusions about angry men and angry people in general.

The story starts on a 104-degree summer day in Phoenix, Arizona. My nine-year-old daughter and I were excited we scored the very last parking space at a Taco Bell. Despite the heavy thickness in the air and the oppressive heat, I was proud of the way I skillfully pulled our red van into the parking spot, leaving as much room as possible for my daughter to exit the car on her side without a worry that she would accidentally allow the car door to touch the car parked next to her. As I finished listening to the spiritual cassette from my favorite teacher, I felt such gratitude for the stories I listened to. This particular spiritual teacher told great stories that were very inspiring to me and encouraged me to listen more to my heart and get out of the bad neighborhood of my mind. I stopped for a moment and appreciated the sense of my open-heartedness with the world, as if a golden yarn-like thread was spreading out from my heart, reaching throughout the world and connecting me to pure, universal love.

I noticed the well-kept and distinguished-looking man in the driver's seat of the gold Mercedes parked next to me. He had the windows down and the air conditioning blasting, and I assumed he was waiting for someone who had gone in to get their orders. I carefully slithered out of the car to avoid touching his car door. I was successful until the last moment when my door gently touched his car door, leaving no mark. I quickly made eye contact with him and said, "I'm sorry." He immediately changed before my eyes and became surly and angry as he replied, "You better be sorry, lady!"

In the past, I'd cringe, cower, and shut down whenever I encountered anyone who seemed angry or upset with me, especially if it was a man. My mind unconsciously replayed the scene with my dad, heard the screen door slamming, felt my body being pulled from the ground, and saw my dad's angry face. Today was entirely different. This post-traumatic reaction didn't happen. Instead of reacting from that old place, using the blueprint crafted in the naïveté of youth, paralyzed with fear and anxiety, I was amazed that my heart remained open. This open heart created a gentle, warm, golden honey that was soothing to my being. Any old intimidation instantly melted beneath its glow, and it was replaced by a deep sense of peace and gentleness. My softened eyes looked into his, and again, I replied, "I really *am* sorry." This time with an even quieter and more loving voice and energy. He became furious and yelled louder, "You *better* be sorry, lady!"

This back-and-forth banter between us continued for some time; he became angrier, and his face looked tighter and more agitated. I responded each time from a more profoundly loving part of my heart, and my eyes grew softer and more gentle. The light and the love in my eyes expanded, growing into an unmeasurable depth of love for this man. This loving feeling seemed to be tapped into the universe itself, and at this moment, a new life tapestry was woven, and his anger was allowing me to manifest a new life decision and story. Now, every time he responded with his prickly, "You *better* be sorry, lady," my love for him grew and expanded as I sent the silent message: *I'm truly sorry for whatever pain you've had in your life that led to this angry part of you.*

This experience continued to deepen and heal the wound in my heart. Now, the stab of fear was replaced by a heart that softened and opened and expanded more than I'd ever known was possible before. My heart's frequency changed at that moment, and the love I felt was channeled from deep within my soul; every cell in my body began to vibrate in this new frequency, and I continued to send him silent, deeply loving messages as if from mother-to-son: *I see you as you truly are and I accept you as you truly are.* Then I switched to the lover, seeing him as the beloved, the essence of deeply accepting him on levels I never imagined existed. Unfazed by the poison anger that no longer could hurt me, my words were laced with deeply kind, unconditional love, and my eyes welcomed him like a long-lost friend as I released my very last sentence: "I'm so, so sorry."

Through that single utterance, I pushed forward all the universal love, joy, acceptance, and healing, and I saw the light of that golden honey drizzle over his anger. I gazed at a face contorted, veins bulging, muscles tight, and my heart responded by breaking wide open in an expanded love I didn't know was possible for me to touch.

He looked into my soft, loving gaze, and his face appeared to change and soften as he responded in a fearful voice, "Get out of here, lady; you're freaking me out."

His reaction broke from anger to fear, and it appeared that in his receiving of my unconditional love, perhaps something also moved to a different place inside him as well. I, myself, knew that my heart was freed to create a new pattern. In that moment, my heart was liberated. It unlocked its chains, and a new me was born.

I had an instant knowing that using my heart, not as the shield forged in childhood but as a scepter of truth and love, made for a potent, laser-like precision that allowed me to see myself in a new, deeply open, divine, free version. My heart initiated me into a new version of myself, and I felt my soul speaking to me, and the new dialogue was clearly saying, "You are home." Embracing this 'I Am Home' created a new way of seeing not only myself but the world and everyone in it. I saw my sensitive heart no longer as a curse but as a blessing, a healing light that could guide me in ways that made decisions that may appear illogical but became ultimately incredibly genius in ways I couldn't have perceived with my logical mind.

This experience ultimately led me to a new level of self-reflection and connecting with my heart and soul in ways that proved beneficial in every area of my life, including my counseling practice. It became easy to invent new ways of empowering clients and assisting them in their assertiveness. Below is an exercise I use with every client on their first visit. I call this exercise stepping into your heart power.

THE HEART POWER EXERCISE INSTRUCTIONS

As a Licensed Clinical Social Worker starting my new career as a therapist, we were taught to tailor our approaches based on our client's needs. As I started my practice and began to listen carefully to my clients' issues and what was missing from them in their lives, I began to experiment with different approaches that seemed to just "come to me" that I felt were given to me by my intuition. Although many of the approaches were so specific to the client that I have not continued to use them with every client. The Heart Power or Stepping Into Your Power technique is one that I often use on a client's first visit. My goal is to empower people immediately and to give them something both tangible and kinesthetic to their feeling nature and also easy and convenient to use throughout the day or whenever they're aware of feeling confused, powerless, anxious, or in any way feeling they cannot find their direction. My experience is that most people are trapped in the "bad neighborhood" of the mind or ego part of their personality. The mind is a useful and powerful ally when it's following the guidance of the heart, but it can be a fear builder when used by itself without the discernment of the heart to process guidance or information coming in.

As I embarked on my career journey, I discovered that this profound approach assisted clients in accessing their heart power and helped them to discern between how to empower themselves and where their focus may be on areas out of their control, leaving them anxious and frustrated that they're not able to make the progress that they wish to in their lives. This spiritual process involves stepping into our power, navigating the heart center as we do this, and then accepting that which is within our personal power and/or responsibility and what we need to surrender to the universe/God/or a higher power. I was guided to this technique after I had the experience with the angry man in the gold Mercedes to help clients and myself discern what is within our control and, therefore, empower ourselves and then realize what is outside of our scope of control and, therefore, a place where we need to surrender or allow ourselves to realize it's not in our current timeline of what needs to be addressed at this moment.

In this instructional guide, we'll explore this transformative process to activate the heart's guidance center, utilizing a powerful energy portal and decipher the significance of our power color in unlocking deeper self-awareness.

THE PRACTICE

STEPPING INTO POWER PRACTICE

By Patricia Elliott, LCSW

Although this is a simple and easy technique, allow yourself to schedule the time for the steps of this journey. As you complete each one, you will find how good it feels to be fully connected to your inner wisdom, which will only make you want to tap more into the beautiful discovery of your inner power.

To allow this process to be understood in easy-to-follow instructions, I've broken this down into steps.

THE STEPPING INTO YOUR POWER TECHNIQUE

1. Your first task is to visualize a beautiful sphere in a vibrant color that inspires power for you.

2. As you envision this color sphere, to enhance the physical experience, bend your arms with your palms extended upward. Then, bend and raise one leg as high as possible to impress upon your unconscious mind the profound experience of stepping into your power sphere. Now, step into your Power Sphere.

3. As you step into the sphere of the colored power energy, this intentional movement intensifies the sensation, reinforcing the connection between physical and spiritual realms. The sensation will be palpable, often manifesting in the hands as warm and tingly, which creates a tangible connection with your personal power.

4. Then, step back out of the Power Sphere, noticing the sensation that power has left.

5. Then bring to mind a situation you want to discern, what is truly yours to do, and what needs to be released; perhaps you even feel powerless and confused as to how to resolve it.

6. Now, step back into your power sphere and notice the information that comes as you bring that situation to mind. You will notice immediately what is yours to do and what needs to be surrendered to God/the universe.

This part of the exercise vividly illustrates the transformative nature of stepping into your personal power. Remember how this feels so you learn to seamlessly transition back into your power at moments when you may feel powerless.

The process of stepping into your power releases a knowledge of what is truly yours to do.

Note: I have found by doing this process, you are actually stepping into a power portal of knowing, and a consciousness of oneness.

After stepping into your power the first time, there is no need to raise your leg high because your unconscious will now remember the sensation of feeling power as witnessed by the tingly and warm feeling in your hands.

CONCLUSION

Simply put, stepping into your power informs you clearly on what immediate steps need to be taken. Stepping back into your powerlessness allows you to see clearly what you have no control over.

At this point, I encourage you to integrate this practice into your daily life. Regularly stepping into your power sphere and connecting with the physical sensation reinforces the mind-body-soul connection. This consistency strengthens the ability to discern tasks, make empowered choices, and surrender to the greater flow of the universe.

Stepping into your power is a journey of self-discovery, guided by the heart's wisdom and empowered by a vibrant energy portal. Through the Stepping Into Your Power Technique, you will unlock the transformative potential within, gaining clarity, purpose, and a deep sense of personal knowing. By consistently embracing this practice, you embark on a profound spiritual journey toward living authentically and aligning with your soul's destiny.

Patricia H. Elliott, LCSW, stands as a messenger of transformation in the field of clinical social work and counseling. With a respected career spanning over three decades, Patricia has a wealth of experience rooted in her education from a Master's degree from the University of Nevada, Reno (UNR). Throughout these years, she has dedicated herself to guiding individuals and couples through profound difficulties.

Patricia is distinguished in her unique approach to healing by seamlessly integrating traditional therapeutic methods with holistic techniques to offer a more comprehensive and tailored treatment for her clients. At the core of her practice is the profound belief that many individuals form "thinking errors" or "survival conclusions" due to past traumas or adverse experiences. Her beliefs are that these conclusions often distort self-perception and create barriers to one's true potential.

Patricia serves and guides thousands of people through a transformative journey to shed misconceptions and reconnect with the purest whole version of themselves. She passionately believes in and advocates for the innate power of the human spirit. She strives to gently and lovingly guide her clients to rediscover passion, purpose, and joy in their lives. Her extensive knowledge, skill, genuine compassion, and dedication have made her an indispensable asset to both mental health and spiritual communities.

As a certified Heart-Thread Practitioner, Patricia advocates for integrating holistic approaches in the mental health and wellness communities. She emphasizes the importance of viewing every individual as a holistic being. Patricia Elliott's name represents decades of service and signifies a holistic evolution in mental well-being.

Contact: https://www.facebook.com/patricia.h.elliott

CHAPTER 9

LOVING MYSELF THROUGH ILLNESS

EMBRACING THE HIGHER FREQUENCIES OF LOVE FOR VITALITY

Kimberly Barrett

MY LOVE INITIATION

Really? I'm still here? What possible use could God have for me to still be on this planet when I have nothing left to contribute? I think this to myself as a stray beam of sunlight finds its way through the blinds in my bedroom, waking me.

I lie in bed for a few moments and assess my energy levels. My body feels weak and slow to respond as I try to peel the sheets off of my body. *Can I take a shower today? Cook a nice breakfast for myself instead of instant oatmeal again? How about vacuuming today? I've put it off for a week now. What can I do? How much can I do before my body sends me back to bed?* Just the thought of doing any of these tasks sends a distress signal out to my body, and my brain says: *Ain't no way in hell we're doing any of that today.*

Frustrated at the possibility of not getting anything done again today, thoughts that have played over and over this last year resurface. *How could this happen to me? I'm only 34! I haven't even had children with my husband yet!* The diagnosis of scleroderma, along with interstitial lung disease, is a moment in time frozen like a picture in my head. Looking at me with concern in his eyes, "You'll have to undergo chemo to stop the attack on your lungs," my doctor said. Then, four months later, I had a massive operation to remove a tumor from my abdomen. *What is the point of even getting out of bed? It's just going to be the same as it's been for the last ten months.*

I was beyond angry with God, my angels, and my guides, and had slammed the proverbial door in their faces. I felt betrayed by my body, a body that won me MVP trophies in soccer, softball, and, yes, bowling is a sport. I used to love my job. I was surrounded by amazing people. Now, I just stare at the same walls every day. The only sources of interaction keeping me relatively sane are my husband and my cat.

The rooms of my two-bedroom apartment I took such care in decorating are now my cage. I feel left behind as everyone I know goes on with their daily lives. I look at the clock at various times, guessing who's coming in for their shift or going home for the day. I find myself reaching for the phone, wanting to talk to someone. Anyone. Yet, as I mentally go down the list, they're at work. I think about what conversation we might have, and I don't want to hear the pity in their voices or to have them ask the same questions I don't have answers to. I also don't want to sour someone's good day. And why should I have to call? The phone works both ways. *Are they avoiding me because talking to me makes them sad?*

The array of prescribed medications is lined up like soldiers standing at attention on the kitchen countertop. Fourteen pills of various shapes and colors meant to restore some semblance of balance and health to my body while also keeping my pain in check. I question some of them: *Do I really need these two? He said they are to counterbalance the side effects of these two. But what are the additional side effects? What do I know? I'm not the specialist.* I feel as though I'm in uncharted waters, trying to fix a broken ship in the middle of a hurricane and desperately trying to make it to shore alive.

Then, I hold the one drug that could take away all the pain. End my suffering. It's as simple as having more than my body needs. *How much is that? I mean, if I'm really going for it, I'm sure the whole bottle will do the trick.* It starts to tease me each day, whispering words I want to hear. *You'll simply sleep and not wake up. You'll be free. No more pain. No more suffering. No more loneliness.* My resolve not to give in waivers daily depending on my pain levels or my mental and emotional states that never seem to rise up to the person I once was.

It's not even myself or my family keeping me here. It's the love and devotion of my husband. He puts his all into everything he does. He is endlessly kind and helpful as he aids fellow veterans in filing claims for injury or illness during their time in service.

I watch the door open, and he walks in, eyes and shoulders drooping, showing me he really doesn't have much left to give. "How was your day, HoneyBunny?" He asks.

"It was pretty much the same as yesterday. I'm sorry that I didn't get to clean the carpet today," I apologize.

"That's okay. It will get done when it gets done. Did you get to shower today?"

"No. I really didn't have the energy to do it today," I respond.

"Would you like me to help you after dinner?" He offers.

"I would really love that, Pumpkin. It's been a hot day, and the AC really didn't make a difference. I feel as though I've sweated through my pj's three times today."

I sit on the plastic shower chair, which sticks to my boney butt, and feel the weight of guilt start to suffocate me as he tenderly washes me. I envision his reaction to finding me unresponsive, gone from this world. His grief would be too much to bear, so he chooses to join me. It isn't romantic. It's tragic. I think of all the veterans he has yet to help. They wouldn't receive the same level of love and care from someone else. I decide then that each time that pill tempts me, I will muster the strength to walk away.

Still, there's nothing wrong with asking God to take me away. Right? I mean, if it's my time to go, then it's time to go. Somehow, in my mind, there's a distinct difference. There's no guilt attached, and my husband would accept it and stay. So, every night, as my head presses into the soft pillow underneath, I close my eyes and pray: *Dear God. Are you really there? Do you really hear me? I don't understand why I'm still here. This isn't a life. I am merely existing in varied states of anguish, suffering, sleep, and repeat. Please, please end this. Please set my soul free from this broken shell of a person I've become. Bring me home.*

My eyes spring open as a loud crashing sound from somewhere outside disturbs my sleep. I knew there'd be construction going on in the development at some point; I just didn't realize it would start today. My heart thumps in my chest from the flight/fight response pumping through my veins. As my heart rate normalizes and muscles unclench, the awareness of my pain level increases. My joints, bones, muscles—places I didn't know could hurt—are screaming, leaving no room for thoughts as my entire system is overwhelmed in agony. I search for a gap in the pain to have a moment of coherence. *What, if anything, can I do to get relief from my current state that doesn't involve the pain medication?* It's already too late. Taking the prescribed amount would be a drop in an empty well. I don't trust myself to know how much would be too much. Each breath I take seems to only amplify my torment, and tears uncontrollably run down my face.

A small thought occurs, and I latch onto it like a lifeline. *My iPod. I have music and meditations on my iPod.* I reach out to my bedside table, only to remember that I left it in the living room. Pulling myself together, I somehow make it to the living room and collapse onto the couch, feeling the springs pressing up underneath me, adding to my discomfort. Putting the earbuds in, I hit shuffle, as anything will do at this point. Familiar music begins to play, and I await the soothing voice I know will begin to speak. I'm trying to hear the voice above the noise of my pain screaming in my brain, but I can't seem to turn down the volume. Drowning in the noise of my pain, tears still falling, I finally surrender to what is; there's just no escaping the agony I'm in. Quietly, oh so quietly, I hear, *just breathe through it.*

Just breathe through it? What's that supposed to mean?

Just breathe through it.

Slowly, an awareness descended, and I spoke aloud to my body. "With each breath, I need you to release the pain. All of it. Physical, mental, emotional and spiritual. With each breath, we're going to release the pain." It feels as though I'm suspended in limbo, that time and space no longer exist. My only awareness is each breath and the release of all I've been holding on to. When reality returns, I hear the meditation still playing, and not an ounce of discomfort is left in my body! Knowing some Divine intervention just happened, I need to investigate. *What happened, and can I do it again?*

I look across the room to my bookcase, and my eyes fall upon the book: *The Masters and Their Retreats* by Mark L Prophet and Elizabeth Clare Prophet. I feel the urge to pick it up and just sit with it for a moment. *Okay, I know I've been angry at you guys, but apparently, I'm ready to listen.* Closing my eyes, I take a moment to get centered, and breathing into my heart chakra, I ask: *Who is present to get me through this?* Eyes still closed, I open the book to a random spot and flip a few pages till it feels right. I feel my finger drawn towards the bottom of the page, and I open my eyes. *You have got to be kidding me! Really? Jesus the Christ!* You must understand that my time in the Baptist church left a bad taste in my mouth. Having since embraced a more spiritual than religious path, I was more than ready to welcome Buddha, Krishna, Kwan Yin, or anyone other than Jesus.

Okay, Jesus, I guess I need to put all that baggage behind me and listen to what you have to say if you're here. Sitting in silence, eyes closed, I take another breath through my heart, willing myself to be open to receive. Slowly, a vision appears in my mind's eye. Jesus appears holding a little lamb in his arms, just like the picture that sits on my altar that my grandmother had given to me as a child. *You are so broken. You are so broken on so many levels. Would you just let me heal you? Stop trying to control what you don't understand. Just come to me every night, sleep in my arms, surrender, and let me heal you. I can not help you if you're trying to control everything, so please just surrender. Even if you have to say surrender till you're blue in the face, to break down those walls that you have built around your heart.* My heart breaks open in that moment, and all of the old, twisted words of the church flee from the love that is now being poured into me at a level I cannot comprehend. I now see Jesus for who he really is, always has been, and reply *YES*, with all of my being.

That night and every night going forward for the next year, regardless of how challenging of a day I had, I called upon Jesus, felt him wrap his arms around me as if I were that little lamb, and I surrendered. As the weeks turned to months, my strength and stamina grew. I felt less tired at the end of the day and found I was accomplishing more tasks. I started a daily ritual of honoring my body and loving it instead of being angry at it. It was as though I was picking up each of those broken pieces, tenderly loving them and, at times, redefining their purpose. Piece by piece, I rebuilt myself, with love being the glue holding each part of me in place, much like a Japanese Kintsugi vase.

On my more challenging days, I found soothing instrumental music or songs to boost my spirit. One that stayed with me most was Josh Groban's "You Are Loved." The key words that stayed in my head were, "Don't give up" and "You are loved." I needed to hear that, to keep putting one foot in front of the other when I'd rather just give in, especially when I started venturing out to do things such as food shopping. It was such a blow to my ego to be using an electric shopping cart. I could feel eyeballs following me. The stares felt like laser beams burning my skin as I made my way down each aisle. It was as if I could hear them wondering why such a young person needed to use something that was typically used by the elderly.

Slowly, more and more love started entering my life. Members of my spiritual family also stepped in to randomly offer reiki sessions, drop off prepared meals, or called just to check in. My local Veterans of Foreign Wars post, and one in New Jersey, where my in-laws live, held fundraisers to help with expenses as I was out of work and fighting to be put on disability at the urging of my doctor. I felt held, loved, and supported—not just by those physically around me but also by those in the upper vibrational realms where only love resides. Most importantly of all, I found love for myself.

Looking back now, I see there was purpose behind what I've gone through. The depth of understanding and compassion I have of what it is like to live with an autoimmune disease, the dark places depression and thoughts of suicide can take you, the toll that chemo takes on the body, and the mental and emotional rollercoaster that comes at you and takes you along without your consent.

My energy healing practice has deepened in ways I never imagined it could. My intuitive knowledge is more sensitive; I often pick up on things never discussed aloud, which helps me hone in and get at the core of what really needs healing. I now hold a deeper space for my clients in my heart, and they feel seen and heard. They look up to me, knowing I came out the other side, and that gives them hope. I'm still astounded that I've come so far and that I now offer transformational sacred pilgrimages to help others on their healing journey! I give my clients tips and tools I used that I was taught or shown by Jesus and my angels to use for themselves. In time, many of these clients reach a place of healing and then become my students, learning the healing modalities I used in their healing process. It empowers them to take their healing process into their own hands. It is then that I feel I've accomplished what I was sent here to do: empower them.

THE PRACTICE

Even though I use terms such as Angels, Jesus, and God, please know that you don't have to believe in them for this practice to assist you. All matter is energy vibrating at a certain frequency. Where thoughts go, energy flows. Negative thoughts/feelings are denser/lower in vibration and, over time, cause illness. Positive thoughts/feelings are lighter/higher in vibration and open the body to heal. Think of Angels, Jesus, and God as higher frequencies that you can tune into, like a radio station. Your intention is all that is needed.

Take a few moments and breathe into your heart chakra, located in the center of your chest. Try to feel as much of your body as you can. Your body has an awareness and will listen to you. Talk to your body. Ask that it surrender all pain that it is holding on to, even deep in the cells of your body.

Tune into the frequencies of your angels, ascended masters, guides, and the Divine Creator, and ask to be surrounded with love. Give yourself permission to feel this love. Allow this love to wrap around you like a thick, cozy blanket. Engage your breath so that with each breath, you surrender more and more. Allow the love of these Divine frequencies to fill every cell, every atom, with the light of that love.

Allow the color of the light to intuitively come to you. It may be different from day to day, depending on what you need most for your highest healing and highest good. Allow this light, this love, to expand within, through, and around you in all directions, filling up the room/home that you're in so you can continue to walk within that love.

Ask your guardian angel to seal this love and light that's around you. Ask for their help in integrating this love into your body to heal what is needed with grace and ease. Give thanks to all who aided and assisted. Thank your body for surrendering and allowing itself to receive the love that it needs to heal. Again, your intention is all that is needed.

To get a free download of this guided meditation, go to https://www.lightuponthelotus.com/resources.html

Kimberly Barrett has two decades of experience helping people heal. She receives wisdom from angels, ascended masters, and spirit guides and draws heavily on Violet Ray energies.

Kimberly practices and is certified to teach the Melchizedek Method, Magnified Healing, Integrated Energy Therapy (IET), Karuna Reiki, 5th Dimensional Bodywork, and various crystal therapies. She is certified to practice Spiritual Coaching, Brain SOULutions, Bars (Access Consciousness), Shamanism, and Tong Ren. Kimberly melds the lightness and mysticism of fairies with the intensity of the violet flame.

She is a big believer in the healing power of nature and has been known to whisper to flowers and trees and hear their guidance. Some even say with her pointed ears, she is an Elfin herself. Kimberly communicates with crystals and has developed innovative, new therapies from the wisdom stored in the stones.

If you find yourself in Manchester, New Hampshire, be sure to visit Kimberly's practice, Light Upon the Lotus.

Website https://www.lightuponthelotus.com/

Facebook https://www.facebook.com/KimberlyBarrett.earthsinger

Meet Up https://www.meetup.com/Light-Upon-the-Lotus/

CHAPTER 10

CHOOSING TO LOVE THE JUDGY ONE

FIND YOUR POWER IN THE MIRROR

Andrea Paquette, MSN, APRN, PNP-BC, APHN-BC

MY LOVE INITIATION

"You should have called; I was waiting," she says in her usual irritated tone, eyes averted.

"I'm sorry," I say lightly, trying to move on, feeling judged and hurt again.

My apology bounces off your concrete wall, not sorrowful enough for you. I'm done trying to break through. I love you anyway. I want so much for you that I fear you will never be able to imagine. I feel sad, wilted hope going nowhere. My path is not yours. You can keep your concrete wall. Your path is not mine. I love you anyway.

"You really should get the vaccine. How can you justify being so irresponsible?" she says with impatience and disbelief.

I respond, "There are a lot of problems with it. It doesn't feel safe to me."

Should I explain more or keep quiet? Will it turn into a fight?

I want to be close to you, but you won't let me in. I bounce off your concrete wall every time. I don't want to argue, so I'll let you have your rigid opinion. I feel sick and sad for you and for me.

Am I judging you for judging me? I don't know.

I know this pattern well. It was handed down from my mother, sitting in her recliner, emanating negativity and fear, keeping the world small. She found fault with everyone in private, smiling to their face in public. Poor Mom, she never did get it.

I see this in you when you say, "I don't like most people. People are awful." Sometimes, I hate to admit, I say that too. I feel restricted writing this because I don't want to offend you. I do love you so much despite the judgment and pessimism. I have such a wider worldview now. I didn't know there was so much love to be felt, so much more happiness, joy, and contentment to embrace. I truly want you to know it and feel it, too. I love you anyway.

Is there such a thing as too much self-awareness? I feel like I've been highly self-aware and intensely aware of others all my life. Phew! Exhausting!

In my childhood, I was known as the smart one, the quiet one, the obedient one—the good girl. As I matured and understood myself more, I realized I was a highly sensitive person. I am also empathic, very observant of others, and very careful to remove myself from hurtful people and situations. This way of being left me alone a lot. I developed a pattern of judging people's behavior, beliefs, and ideas to keep myself emotionally safe.

Why doesn't anybody like me?

Well, I really didn't like anybody either, finding fault, tuning into their negative, difficult parts only. I made my own prison cell.

Light bulb moment: *Oh, I carry judgment in me, and that's why I hate it in you!*

Ugh! It feels so true. I feel it all the way through my body, like contaminated water. You are my mirror, lesson, and wake-up call. Protecting my sensitive heart restricts me—insulates me from possible hurt. My heart is in a lockbox.

Whoa! Judgment really does keep us isolated.

Being highly sensitive and empathic, I feel you, and I feel me, all the time. How can I accept love as it comes, not flowing and easy, but glitchy and awkward? How can I give love to difficult, rigid people? How do you flow like a river, easily and gracefully around the rocks? Your judgment of me jars my nerves and makes me want to run and hide, avoid you. I can't imagine calling out this behavior. I hate conflict! Breathe and breathe again. I love you anyway. Stay, don't run.

This sounds hard!

Well, I can work with myself easier than trying to change you. There's one good thing!

This practice of loving others without conditions is new to me if you consider ten years of working on it new. Extending love and peace in disagreements. Finding and remembering what there is to love about that person, even when you have to walk away. It's hard! How can I practice non-resistance? How can I allow you to be you without judgment? I'd love to be able to let things flow, have easy conversations, and make quick compromises. Can we find ease and grace even when we rub against each other? A kayak stuck on a rock always comes loose with more water flow.

Hmm, does that work for relationships?

Can I love you even when you hurt me?

I've been in a deeply unconscious pattern of protecting myself from emotional wounding since I was a young child. It turns out that blaming and trying to change other people is not the way to freedom. Neither is running away, which I did a few times. I had to learn to love myself fully. No more self-judgment or self-criticism. I had to have my own back, do my own work, and feel into my power, strength, and confidence.

Oh it's my journey, my personal growth. I'm responsible for my happiness and well-being. Yikes!

I get irritated and judgy with others who have the same characteristics I don't like in myself, such as changing plans at the last minute, being late, being disorganized, being unprepared, not getting work done, and not following through on commitments, to name a few. When I pay attention to that mirror, things become clear. I'm steered directly toward where I need to give myself some leeway, forgiveness, and grace.

Geez, where is my compassion for myself?

It's been a lifetime of cutting out negativity (I was voted class pessimist in high school. Nice, huh?). I committed to refocusing on my positive attributes to start believing I was lovable. I ended up finding a pretty awesome person. Once I shined the light on my true, loving, capable self, I knew in my bones, gut, and mind that I deserved kindness and I was capable of protecting myself without shrinking.

I started by using my talent of self-awareness to notice where, how, and when I judged people. I always thought my way of thinking and behaving was right—*follow the rules, help others, and don't bother people.* I silently, or sometimes sarcastically, judged anyone who dared to step outside these lines. Pretty strict lines. I felt the restriction in my body, tight muscles, shallow breathing, and constant vigilance. I remember thinking my college roommates were way out of line in each of their own ways. Secretly, I envied their bravery and freedom, but I judged them nonetheless. And I wondered why I had no friends! It took me 30 more years to go from noticing to purposefully working on shifting my outlook.

THE PRACTICE

FIND YOUR POWER IN THE MIRROR

Being wary of others keeps your world small and scary. Lots of self-awareness and introspection are needed as you turn the tables and look at yourself rather than others. Noticing patterns of thinking, such as how quick you are to categorize, assume, and judge. Noticing how you do this to yourself and others. Noticing how this habit has developed for self-protection. Then, writing about what you notice is a powerful way to bring thoughts through your body out onto paper. As you read your thoughts back to yourself, you can clearly see and feel what needs to shift.

How do I judge others? In my thoughts with a know-it-all attitude? Out loud with condemning comments or helpful/unwanted advice? Ick!

If these patterns started when you were a child, you may also feel helpless at the mercy of unkind people. You may label yourself as introverted, highly sensitive, and/or empathic. These are not weaknesses. When you understand yourself better, you will feel into your unique skills. You will know how to use them wisely for your own enjoyment and the benefit of others. A balanced feeling of empowerment will rise in you.

Your commitment to viewing yourself with compassion and patience is pivotal as you practice breaking old patterns of thinking. The following practice will help you stay on track and stay aware and mindful of your programmed thoughts. You'll discover your view of others and yourself becomes wider, more flexible, more forgiving, and even more curious. The effects will ripple out into all your relationships. With this practice, your world will look new and shiny, I promise. Compromises are easier. Asking for what you need and want is easier. Forgiveness comes more quickly. You'll breathe easier.

Be like the kayak in the flowing river; keep paddling around the rocks!

DAILY PRACTICE

Listen to yourself for the use of the word should. It was a clue for me to show me when I was in judgment.

Notice any negative comments or thoughts you have about other people or yourself.

Practice extending grace instead. Allow yourself and others to be human with all of our flaws.

Get neutral. Practice a relaxed, neutral tone. Offer your own opinion and ideas without trying to convince the other person.

Try silence. Not everything needs a response. Let the river flow without contributing to the turbulence.

Notice your emotional and physical states by tuning into your body. Where do I feel this emotion in my body? Do what you can to take care of yourself. Do I need to breathe, move, or go outside? What would feel good, calming, or stabilizing? I like dancing, stretching, getting out in the sun, and walking in the woods.

Forgive your slip-ups quickly. Allow yourself to be human!

NIGHTLY PRACTICE

Calm your nervous system with a breathing practice. I use pranayama breathwork (in through your nose, out through your mouth). Notice peace wash over you, your mind slowing down, your body relaxing.

Find your gratitude for the love and abundance present in your life now. Judgment comes from a lack mentality. Reverse your view to focus on every little thing in your day that makes you happy, content, or grateful—that yummy cup of coffee, a smile from a friend, your home, your children.

Journal what went well each day. Compliment yourself on your successes, even the small ones: "I was able to be patient and calm for 5 minutes with the one who talks about and judges others, and I walked away without guilt."

Journal what you are grateful for. Notice what a rich life you have already. You just need to dive into it fully. All your relationships are blessings. All your accomplishments and contributions to your family, your work, your community, and the world are extraordinary.

Now, when I witness judging from others, I get quiet and breathe.

Can I find my compassion and stay? Or do I need to excuse myself?

Do I have the bandwidth today to challenge them on their views, or just state my view?

Most of the time, I feel myself happily floating through my day. My mind has been trained to focus on what's going well. I can access compassion and gratitude easily. My emotions are on an even keel. I flow like the river around and over the rocks. I expect the rocks; they are a natural part of the river. When you adopt this peaceful approach to life, you attract more peace. You can enjoy the people in your life and form deeper, more meaningful relationships. Then you'll feel true human love, messy and glitchy and wonderful! The best part is that judgy, negative, reactive people simmer down around you, or they just don't show up in your life anymore. Really, you'll see!

If you resonate with the chapter and are longing to dive deeper into this healing work, I invite you to take a look at my book, *Lovable.* I wrote it for women like you, who are ready to heal their emotional wounds and become the leader of their lives, living and loving as their true selves. You can find *Lovable* on my website: https://andreapaquettenp.com/order-my-book

Andrea Paquette, MSN, APRN, PNP-BC, APHN-BC

Andrea Paquette is a Pediatric Nurse Practitioner, Holistic Nurse Practitioner, Life Coach, professional speaker, and author. Her mission is to elevate balanced feminine energy in the world by helping women heal their chronic emotional health issues. Andrea's work shines a light on hidden childhood wounding that is a major cause of chronic emotional instability.

Women who have been on a path of personal development and/ or spiritual growth but have stalled out or keep spiraling backward will benefit from working with Andrea. She helps them uncover stubborn subconscious beliefs that may be holding them back, caused by childhood emotional wounding.

Currently, in her private practice, she treats emotional health issues in women and children using a holistic approach, meaning the mental, physical, emotional, and spiritual parts of the self are all considered. Andrea's treatment methods include breathwork, mindfulness, specific meditations, several types of journaling, and communication skills. Most importantly, she provides a sincerely caring, supportive, and safe space.

Over her 35-year career as a nurse practitioner, Andrea has worked in primary and specialty care practices, home healthcare, and private practice. She has developed several programs and presentations on child health topics; her passion is women's and children's emotional health. Andrea also enjoys teaching and speaking to community groups about women's personal development, parenting, and child emotional health.

On her website, Andrea offers private coaching sessions along with her other services: author of her book Lovable, feature writer, guest speaker or podcast guest. Andrea lives in Manchester, NH, and has two grown children she adores. In her free time, you will find Andrea at a yoga studio, on a beach, or eating delicious food.

Links:

Coaching:

https://andreapaquettenp.com/

Counseling:

https://www.choicescounseling-nh.com/andrea-paquette-pnp-bc.html

Lovable Book:

https://andreapaquettenp.com/order-my-book

Facebook:

https://www.facebook.com/andreapaquettellc

Instagram:

https://www.instagram.com/womantowoman_lifecoaching/

LinkedIn:

https://www.linkedin.com/in/andrea-paquette-msn-aprn-pnp-bc-aphn-bc-08b50822/

Women's Wellness Exchange:

https://www.womenswellnessxchange.com/new-hampshire/services-products/woman-to-woman-coaching-andrea-paquette-llc

American Holistic Nurses Credentialing Center:

https://www.ahncc.org/certificants-in-action/cia-overview/cia-business/

CHAPTER 11

THIS LITTLE LIGHT I AM

I AM GOING TO LET IT SHINE

Deborah Olson

MY LOVE INITIATION

I set the alarm for 2:00 AM. We had just arrived at the hotel. I ordered a quick bite from room service, took a long hot shower, and lay down for a brief 40-minute sleep before my alarm startled me awake.

Yup, the bus is leaving at 2:15. Rise and shine, Buttercup!

This was the day I had been awaiting. I was returning to the Great Pyramid.

Oh, the Queen's Chamber; that was so supportive yet empowering. It filled me with that snuggle-up, warm, cozy, fuzzy blanket feeling and gave me wings to dive deep for that inner love. It whispered: *Open, open, dear one. The strength you seek comes from the nectar of love within your open heart.*

I remember it like it was yesterday. The overflowing with love feeling, as I climbed on up, up, to the King's chamber, where I gently slid into the King's sarcophagus. The moment was mystical and life-changing. These were the memories that brought me back to Egypt. It had been five years, five life-changing years. I had been here for over two weeks, but this was the moment for which I waited.

Beep. Beep. Beep.

The alarm startles me. As I awaken, to my surprise, everything is screaming inside of me.

No. No. Don't go!

Despite the message, I pull myself together. This feeling of fear and anxiety is not what I expected. I try a sip of the cappuccino that was delivered less than two hours before. Yet my body is having none of it. *Only small sips of water this morning.*

It's time to go. I'm having a hard time moving forward as I climb into the bus that will take us to the pyramid site just a few minutes away from the hotel. This is the awaited moment.

Why am I in turmoil? Nauseous?

I try to drink a little more water. The bus arrives. There is a rush of excitement from the others as we finally climb down in the darkness and walk slowly toward the Great Pyramid.

I should have stayed home in my hotel room. I should never have come!

As I put my hand on the first great stone to start my ascent, I notice my palm is cold and sweaty. My whole body has a sheen of sweat. My nerves and anxiety are rocketing.

This should be exciting. I am light. I am surrendering. I am here!

My body moves forward. My legs are like jelly. People around lend me a hand as I climb up the huge, uneven rock steps to the pyramid's entrance. It's all so familiar—the entrance carved out through the pyramid and the curved walkway area before we bend down and start climbing through the upward shaft, leading us first to the Queen's Chamber and eventually up to the King's Chamber.

I'm number fourteen. We each have a number, and we enter the pyramid in that order. This is a love initiation of unity. We each have a particular task to do, supporting the whole. We each contribute our own unique, beautiful light. As we allow ourselves to fill to full capacity, we overflow— sharing with our brothers and sisters, we come together as one.

I know this. I teach this. I don't want to let anyone down. I don't wanna let myself down, yet over the past 20 years, I have learned to listen to my body. This morning, so far, it has sent up red flag after red flag and cold sweats!

We start heading up the shaft, each bent down in a squat, climbing slowly through the pyramid one after the other. Up, up, up we climb. When

I need to, I stop for a breath, and I know those behind me are grateful for the chance to take a break. I try to stay in my light, which seems to get stronger the higher we climb, yet I notice my legs shaking and my hands sweating on the wooden rails that line the wall beside me.

I focus, putting one foot in front of the other. Up, up, we climb. Near the Queen's Chamber, there is an open space. I can see it ahead.

We will be standing up soon. Oh my gosh, it will feel so good to stand up straight, so expansive!

However, when I get to this opening and finally stand up, the walls begin to slowly close in around me. I'm silently crying, tears streaming down my face. My breathing is shallow as I walk into the Queen's Chamber, touching the walls. I will myself to slow it down with each breath.

Slowly, slowly, just breathe slowly. Rekindle the light within.

Yet again, there are fire station alarm bells going off in my head.

Alarms are blaring inside of me. I'm visibly shaking. I'm picking up thoughts of others and from others, even other times around the world. These are not mine, bubbles of fear, fighting war images ancient and modern. This is a full-body experience. I'm queasy now; there is not much air movement with so many people in this chamber. My shirt is sticking to my body.

The next bubble of awareness is exuberant, happy, joyful, and ready for the mission of being light. As quickly as it appears, it bursts. Other bubbles of fear appear.

Is it safe to be in this pyramid? It's like I'm reacting to headlines. What if the pyramids are bombed, and war is at hand? Are we safe?

Anyone who knows me knows this is not my thought process. I normally turn my light on in the dark space inside and breathe angel light and grace with intent for all involved. I breathe deep, slow, and steady with the intention of planting peace within myself and allowing it to blossom out to others. Usually, I live in the moment. I'm a grace-be-with-you type of person, and then move on.

Here in the Queen's Chamber, I'm desperately trying to stay in the moment. I'm breathing; I'm trying to be of service to myself and others. Normally, I just turn on my light, call in the angels, and my fear vanishes. But this is like walking into a dark room.

Oh my gosh, oh my gosh! Are there any light switches in this big empty room? No, I must turn my light on. I must go inward, but it's not happening here!

Everything is banging up against me on the inside. I reached out to our leaders—Julianne and John. I trust them on a foundational level, and I have this with so very few.

I tell Julianne, "I need to leave; I can't stay here," yet she seems to already know.

This is our group love initiation. I do not want to miss it, yet I am being strongly guided to leave. Compassionately, she asks if I can hold on for a few more minutes.

John sees my distress, saying, "Do what your body can do; listen to your body."

John is my sergeant. We've walked this journey before, and I trust him. I feel affirmed, but even with this confirmation, I'm left wondering.

If I unzip my pocketbook, can I puke in it? And am I going to regret not going on to the King's Chamber this time?

As the walls of the small chamber continue closing in on me, Julianne walks into the closet-like space, and the room appears to illuminate. I see beyond, before, beneath, above. I'm frozen in place, bombarded by light shapes and number codes.

I know this feeling. I should understand it. Oh my gosh, my body is responding.

Yes, the walls are moving; yes, the chamber is multi-chambered, aspects of life, worlds, oh my, I am rambling.

I can hear the vibrations of the stones moving; I can feel it in my system. In reality, I know there is not a stone moving. The pyramids are completely safe. They have been here for thousands of years.

Yet, the red fire bell is still clanging. I look around at all the people.

Bless you, bless you all, but get me out of here right now. I need to be out of here!

The inspector is waiting to help me out. I follow him slowly to the shaft that leads back down. Here, I turn around and get into the squat position and back down the shaft. Down, down, down I go, my body shaking. Again, I notice my wet hands slide down the wooden railing. I'm so confused. At this point, I'm a hot freaking mess. I don't know what's going on. It takes forever to reach the entry, and yet here I am, down in just seconds. I sit next to our guide.

"Debbie, are you here?" he asks, rubbing and tapping my hand. "Are you okay? You are okay, yes?"

I say nothing, but I want to say, *I'm not here, I'm not here, I do not know where I am, but I'm okay.*

At that moment, I just breathe, and he holds space for me there just to breathe and slow it down.

After a bit, he asks if I would like to sit outside in the fresh air. I get up slowly, and he guides me through the pyramid opening. Guards are sitting by the entrance, and one stands to offer me a seat. It's still dark, but I notice they're carrying guns.

Just breathe, Deb, just breathe. They are not only guarding the monuments, but they are also protecting us. Just breathe. Everything is okay.

I sit down on a huge stone at the entrance to the Great Pyramid of Giza. There is a slight breeze of air on my skin. My entire system starts to recalibrate. It feels like I have been in a very hot room and now step outside in wintertime. It takes my breath away, yet I notice everything falls into place.

I know there's a reason I'm here, why number fourteen is sitting at the entrance of the pyramid rather than in the King's Chamber. We all have a part to play. Thy will, not mine, be done. We each must step forward in our own light and share it with the rest of the group. This is our love initiation. It brings us all together as one and oneness in the light. It's now time for me to share my light, to do my part, no matter where I am.

As I sit here on this giant stone, still high up, at the opening of the Great Pyramid of Giza, I rest easily in the presence of the guards. I take a few minutes, as I often do, to breathe in the light of the angels.

Angels, please merge your light with mine. Guide and protect me.

I submerge myself, the pyramid, this sacred land, and all the people inside and out in this unique beam of sparkling, luminous light. I see people and things everywhere connected by light. In this unity of light, a sense of oneness surrounds us.

I sit for a few moments in the cool night air, quietly being the light I am. I close my eyes and offer love to the angels, and I breathe in the light that they share. I allow it to fill every fiber of my being until I'm overflowing with light.

Softly, I feel I'm being drawn back inside the pyramid. The light of the others calls to my light to be with them as one. I very carefully stand, thank the guards, and move slowly through the carved-out path to the base of the shaft that leads upward.

Breathing slowly,

I love you

I allow myself to expand my own light.

Above me in the King's Chamber, the others are standing in their unique lights. In the mysterious way of the Divine, in this love initiation, our lights merge.

In this moment, I feel a sense of profound belonging and alignment. It's a homecoming of the soul, not just within the pyramid's walls but within the vast universe of interconnected souls.

Our journey through the pyramid has deepened our connection, and I carry this newfound unity within me as a guiding light for the path ahead. It is a reminder that love can unite us all "as one."

All offer blessings, and all are blessed, experiencing this love initiation in unity as one. I am home!

THE PRACTICE

The energy of the angels always feels like home to me. Years ago, I learned a profound technique from Julianne to connect with the energy of angels through Integrated Energy Therapy® called Heartlinks. It's a technique I continue to use today and love to share with others.

No attunement is needed to connect with the angelic realm, just a heartfelt request. It's a foundational exercise and brings in an immediate sense of safety, love, and compassion. This is a wonderful practice to become familiar with working with light.

Lean into the energy of the angels, and you may learn the language of your soul. The angels continue to work with me and share other light practices like the "Atom Exercise." Who knows what they will teach you?

This is my version of the heartlink practice called "Bubble Up!"

- Bring your awareness to your heart and breathe.

- Breathe as though you can breathe right through your heart, activating the heart chakra.

- Notice something you are grateful for. It can be anything. Something little or something big.

- Whatever it is, love it! Be so grateful for it. When you're grateful, the heart opens.

- From this place of heart-opening, offer a prayer of gratitude to your higher power and angelic realm. This opens the heart even further.

- Imagine, feel, sense, or perceive yourself sending a golden cord from your heart up through your throat, third eye, and crown, to what may feel like the far reaches of the universe, and connect to the heart of your guardian angel.

- Start by sending your love and gratitude up this golden heartlink saying, "Thank you, angels, for coming when I call."

- Visualize your heart like a cup, a chalice, or a fountain as you open your heart and receive the magnified love your angel sends back down to you.

- Allow your heart to fill to overflowing. Sit in the overflowing energy for one to five minutes.

- Become an observer and watch where this energy goes in your body, chakras, and aura.

- Allow it to fill the aura until you see yourself in a bubble of light!

- I like to use this practice and "bubble up" morning, noon, and night or whenever I need a little extra light.

- I ask my higher power and angel guardian to guide, direct, surround, and protect me in my bubble of light. What is your heartfelt request? What do you need? How would you like to work with the angels?

Deborah Olson — Intuitive Coach, Energetic Healer, and Medium.

Deborah has been internationally trained in Egypt, India, Peru, Ireland, and England. For over 17 years now, she has been immersed in angelic light, working with energy. She is an energetic healer, Law of Attraction leader, intuitive coach, medium, Reiki master, Integrated Energy Therapy master instructor, a practitioner of mindfulness meditation, Emotional Freedom Technique, Theta Healing, Shamanic Journeying, Egyptian Activation Alchemy, and a Transformational Travel Guide.

She blends psychic mediumship with intuitive healing. In a session with Deborah, she receives a stream of information through pictures, feelings, and soul-infused messages. She enjoys being a voice for Spirit and assisting clients in learning the language of their own souls. Sessions always end with an Intuitive Healing Blessing.

Deborah truly shines when she is teaching! If you'd like to learn how to activate your angelic heartlink using an automatic activation technique, share angelic energy with another, or study an angelic hands-on energy modality, come learn Integrated Energy Therapy®. She'd love to be your guide.

Deborah's happy place is in the kitchen. She likes to ask, "What if you could create your life like a chef creates a holiday meal? If you could create your life any way you desire, would it be comfort food, sweet and salty, savory, or a bit of spice? Each morning when you wake, it's a blank menu. So, too, in life!

Creating recipes in the kitchen is one of Deborah's passions. When she's not with clients or students, you can find her visiting small farm stands, growing herbs in her garden, or creating healthy teas and juices.

Connect with Deborah Olson:

Email: Deborahhume7@gmail.com

CHAPTER 12

DIS-EASE AS THE DOORWAY TO LOVE

THE GIFTS OF CANCER

Judi Raiff

MY LOVE INITIATION

For over sixty years, I lived in fear, not confidence; this changed in an instant.

I cowered, determined not to cry, in the corner of the school's gravel, fenced-in playground as the quietly whispered taunts came at me. "Look at her; she looks like a poodle; what is that on your head, a bird's nest?" The dirty, smelly third-grade boys laughed uncontrollably at my discomfort. It was the 1960s, and adults did not spend time outside of the classrooms monitoring the playground. For me, relief came when the school bell rang, and we filed, single file and silent, into the boxy, white-walled classrooms with multiplication tables and grammar lesson posters. There, I could be the smart one and show them all up.

I was the oldest of four in our house and the only girl. I grew up, the quiet, insecure child, in the shadow of the stillborn boy born two years before me and my three younger, louder, active brothers. I was adored and doted on by my grandfather; he was the person who taught me what unconditional love felt like. His death, when I was eight, moved the already painfully insecure girl even more into herself. Tears streamed down my face when I learned, only recently, that he was nonverbal from a stroke by the time I was born and never actually uttered the words "I love you" out loud to me, though I know I heard them from him regularly. His love was evident in every action: apple slices with sugar when I was sick, walks to the corner store where I was allowed to pick out candy from the penny candy counter, and visits to his friends' businesses on Saturday mornings.

Life moved on, as it does. My little girl self with great grades hit middle school and had a group of friends; puberty hit, and so did my learning issues. As I entered high school, I was a quiet, insecure, straight-A student who could no longer keep up. Every struggle created more doubt, my belief in myself plummeted, and my coping method was to remove myself from the group of "smart," good kids and gravitate to those who were into drinking, drugs, and trouble. I look back and realize how much I felt I did not belong anywhere.

My home life, where I had way too many responsibilities for a teenager, was disintegrating. My weekend mornings began with my yelling: "Get up, you are going to be late for hockey practice," as I dragged my brothers out of the house at 6 a.m. as my parents slept in. While my friends were hanging out at the local burger place or had part-time jobs, I was expected to be in the house babysitting my mother. Her anxiety and my father's agoraphobia limited our life as we never left the town we lived in, and their fighting, which had always been a constant, was escalating.

After a rough start at college, filled with ups and downs, a major health issue, and academic failure, I landed somewhat on my feet. That looked like moving to a state university and getting high all the time to try to negate the talk in my head. *You are not good enough to be here. You are not as smart as everyone else. You are a waste of space.*

Along with that was the guilt. *I should be home taking care of my mother. She is my responsibility. I have left my brothers to handle it.* Then I met Neil. For the first time, I felt loved and cared for and that someone had my back and would stand with me and for me. He was also the first person I dated that my family approved of. We married with visions of two-point-five children and white picket fences. There was security but no passion in our relationship. As an aside, I know now that he filled a need in me that saved me from the life I was heading into. One of living in a town where I would never feel good enough and would never have removed myself from the constant needs of my mother.

We divorced fifteen years and two children later. In a notebook, I poured out my anger at him and at myself for not being strong enough, good enough, or willing to put in the work. I found a therapist who helped me move beyond my anger at myself for not ending the marriage earlier and allowing yet another person to control my future. I threw myself into being a good mother, sometimes at the expense of my own well-being. I'm forever grateful Neil and I resolved our issues and became the friends we were meant to be before he passed away from leukemia twelve years later.

I started my own spiritual journey after my divorce, taking classes and going to workshops every summer when I had a week off from parenting. I took baby steps but was never able to get the *you are not good enough* voices out of my head. To say I was fearful of making any type of mistake would be an understatement. I bowed out of conversations and social events for fear of saying or doing the wrong thing that would allow people to see my "not good enough." I plugged along, putting on a great show to the outside world and internally, never, ever seeing any good in myself and definitely not allowing anything positive to penetrate.

Somewhere along the way, a tiny flicker of light entered my soul; after years of soul sisters telling me what a good coach I was or people telling me I was funny, I started to let just a little bit in. In my early spiritual training, I learned to pray, not that I always believed or trusted it would make a difference. I was an expert in not recognizing the changes in myself.

I continued to take a mish-mosh of classes, meditation, shamanic journeying, Laugh Yoga, Reiki, intuition, and mediumship and started to build a foundation to keep me safe and to protect the little girl in me who continued to be afraid. During a shamanic journey, on my first ever international flight, I met a spiritual guide I named Grandmother Ayahuasca, not because of any plant ceremony but because of a picture I was given that looks just like her surrounded by ayahuasca plants. She shows up at the times I need her most.

In June of 2021, I received the call that women dread, "We are concerned about something we see on your mammogram and need you to come in for some additional testing." As I drove to the mammogram center, shaking from head to toe, the ABS braking system on my car failed. In an instant, my concern changed from the possibility of cancer to getting myself to a safe place and getting the car to stop. The universe had a very strange sense of humor that day.

I had an MRI where Grandmother Ayahuasca climbed into the MRI tube and held me while I sobbed in physical pain through the entire procedure. I went numb through all the testing over the next month and a half and, like an ostrich, kept my head firmly in the sand to try and block out the fear. The voice in my head was brutal. *This is nothing. It can't be cancer. What about my kids? They can't lose a second parent. I can't leave them now. God would not be that cruel.*

Then something changed; I don't know exactly when or how, or if it was delusional on my part, but I started to believe this was just a blip in the road. As I had so many times before, I stopped feeling and just went into action mode. It was the only way I could keep the fear that appeared as an internal shaking in check.

I advocated for myself before my second lumpectomy like I did during my first procedure, which should've been an easy day surgery. It became complicated because the medical staff didn't take my concerns about sleep apnea seriously. All through this, I was numb; I did not cry or feel. I shared this with only a few people I trusted. I asked for prayers and to be put in prayer circles. I recognized there were lessons for me to learn: to allow myself to be vulnerable, ask for help, and to accept it when offered.

I'm very blessed. My second lumpectomy removed all the cancer cells, not without its own complications. I woke totally covered in sweat and in a fog to the surgeon on the bed yelling: "Get me a syringe and a bucket. Judi, this is going to hurt." I had started to bleed internally and ended up back in the operating room. Grandmother Ayahuasca, standing guard next to the surgeon, was the last thing I saw as I was wheeled back into the operating room.

I recognized this was a do-or-die moment, thank goodness not literally, but clearly a time for me to make changes. I reached out to folks and actually asked for help. To say I was surprised by the response would be an understatement. I cry as I write this as it has finally pierced my walls, and I now know how many people really do care about me. Through all of this, I still had the scared child inside, quivering with fear and doubt that she wouldn't do it right.

Six weeks later, I started radiation treatments. The cancer was found very early and didn't require chemo. One fear that popped up continually was that I'd lose my hair. My hair—a source of distress and frustration for me since my second-grade experience—was not going anywhere.

In January 2022, the surgeon and oncologist pronounced me cancer-free.

During my cancer journey, I learned many lessons. A few I share with you here.

I knew I wouldn't retain anything the doctor said if I was stressed, so it was important for me to have everything in one place. I started a soft-covered notebook to keep track of everything. I also decided early on: *When I'm five years cancer-free, I'll burn this book.* Come join me for the fire on September 8, 2026, five years from the date they removed the cancer from my body!

I reached out at the beginning of my journey to two trusted cancer survivors and asked them one question: "What are the three things I should know?"

They basically had the same three answers.

1. Ask for anti-anxiety meds; even if you do not take them, have them on hand.
2. Your doctors are your partners; if they don't act that way, find a new doctor.
3. You should not do this alone; ask for help.

I thought I could do the first one easily. Number two shouldn't be a problem, but number three was a challenge to even think about.

Take baby steps; who do you trust will be there for you? Think about how you interact with the people in your life. Do they tell you what to do? Do they ask for your opinion? Will they be there for you emotionally or just physically? Do they have similar beliefs as you? What type of support do you think you will need? Each person and each situation is different.

I asked my daughter to come take notes at each of the doctor's visits until I felt strong enough to do it myself.

Reach out to others. I'm a talker, but realized I wasn't up for telling the story over and over. I emailed the people I knew would support me, asking for their patience if I didn't return calls, and screened every phone call I received.

Talk to a trusted friend or two. Ask them to just let you talk. Getting out all your thoughts, even if you think they are crazy, gets them out of your body. You may surprise yourself and maybe come to a conclusion or two about your life.

There were many things I learned along the way that I wish I knew at the beginning of my cancer journey. You can find them all here: https://judiraiff.com/resources

As happy as I was to be cancer-free, there was still a piece of me that held onto all the childhood fear and doubt. *Can I put myself out in the world? Do I have anything of value to offer others? Who will pay ME to help them?* I stumbled back and forth in my mind, from a confident knowing I was on the right path to, more often, *I'm not good enough to do this.*

The cancer did not take away my curly hair. For years, I had twice-a-week battles with a blow dryer and a round brush, along with having my hair chemically straightened every three months. For the first time in my life, as I prepared for a trip in the summer of 2023, which I knew in my gut would be life-changing, I decided to embrace my curls.

I took my second-ever international trip, a collaborative writing trip, a sacred pilgrimage that would lead to a most amazing experience for me. In a writing workshop, we were given a prompt. I don't even remember the prompt. I found myself writing, "What would my life look like if my first reaction to every situation was confidence, not fear?" My life shifted in an instant.

I held this close and repeated it many times on the trip and since. The terrified seven-year-old was able to breathe, and the adult me took over. As we approached the boat at the start of the journey, I saw the steep stone steps and the two-foot-wide wooden ramp with a rope railing, and the always-present terrified seven-year-old in me stopped me in my tracks. I needed help crossing the ramp and getting on the boat. I was sure I'd have severe rope burns by the end of the trip if I could even get on and off the boat for the day trips. On one of the last days of the trip, we went by water shuttle, and the only way to the waiting buses was to cross an eight-inch ramp with only a hand to support me. I took a breath, and with no fear, knowing and believing others would support me, I crossed the ramp.

I went from a scared seven-year-old to an insecure teen to an even more insecure young woman to a divorced, single mom, to a cancer survivor, to a curly-haired independent woman who loves herself and feels all the love in her life and is ready to take on the next adventure in my life. I now stand in courage, confidence, and a deep knowing that if I could find myself and the courage to love myself in an instant and "cross the ramp," so can you. I will stand with you and for you in faith, hope, courage, belief, and love.

THE PRACTICE

I offer you these easy first steps on a life-changing journey that can lead to instantaneous change when you least expect it.

Get yourself outside, put your feet in the grass. Ground yourself. This is something I want to encourage everyone to do. Imagine you have roots growing out of the bottom of your feet deep into the Earth. Allow yourself to feel the Earth's energy pulsating up into your body. This was a technique I've used along the way in my own healing journey. Feel the energy as it moves up your body to the top of your head. Allow the top of your head to open to the energy of the sun and sky. Feel the sun's energy come in through the top of your head. Imagine the two rays of energy from the Earth and the sun running up and down your body, healing, clearing, cleaning, and energizing you. If you would like to listen to and follow this process, you can find it here: http://www.judiraiff.com/resources.

Meditate every day. Meditation or focused breathing can take on many forms. For those beginners whose immediate reaction is *I cannot clear my mind; my brain won't stop:* Close your eyes, take a few deep breaths, in through the nose and out through the mouth. Try a guided meditation where you have to concentrate on listening and visualizing what is being said. Or simply set a two-minute timer and just breathe; stay at two minutes for a few days. Then add a minute. Make slow and steady increases. Find a favorite instrumental piece of music to listen to as you breathe. You'll find it gets easier the more you practice. If closing your eyes makes you uncomfortable, find a focal point; it can be anything. My favorite one as I was starting my practice was an electrical outlet. I imagined it had a face and was looking back at me. You can find an easy beginner's guided meditation here: http://www.judiraiff.com/resources.

Write it out. A journal can be a simple spiral notebook or a beautifully bound book. Choose what calls to you. Use the writing instrument that feels good in your hand. This is for you and no one else. Don't worry about grammar, punctuation, or even if it is legible. This is for your eyes only. Get it out of your mind and body.

Play around with these tools. There is no right or wrong way, choose one, if it doesn't feel right, pick another. I believe in you and know change can happen in an instant.

Judi Raiff is a mother, healer, and spiritual life coach who opened to her life's purpose and journey upon becoming a single mom at 40. She has a diverse range of skills and experiences and has overcome numerous challenges and adversities. With her unique blend of expertise as a Director of Human Resources, Shamanic practitioner, Integrated Energy Therapy practitioner, and spiritual life coach, she assists individuals in tapping into their inner wisdom and connecting with their true selves.

Born and raised in Massachusetts, Judi was the oldest child of four in a family with parents with depression and anxiety issues. This dysfunction shaped her into a resilient and compassionate individual committed to helping others find their own strength and resilience. One of Judi's greatest joys was becoming a mom and knowing she could raise her children to be strong, caring, resilient adults. She draws inspiration from her own journey, challenges, and triumphs to help others realize their true potential and achieve spiritual fulfillment.

A cancer diagnosis in 2021 was a pivotal turning point in her personal growth and healing, with many lessons learned.

Judi began her spiritual journey after seeing Iyanla Vanzant on the Oprah show in 1996. Listening to her intuition, she took a five-day workshop with Iyanla and the staff of Inner Visions Institute for Spiritual Development at the Omega Institute in Rhinebeck, New York. She continues her spiritual development and education with many classes in various modalities with a variety of teachers, each bringing a different strength and skill to life.

Judi's diverse experiences and skills make her a valuable resource for individuals seeking guidance, looking for the next steps in their own personal growth, and supporting them through life's challenges.

Connect with Judi:

On her website: www.judiraiff.com

On Instagram:@judiraiff

Email: Judi@judiraiff.com

CHAPTER 13

THE QUEST FOR JOY AFTER LOSS

WHAT TO DO WHEN EVERYTHING FALLS APART

Tiffany McBride, LCPC, RMT, ORDM

MY LOVE INITIATION

I did not want my friend to die, but I certainly didn't want her to suffer any longer. Susan already endured so much. She was like a sister to me, and her presence was profoundly significant.

I have to go. I have to be there for Susan.

The thought weighed heavily on my mind as I wrestled with the emotions that surged through me.

Can I really do this? Can I really say goodbye?

I picked up the phone with trembling hands and dialed Mary's number. Her voice greeted me, "Hey Mary, can I go with you to see Susan tomorrow?"

Mary explained the situation with a heavy heart. "The doctor says she can't go to hospice unless she isn't on her ventilator anymore. So the doctor tried to take her off the ventilator today, and he thinks she will pass away within hours. I was going to ask Susan tomorrow if she was ready to go since you and I will be there."

"If she can breathe without the ventilator, she'll be moved to hospice?" I inquired, trying to grasp the gravity of the situation.

"Yeah, but then the fungus-eating infection will fill her organs and slowly kill her, and I don't want her to suffer like I witnessed others did in the ICU in Texas."

My heart ached and I whispered, "I don't want her to suffer like that."

Mary's voice was somber, "Maybe she will pass while we are there tomorrow. Let's hope for the best. I'll see you at ten tomorrow morning." As I hung up the phone, tears welled up in my eyes.

Susan had a rare heart defect and, at forty-two years old, was lucky to be alive. Her prognosis, however, was bleak, with only a few years to live. She had to travel to a hospital in Texas for the needed treatment, and there was a glimmer of hope that she could continue to live a good life.

I remembered how Susan and I met in 2013 at an intuition class, instantly connecting with her vibrant energy. We crossed paths in the yoga and spiritual community, and I had the privilege of coaching her. Susan attended my spiritual classes, drum circles, and Halloween parties, always spreading love and kindness to everyone.

At one of my parties, I heard a sultry voice from behind. "Well, hello." I turned around, and Susan was in a red wig and a suit, dressed as Scully from The X-Files.

I laughed, "What a great costume. It suits you just right."

"Why, thank you," Susan said confidently. Susan had such a great sense of humor and always made me laugh.

Susan grappled with depression and loneliness. Losing her parents at a young age was challenging for her. She struggled to feel included until she joined the sisterhood. Mary, who became like my older sister, extended the same warmth and care to Susan. We celebrated holidays and Sundays together, enjoying our shared laughter and witty banter. Our connection deepened through our shared interests in spooky and witchy things.

The surgery partially succeeded, fixing Susan's heart but bringing about further complications that challenged her health. Susan's condition fluctuated in the following months. She relied on a ventilator to breathe, which also came with complications. She died and was resurrected many times, and we waited for the next disaster. She couldn't eat or drink and was sustained through a feeding tube. Her life became confined to a hospital bed for four months. Her body became frail and thin, limited to hospital gowns and socks.

Mary, who became her caregiver, did everything she could to uplift Susan's spirits. Susan, who was on the autism spectrum, struggled to comprehend the complexities of the medical situation. As Susan's condition deteriorated, Mary needed to find a way to bring her back to Illinois from Texas. It was costly and arduous, with insurance and the medical system often failing them.

The following morning, I woke up with a heavy heart, my eyes swollen from crying. I joined Mary and Tonya, and together we drove to see Susan in Chicago. As we made the journey, I visualized a peaceful end for Susan, a departure marked by serenity and love.

Upon arriving, we were joined by a fourth soul sister who came to support Susan in her final hours.

I overheard Mary converse with Susan, "I talked with the doctor, and he says that once you are off your ventilator, you could go within hours. They can make you very comfortable with drugs and make it peaceful and painless for you. What do you think about doing that today since we are all here?"

Susan, gasping and gargling due to the ventilator in her throat, responded with a clear and resolute: "YES! Yes! I'm ready. I can't stand this thing anymore. I'm ready to go on my next greatest adventure." She winked, "I'm going to haunt the fuck out of all of you. Now, can I have my Coke slushy and chocolate shake?" We all busted out with laughter and tears.

We granted her every wish and pampered her like royalty. Even though Susan was not allowed to eat with her ventilator, I offered her a cold, creamy chocolate milkshake alternating with a slushy Coke and ice water. She was so desperate for the coldness of the ice and the taste of sweetness on her tongue that she eagerly drank as if she had been in a desert for an eternity. She was thirsty from the absence of joy and lack of life she had experienced over the past few months, and my heart ached for her.

No one should have to suffer like this. Why was this happening to such a kind-hearted person?

Susan hummed with pleasure as she gulped down her cold drinks and chewed the ice.

"This is better than sex!" She exclaimed, treasuring every sip and bite. I chuckled at her enthusiasm.

"I will take you to Egypt with me and write about you in my next chapter. I want to honor you and your life," I told Susan, warm drops welling in my eyes. I couldn't hold back the tears, and she looked at me with compassion and love as I wept for her.

This isn't fair. This isn't Fair! This can't be happening.

My tears turned into rage, and as the steaming drops fell, the fire rose from my belly into my chest. Shortly after, I was numb. I felt so much pain, sorrow, and anger in a short time. My mind was lifted out of my body watching the scene play out as if it were a distant movie.

I watched the other ladies wipe down Susan's dry, cracked feet, applying lotion and slipping on her fuzzy socks. I held Susan's hand and watched her face light up with pleasure. We sang to her as they prepared to unhook the ventilator. She became calm and comforted in hearing her favorite band, the Indigo Girls. Then she drifted into a comatose state as the drugs took effect, and her breathing became labored.

Moments went by, but time stood still. The room's energy felt heavy; the smell of death overcame me, and an awkward silence filled the room. The energy began to shift, and I felt a tingling in my chest and upper back. I sensed Susan's spirit departing as her breathing slowed, and her presence seemed to exist in the spaces between breaths. The four of us surrounded her with love and light, ensuring she didn't feel alone in her final moments.

At the moment just before her last breath, the light flickered and then turned off abruptly, leaving us in the dark. Mary stared at me, sharing a moment of astonishment. I automatically knew it was Susan, and I faintly smiled back at Mary. Susan was giving us a sign that she would indeed haunt us, a playful farewell.

Then she took her last breath, and her soul departed from this earthly plane.

Her hand that I held became cold and stiff. An overwhelming emptiness filled my heart as I sat there with her lifeless body. The loss left a void, and I realized that everything would change, and life would be forever altered.

It was hard confronting my grief, as I felt responsible for holding those who grieved for Susan.

I'm the therapist and minister. I have to be strong for others as they struggle.

Eventually, though, I was forced to confront the hollow abyss of my own grief.

Life is so short, I often pondered; *why have I allowed myself to live in suffering for so long? I feel trapped in a box, enslaved to the fear that ties me to it. I need to find my way out of this prison cell and find freedom.*

I lived in depression and trauma most of my life and dedicated twenty years to healing myself and others. The grief around Susan's death only highlighted my own suffering. This gift motivated me to find a way out of the suffering and into finding moments of joy.

I was close to my fortieth birthday, and I yearned for a different way of living, one filled with simple joy. But I wondered, "How can one find joy amid grief?" I posed this question to one of my spiritual teachers, tormented by the guilt of seeking joy while others suffered.

Amidst the heavy weight of grief, I couldn't help but reflect on the profound lessons Susan's journey had imparted. As I navigated the raw emotions of her passing and the void left in her absence, I was drawn to finding joy in the sorrow.

The days following Susan's departure were a blur of condolences, arrangements, and shared tears with loved ones. It was a time when pain was palpable, and our hearts ached for the laughter and warmth we had lost. But Susan's parting words echoed in my mind, "I'm going to haunt the fuck out of all of you." Her playful and brave spirit planted a seed of understanding even in her final moments.

It was a reminder that joy could still find its place in our lives, even in the shadow of grief.

My teacher emphasized, "It isn't selfish to strive for happiness; it is a way to honor Susan's memory. She had been a source of joy and love for so many, and the best way to pay tribute to her is to carry that light forward."

The following month, I began my journey to Egypt, carrying a medicine bag of Susan's ashes. As I set on this journey to find joy among the sorrows, I slowly started to notice the small moments of beauty and serenity around me.

The vibrant colors of a sunset, the gentle touch of the breeze, the sun shining on my face, the sweat running down my spine, and the laughter of friends gathered for a meal all became reminders that life was meant to be lived with gratitude and joy, even in the face of sorrow.

I discovered the power of rituals and practices in the sacred temples and sites of Egypt and the healing power they held. This allowed me to cope with the grief as I found solace in releasing Susan's ashes into the dust and waters of these sacred healing places. Singing and breathing into these moments helped me to stay present, acknowledging the pain without becoming overwhelmed by it.

Over time, the heaviness of grief began to lift, revealing moments of peace and joy. I learned it was okay to smile, savor life's simple pleasures, and continue pursuing my dreams. Though marked by suffering, Susan's journey was a testament to resilience and the enduring power of kindness and love.

As I looked back on my journey with Susan, I understood that she gave me a precious gift—a reminder that joy was not only a destination but a companion for life's most challenging roads. Susan's memory became a beacon, guiding me toward a life filled with simple joy, even in the face of grief. I found solace in the idea that I was not leaving Susan behind but carrying her spirit with me, allowing it to inspire my pursuit of happiness. In honoring her memory, I discovered that the quest for joy was not a betrayal of my grief but a tribute to the resilience of the human spirit.

Susan's journey taught me that life was too short to waste in suffering. With her memory as my guide, I was determined to embrace joy, cherish every moment, and live with a profound appreciation for life's simple pleasures. It was a journey I knew Susan would be proud of, and her playful, haunting spirit would continue to remind me that joy could always be found in the darkest hours.

THE PRACTICE

Finding joy when your life is falling apart in grief can be a challenging and personal journey. While everyone's experiences are unique, here are some strategies and guidelines to help you navigate these difficult times.

For the complete list of 20 things you can do to navigate your grief, go to www.tiffany-mcbride.org/questforjoy.

ACKNOWLEDGE YOUR GRIEF

The first step to finding joy during grief is acknowledging and accepting your feelings. Grief is a natural response to loss, and giving yourself permission to grieve is essential. Understand that it's okay to feel a wide range of emotions, including sadness, anger, and confusion.

SEEK SUPPORT

Reach out to friends, family, or a support group. Sharing your grief with others who have experienced loss can provide comfort and understanding. Feel free to ask for help when you need it.

If your grief is overwhelming and persistent, seeking the guidance of a therapist or grief counselor can be beneficial. They can help you explore your emotions and provide coping strategies. For more info on how to find support or a therapist, go to https://www.tiffany-mcbride.org/howtofindhelp.

PRACTICE SELF-COMPASSION AND CARE

Be kind and patient with yourself. Grief is a complex process, and it's crucial not to rush or judge your emotions. Treat yourself with the same compassion you would offer a close friend. Take care of your physical and emotional well-being. Self-care routines, such as eating, movement, and sleep, can help build resilience and make it easier to find moments of joy.

CREATE RITUALS AND REMEMBRANCES

Establish meaningful rituals to honor the memory of the person you've lost. Light a candle, plant a tree, throw a party, or create a scrapbook with memories. These rituals can provide a sense of connection to the person you've lost. Embrace their positive qualities, values, and passions, and incorporate them into your life. By doing so, you keep their memory alive in a joyful way.

EXPRESS YOUR EMOTIONS

Find creative outlets for your emotions, such as journaling, art, or music. Singing or writing your own songs can be a way to express your feelings and experiences. You don't need to be a professional; it's about finding your voice. Incorporating art, music, and writing into your grief journey is a deeply personal process. Explore different methods and see what resonates with you. These creative practices can provide a means of self-expression, healing, and finding moments of joy as you navigate grief.

SPIRITUAL OUTLETS

If you have a spiritual or religious community, attending services, meetings, or gatherings can provide support and a sense of healing and belonging. Maybe you don't have a spiritual community, but connect with nature. Many find a spiritual connection in nature. Spend time outdoors, whether in a park, by the ocean, or in the mountains. The beauty of the natural world can be a source of spiritual solace.

GO TRAVEL

Travel can be a powerful means of finding joy after grief, offering healing, perspective, and new positive emotions. It allows for a refreshing scenery change, physically and mentally distracting you temporarily from your sorrow. Novel experiences, self-discovery, and encounters with nature contribute to personal growth and healing.

Visiting culturally or spiritually significant places can bring comfort. Travel also encourages mindfulness and reflection, and it can be a way to honor the memory of a loved one. However, it's important to remember that travel should not be an escape from grief but a tool for coping and healing. Grief may resurface during your travels, and self-compassion and self-awareness are vital throughout the journey.

PURSUE YOUR DREAMS!

Don't wait to live your dreams! The time is now, dream wildly and then go!

Embracing new beginnings and pursuing your dreams after losing a loved one can be a transformative and healing process, driven by a desire to honor their memory and find joy once more. This journey may bring unique challenges, as not everyone in your life may understand or support your changes. While it's natural to undergo a profound transformation in response to grief, some may express concerns about your decisions stemming from their suffering and fear of losing a familiar connection.

To navigate these dynamics, maintain open communication with your loved ones, explaining that pursuing dreams and personal growth is a way to celebrate your loved one's impact and embrace life. Setting healthy boundaries and surrounding yourself with supportive individuals who share your vision and values can provide crucial encouragement. Pursuing your dreams after grief is a deeply personal journey that can be a testament to your resilience and a way to continue your loved one's legacy, ultimately leading to a future filled with meaning and purpose.

Finding joy during grief is an ongoing and entirely personal process. There is no one-size-fits-all solution, but with time, patience, and self compassion, you can gradually reintroduce joy into your life while honoring your grief. Remember that seeking professional help and support is okay when needed, and don't rush yourself through the healing process.

Tiffany McBride is a Clinical Psychotherapist, Life Coach, Energy Master and Teacher, Birth and Death Doula, Ordained Shamanic Minister, Expressive Artist, and Author. Tiffany runs a private practice named Holistic Vibrations, LLC, utilizing holistic remedies and altered states of consciousness for those who struggle with trauma, addictions, women's issues, LGBTQAI+ support, and those seeking a deeper spiritual connection.

These holistic and altered states of consciousness modalities include Emotional Release Therapies (utilizing EMDR and Shamanic Breathwork), Expressive Arts Therapies, Energy Healing, Womb Healing/Doula Services, Sexual Health Education and Empowerment, Attachment Trauma Recovery, Internal Family Systems, Inner Child Healing, Codependency Recovery, Emotional Freedom Technique, Motivational Interviewing, Transitional Life Coaching, Spirituality, Breathwork, Hypnosis, Somatic Psychotherapy, and Psycho-education.

Tiffany is currently working on their Doctorate in Shamanic Psycho-Spiritual Studies and training to be a Yoga Teacher and a Clinical Hypnotherapist. Tiffany hopes to travel the world offering empowering and healing retreats and workshops in different countries. Tiffany is growing a Virtual Community and a Healing Arts Studio to help people access healing tools and resources more easily in order to heal from their traumas and enhance their lives and spirits. Virtual classes, workshops, online groups, reading material, and healing music coming soon! If you want to keep up with the latest events, please sign up for my newsletter at https://www.tiffany-mcbride.org/contact.

Tiffany loves to write, blog, paint, draw, create digital art, play the ukulele and guitar, sing, be in nature, take photographs, read, go to concerts, hang with friends, and learn more about psychology and history.

Stay connected with Tiffany on the following sites:

Website:

https://www.tiffany-mcbride.org

Egypt Journey Blog:

https://www.tiffany-mcbride.org/post/the-magic-of-egypt

Facebook:

https://www.facebook.com/profile.php?id=61552573784401

Instagram:

https://www.instagram.com/witchycrowwmn83

Susan's story and donation link:

https://www.caringbridge.org/visit/saving.susan.crowe

How to find a therapist/coach:

https://www.tiffany-mcbride.org/howtofindhelp

CHAPTER 14

MOVING TOWARDS WHOLENESS

AWAKENING TO THE POWER OF THE INNER HEALER

Jeffrey Warren

MY LOVE INITIATION

My love story hurts like Hell. I've got a secret I've never told anyone. I'm 29, and I'm in love with my best friend. He doesn't know, but I'm going to tell him tonight.

It's New Year's Eve, and I refuse to step into another year carrying the weight of this secret. My love has become sharp like wild roses. Twisting through my heart and lungs, their dark roots reach down into my guts. I love this man, and I can't suppress it any longer.

For the last three years, I've held these feelings hidden within the secret chamber of my heart, waiting for him to get sober. I didn't want to make his life more difficult. In the beginning, I did it out of compassion and care, as I wanted him to have as much stability as possible. He stayed sober as the years progressed, and in time, I realized my motivation in keeping this to myself shifted. I wasn't still afraid I would hurt him. I was afraid of being rejected.

He arrives as the sun sets beyond the trees. My apartment, an old castle, perched high on a snowy hill. It's January 1st, and today is the day. We step onto the stairs.

"Do you know what this is about?" I ask.

"I think so," he tells me, looking worried.

I am nervous as Hell. We enter my apartment and sit down together on the faded faux leather couch.

"Okay, Jack. I'm just gonna say it," I tell him.

I bite my lip gently, afraid the words won't come out, sweating, heart racing. I was too scared to say it but even more terrified to keep it to myself.

Years of hiding rushes to the surface, and in complete vulnerability, I hear myself admit, "Jack, I love you. I've loved you since the moment I first saw you, and I just want to be with you."

I thought I'd feel relieved, but I'm only more scared. I sat nervously, waiting for his response. I finally hear him say, "Jeffrey, I love you too. I've loved you since the moment I first saw you, but I can't."

My glass heart falls to the floor and shatters. I cried for days.

I force myself through work, doing the best I can. I manage a natural food store. I like my job, but these days, my friendly face is as fake as the leather I was just destroyed on. A buddy stops by the store one day and convinces me to join him at a group gathering—some psychic thing.

"We're all psychic," he says with enthusiasm.

"Yeah, sure we are," I respond a bit sarcastically.

Despite my apathy, I submit to the invitation. I never would've agreed if I had just begun a new romantic relationship. Everyone in attendance is nice enough, but it's not really my scene.

A few days later, that same friend tells me stories about a practice called shamanic journeying. It sounds unbelievable. I'm deeply intrigued by what he describes and am immediately hooked on the idea. I know this is something I have to explore. He gave me the name of the woman he studied with, Julianne Santini.

I found her website and discovered she's teaching the next journeying class in a couple of days. It's not possible to take a Saturday off on such short notice. My heart is screaming, calling out in desperation.

I have to get in touch with her! I have to meet her!

Saturday arrives, and I'm out back at work, feeling underwhelmed and disappointed, questioning all of my recent choices, when suddenly, it's as if a bell or an alarm goes off in my head. Something becomes awake and alive. Without thinking, I burst through the swinging double doors and charged to the front end of the store. A cashier is checking someone out, and there's another customer waiting in line. I jump onto the other register and wave the woman forward.

"I can help you over here. Do you have a rewards card?" I ask.

I tap her phone number into the keypad as everything in my life prepares to change. My finger strikes the enter key, and her name appears on the screen. It's Julianne Santini! My brain makes the connection, and I immediately recognize her face from the tiny photo I saw on her website.

Oh my god! It's her! She's here!

My mouth drops open, and for a moment, I can't speak. *I must look like an idiot.* Her eyes are wide and welcoming, with a subtle sparkle. My ability to think comes back online, and I introduce myself, hoping to appear normal and sane.

I began studying with her right away. I journey through mystical worlds and make contact with my own heart and healing. I'm amazed at the easy access I gain to the spiritual realms through her guidance. It feels like I've found my way back to a part of myself that was lost. It feels as though I've found my way home.

One day, at the close of our session, she asked, "Have you heard of Holotropic Breathwork?"

I was clueless.

"There may be something important there for you because of how you like to journey so deeply," she explained.

It takes a couple of months before I find my way into my first Holotropic Breathwork session. I don't know what I'm getting myself into, but I'm ready.

Holy shit!

My body drops from the safety of the soft carpet and sinks into the raw earth below. Adrenaline rushes through my spine. The surge forces me to catch myself from falling and disappearing into the floor forever. I return to the carpet. The pounding of my tender heart rattles the inside of my rib cage. The music is so loud I can barely hear myself think.

Okay, I'm still here. That was strange.

I take another deep breath. A subtle tremor awakens gently in my hand, slides up my arm, and disappears into my shoulder.

Should I move my hand? Should I lift my arm? What if I look stupid?

My self-doubt has arrived. I lay paralyzed on the floor, wrestling with my indecision. A recurring theme I know all too well in my life. I remember the woman leading the event said everything was allowed as long as I didn't intentionally hurt myself, the property, or someone else.

But what about this? Is this what I'm supposed to do? I just don't want to look stupid!

I remember her words from the intro talk. "Whatever is happening, do more of it. Make it bigger! Healing happens through intensification. Just go with whatever it is. Allow it. Breathe into it," she said.

I'm almost comforted and encouraged as I remember her words.

But what was that last part? What did she say?

Suspended in frustration, trying to remember, suddenly, her words strike me with the power of thunder.

"Breathe until you're surprised!" She had said.

That's it! Just let go!

My hand continues to shake gently. I stop worrying about what it means and how it looks. I stop trying to control every little thing, and I surrender.

I breathe deeper and faster, eliminating the pause between the inhale and the exhale. A buzzing sensation radiates from within me, moving down my arms and legs. My fingers tighten, cramping and curling over themselves. My body has become electric.

The vibration increases, and the movement gets bigger. My hand flails at the wrist as I breathe deeper into the body. My whole arm shakes violently in the air, no longer concerned with how it appears to the outside world. My shoulder shrugs as the movement gets bigger, energy amplifying. Each breath is like a gust of wind, rising and falling with great power. My heart pounds as the motion intensifies. Just a little more breath now. Deeper and faster and faster and deeper until suddenly, there is no sense of my body at all.

A warm energy fades gently into my awareness. It glows with strength and softness. I feel the presence of all of the mothers of India. They are calling to me. Cheering me on. Welcoming me forward. Whispering me into their world. Their arms outstretched, encouraging me to merge with them. I become the breath, and they breathe me in.

I am no longer me. I disappear into them as my heart swells in disbelief, with tears and with joy. I vanish into the cosmic embrace of her infinite love. Merging completely with her essence, I become the unbounded love of the divine mother.

I dissolve deeper and deeper. I become aware of a landscape as it flashes by. The glow is gone, and I'm moving quickly now. I'm moving faster and faster, my bare feet hardly touching the ground. I gain enough awareness to realize I'm sprinting through the streets of a marketplace.

No more than eight or nine years old, my youthful body leaping over stone steps. I am in India. I remember who my mother and father are in this life. They're gone now, but I remember who they were. My life is both hard and playful. I have to take care of my younger brother. We have to steal food to survive. I'm not proud, but I'll do anything to keep us alive.

One more leap through a doorway, and I land in the woods. I'm a young native boy running through the dense forest of early America. In a moment, I remember who I am and who my family is. I see a herd of deer running beside me, and I become them. I continue on four legs, picking up speed as I charge forward through the fading light of dusk.

The landscape shifts again, and I emerge in an open meadow. Standing still. Snow-capped mountains in the distance. Green and golden blades of grass stand tall in the warm light of the sun. Flowers grow wildly in the field. Butterflies and other small insects dance and play in the open air. Nothing but nature surrounds my slender frame. I am eight years old again. This time, a young blonde boy. Somewhere in Europe. Maybe Switzerland or Denmark. I'm not sure.

I step towards the gentle crest of the hill, and I see it sitting there, waiting for me in the distance of the shallow valley. My heart explodes gently, rippling deep with gratitude at the revival of this memory. This was my home. I haven't seen this place in a hundred years.

How is this possible?

Filled with wonder and curiosity, I run down the hill, remembering my mother's name in this lifetime. I remember her long, sandy brown hair, her soft, simple clothes, and the details of her face. Praying and hoping that she or anyone else will still be there, I enter the house. No one is home, but it all remains, just as I know it. The dark wooden cabinets and drawers are exactly where I remember them. The familiarity of the floor assures me that I've found my way home.

Waves of experiences come and go. Arriving and vanishing back to the place from which they were born. Each brings varying degrees of wonder and awe. I remember something the facilitator said before we started, "Once you're in the waves, it's time to come back home."

Laying on my back, I slowly became aware of the sound of the waves. Rolling in gently through the speaker system, encouraging me to come back to the place I call home.

I eventually make contact with the darkened room I'm lying in and slowly peel back the blindfold. A smile spreads across my face as I awaken. The facilitator crouches reservedly near my mat on the floor. She gets a little closer and enters my space with incredible skill so as not to startle me or interrupt my process. I lift my head to meet her eyes as we make contact for the first time in several hours. Her gentle gaze holds me with comfort and care.

Filled and overflowing with pure joy, my mouth opens, but no words will emerge. I laugh quietly as I begin to sit up, gently shaking my head from side to side in pleasant disbelief at what I've just been through.

She smiles with warmth and wisdom, leans in just a little bit closer, and says, "We're all just a few breaths away from a whole other world!"

That first Holotropic Breathwork session was one of the most incredible things I've ever experienced in my life. I knew from that moment that this type of work would become an important part of my own journey. I also knew I wanted to become a facilitator and support others in it as well.

Though the session was quite mystical on the mat, my ordinary world began opening in new ways as it integrated over time. It served as the catalyst for deep change I didn't even know I needed, and couldn't have coordinated better if I had tried.

It's been many years since that first session, and I've had countless experiences on the mat since then. Many have offered beautiful insights and openings, while others have forced me to face my darkest shadows and deepest pain.

Through this work, I'm learning how to embrace the full spectrum of the human experience with open arms. I'm learning how to stop dissecting and discarding all of the aspects of life that I declare are undesirable. I'm discovering there is great value in all experiences when I allow myself to be awake to their gifts. I can say with great honesty and clarity that no other body of work has enriched my life so much as Holotropic Breathwork has.

As I look back to the beginning of this chapter, I can now see how that first heartbreak ultimately led to my heart opening. I realized how present my inner healer was, guiding the entire process and bringing forward the experiences that were needed to create the most profound changes in my life.

This entire experience is my love initiation. It's an ongoing process and awakening that continues to unfold over time. Every day, I am gifted an opportunity to be initiated more deeply into the energy and experience of love. The truth is that my love story isn't over at all. In fact, it feels like it's just beginning.

THE PRACTICE

Holotropic Breathwork has many unique components that make it a rich, deep, and powerful experience. A supportive environment, along with well-trained, world-class facilitators, is what creates a safe space for our participants. While it's not safe or wise to attempt Holotropic Breathwork alone at home, I can offer you a powerful practice to help you awaken to your own inner healing wisdom. This practice is based on deep presence and allowing. If you're truly listening, it can help your inner healer to become powerfully awakened and activated.

1. Preparation

    Find a comfortable place where you can sit or lie down undisturbed. Set aside ten to 20 minutes to fully experience the practice. Allow about half of the time for the active practice and the other half for integration.

This can be done with or without music. If using music to support the experience, select one or two tracks that feel interesting and evocative, with some emotionality, preferably with no lyrics in any language you understand.

2. Practice

Play your music or set a timer and take ten slow, deep, gentle breaths. Breathe in through the nose and out the mouth. You don't have to try too hard. Simply inhale a little bit deeper, and on the exhale, just let it go. After ten breaths, relax and allow yourself to sink into the experience.

Try not to analyze or search for meaning. Simply allow whatever wants to come forward. What do you notice? Are there physical sensations? Vibrations, tingling, hot or cold? Does the body feel tight or spacious? Just observe and allow.

Is there an emotional quality? If so, allow the emotion to be present. Don't try to change it. Just let it be exactly as it is.

Is there a vision, color, or imagery? Perhaps you feel inspired to move your body in some gentle way. Whatever it is, just allow it.

Allow the process to continue until your music is over or the timer is up. Bring your awareness back to the room and make sure that you feel grounded and back in your body.

3. Integration

There are many ways to integrate an experience like this. Choose what feels right for you today.

You can write a few paragraphs in a journal about what you felt or observed, or perhaps it would feel more free to use art to express yourself non-verbally. You don't need to be an artist to enjoy this practice. Simply allow some splashes of color or other marks to be offered to your blank page as a representation and reminder of your experience. You could also spend a few minutes outside in nature. Connect with the world around you and see what additional insights may be there for you.

4. Final Invitation

I invite you to use this practice to connect with your inner healing wisdom and discover how just a few minutes of authentic personal presence can offer you powerful self-healing, meaningful insights, and beautiful gifts. May the journey serve you well.

Enjoy a guided version of the practice
at https://www.jeffreycharleswarren.com/awakening-breath

Jeffrey Warren is an artist, musician, and healer trained in more than 20 healing arts and spiritual traditions. He is wildly passionate about helping people awaken to their inner healing wisdom and highest potential.

His warm heart, humor, and passion for deep inner work make him an excellent facilitator, guide, and teacher. He is deeply committed to supporting his clients and students in their personal discovery, spiritual growth, and conscious evolution.

He is a GTT Certified Holotropic Breathwork Facilitator, Fire Walk Instructor, Ecstatic Dance Leader, Kundalini Yoga and meditation teacher, sound and energy healer, and shamanic practitioner.

Jeffrey offers personal healing sessions, dynamic workshops and retreats, sacred travel, and energy therapy training and certification across the United States and abroad. His online programs and courses offer students the opportunity to learn, heal, and awaken from absolutely anywhere in the world.

Jeffrey Warren is a New Hampshire native, a proud uncle to baby Grace, and enjoys time with his family on the East Coast between his travels. He spends his free time sipping espresso, lounging on the beach, playing electronic music, and chanting.

Connect with him on social media @jeffreycharleswarren and learn more about his work at https://www.jeffreycharleswarren.com

CHAPTER 15

SACRED SOBRIETY

THROUGH SPIRITUAL SABOTAGE AND ADDICTION TO ILLUMINED SOBER LIVING

Marion Noone

MY LOVE INITIATION

Please just stop breathing. Fuck. Every second hurts. My babies. I can't live without them.

I knew it was coming. The shakes set in. My plan was coming to fruition. I couldn't function without it. The spirits reached possession. There is a reason alcohol is termed "spirits." I'd be dead soon.

There I was, on the majestic Big Island of Hawaii, with my soulless stare and victim-hood championship medal draped around my neck, weighing me down like boulders tied to a corpse tossed out to sea. I physically ached for freedom from a lifetime poured with every liquor of human pain tastefully infused with shame and loneliness. It's the perfect cocktail for the suicidal drunk.

I sat alone in the jungle, 3,000 miles from everyone I loved and everything I had ever known, lifeless. Dead in every sense except the auto-programming my avatar set on repeat. Rainbows in my view obscured by tears and alcohol-infused sweat wept from my pores, tracing hauntingly down my skin.

Hawaii—a place most people pray for their entire lives to experience—was Hell to me. Every waking breath was painful. The pain felt as if every inhale was a stinging poison, and every exhale was a gut-curdling desperation to leave this earthly plain.

I made the conscious decision to unalive myself, and alcohol seemed the best solution. When a person experiences the loss and heartache I have, living loses its point. No mother should know the pain I endured—parental alienation, emotional abuse, and gaslighting to the end of no return. I didn't trust my reality anymore. I didn't trust anyone. Everything I thought to be true and real was a lie, and everything I ever loved was gone. It was five years of fighting. I was financially, emotionally, and spiritually shattered and riddled with relentless anxiety, PTSD, and depression.

I turned my cheek and began taking notice of the green sea turtles surrounding me in their off-trail lagoon. I watched each of them care for their needs with ease and an innate self-love. They sunned with pure hearts, grazed with intentional hunger, and nurtured one another without fear. Each was swimming freely without agenda in a perpetual baptism. I remembered a past version of myself when these actions were just as natural for my self-loving practices.

I miss her. Where did she go? What happened to her? How did I get here?

In Hawaii, the locals refer to the sea turtle as Honu and regard them as an Aumakua, a spirit animal guide. These sentient beings, in both native American and native Hawaiian cultures, are revered and symbolize creation and Mana (spiritual energy). I suddenly remembered these learnings and leaned into that creator's love. I heard my quiet yet persuasive inner voice whisper,

Get in!

I surrendered into the waters with a slow, mindful descent. As the icy water met my skin, shivers shot quickly up my spine, and my breath almost instantly came with greater ease. I sunk deeper into trust. The bite of the ice floated out of my awareness, and a sense of safety overcame the wholeness of me. My soul dropped back into my body as the weight of gravity and life were carried out to sea joyously on the backs of my reptilian friends. My very own Baptism and rebirth.

I left the womb waters with a renewed sense of clarity and a piggyback of strength. Without hesitation, I picked up the phone and called a friend who later became an angel on my path back home to me— Colin Aspin.

"I need help! I changed my mind. I don't want to die anymore."

"What! Where are you? Are you okay?"

"No, and I don't know how to explain to you how to find me. I have no energy to figure it out."

Words left me entirely after that. All I could do was sob, scream, and cry.

"I'm coming to find you."

Everything after that was a blur. Mr. Aspin miraculously found me out there, far off in the jungle. The next moment I can recall, I was sitting on his porch, watching him speak inaudible words on his phone. I could only make out the word Honu. My ears perked up. Someone recommended a man named John. John, he was the man to help me. John answered, and when he started speaking, I almost left my body. I couldn't believe what I heard.

"I am the owner of a local treatment center here called Honu House Hawaii."

Suddenly, I realized I was in the presence of a long-lost friend. This friend goes by many names, but for this chapter, I will call it "God." Let's jump back a few years of my lifetime. I'll explain how exactly I know this coincidence was no coincidence at all but instead a divine miracle.

It was 2016. I was pregnant with my fourth baby, attending a Christian workshop. I wanted to save my marriage and family. Minimally, I wanted to save myself and my children. It was clear my husband had no interest in taking ownership of his multiple family-destroying affairs. I was desperate, grasping at straws. I had three young children, one on the way, no money of my own, and nowhere to go.

Even though I'm not affiliated with any religions, I do love and respect them all. I go where the love is, and the Christians know a thing or two about love. The workshop was a prayer meditation to meet God or Jesus Christ.

The Pastor was great! He was well-spoken and energetic with a tasteful charisma. He was a bit younger than I expected, but his old soul made that easy to overlook. You could almost physically see his golden glow of love for his people and his Lord God. He guided us through the prayer meditation.

I don't remember his wording, but I remember entering with butterflies in my stomach, ready to meet Jesus or God or anyone divine. I needed love and support from something that wasn't human. I wanted the glow that Pastor had. I needed my creator.

In my meditation, a vision entered my inner sight. Tall grass swept the land, glimmering with the golden rays of the setting sun. A broad-shouldered oak tree poised cliffside like a wise observer in the near distance. The foreground grass whispered gently as the wind sweetly kissed it. I began to walk towards the wise oak, and white butterflies swept up from the ground like celebration confetti. I swear I heard them giggling. Caught by the wind, my celebratory companions formed a visible swirl aimed in the same direction as my gaze. I felt a gentle smile meet my lips, and an inhale soothed me with a warm hug. I met the oak and rested upon a patch of rich, forest-scented moss just under the kind shade offering bough. Wildflowers came into view now and then, and I felt a deep appreciation for their pop of color and excited dance. I heard birds off in the distance singing tunes of harmony. I noticed sparkles on the white-tipped waves riding the ocean down below. Peace, I felt peace.

The Pastor led us out of the meditation, and I carried the peaceful heart space over into reality. People began to share their excited experiences of how they met Jesus or God. Suddenly, my peaceful state left me, and my heart rate rose.

What? Does God not love me? Is it because I don't claim a religion? I love Jesus, why didn't he come?

I waited for the shares to end and room to clear out. I walked over to approach the Pastor.

"Sir, can I ask you a question?"

"Yes, ma'am, you can."

"Why didn't God or Jesus come to me?"

I explained my experience to him and how I felt. How perfect it was in every way except I wanted to meet them, and I didn't understand why I wasn't chosen.

You know how sometimes you meet certain people without cause, and they say or do something so profound it changes your entire life trajectory or outlook on the world? On this day, this Pastor did this for me.

"Have you ever been raped or beaten by a man?"

Shocked and slightly perturbed, I curiously replied, "I was molested and raped, why?"

"God nor Jesus would not show up to you in a way that would cause you fear or pain. Would you say seeing men scares you?"

"Sometimes, yes."

"Look for God and Jesus in the places and things that bring you the most peace and joy. Would you say this vision you saw is a place you would go to feel solace, peace, and love?"

"Definitely, Yes!"

"Then, sweet sister, you saw God today."

OH MY GOD (Duh! Pun intended haha)!

Explosions of lightbulbs in my head! God always has and still speaks to me through the Earth; I just wasn't listening.

Now that I've explained how this Honu coincidence is no coincidence at all and hopefully inspired some of you atheists out there, let's talk about why I wanted to die.

I could say it was because of all the human life pain. I could blame my rapists or my ex-husband. Shit, I could even pull the classic addict card and blame it all on my parents. Yes, the difficulties in one's life story contribute. Still, the absolute truth was that I didn't have my authenticity. I didn't even know who I was. This happens when you become a mother at 18. That led me to make the wrong choices in a partner and, subsequently, life in general. I chose a path and direction that did not align with my soul's purpose and divine mission. I was stifled, uninspired, directionless, loveless, purposeless, and Godless (so I thought).

Guess where I had to go to learn this? If you are in active addiction, sober, or a family member/loved one to an addict, I bet you can guess what I'm about to say.

Rock bottom.

A suicidal drunk in the jungle.

At this point, I'm sure one might be wondering how to find one's own authenticity. It was a long journey for me to discover this secret formula, which I will share in the practice section. I didn't have any resources or people present in my life that could guide me in this direction. When I lost everything, and my identity as wife and mother was stripped, I didn't even know what I liked to do or eat. My whole existence before this was being of service to the other. Initially, this was deeply painful. I spent many days and nights in a ball on the floor crying, feeling lost. I was husbandless, childless, and without identity. Prioritizing myself, nurturing myself, and learning myself was completely foreign.

I spent 90 days in the treatment center of Honu House. This is where I combined my baseline self-obtained knowledge with the knowledge of the experts I had access to in this healing chamber. I realized through inner-child work, internal family systems therapy, and EMDR, provided by various experts in these fields, that I had a lot of trauma to unpack and PTSD to unravel. Honu House is also where I learned the root of all addiction is trauma, and if that trauma goes unmet, the risk of relapse is much higher.

After graduation, I was hired as a manager at Honu House. At six months of sobriety, I took our clients on an adventure. I found myself in the same lagoon, floating with many sober friends in the local community. We shared our sobriety stories, and as I was sharing mine, a large Honu swam underneath me and grazed my legs with the tip of its shell—a precious high-five from God. During the early months of my sobriety journey, I was also divinely guided to attend a retreat on the Island of Kauai led by another angel on my path, Dr. Aurora Ariel, Ph.D. The message came through in a local email chain titled "The Oracle of Love, a pathway to your inner freedom."

I heard that quiet and persuasive whisper again.

Go!

I booked the retreat, and that is where my life path and purpose became clear. Shortly after the retreat, I joined Dr. Ariel's mystery school, sponsored by Mother Mary. I became a certified life coach in TheQuest 7 steps. This training took me deeper into the layers of the psyche. I went through all of my patterns and programs with a fine-toothed comb. This is a level of inner work you rarely see people practicing. The goal is to meet all shadow aspects of self and alchemize these traumatized parts of the psyche to one's illuminating gifts. I'm proud to say I can now offer these sessions to others and help them actualize into a fully authentic, illumined path and a divinely abundant life.

THE PRACTICE

Now, moving into the practice, let's explore the formula on how to begin to find the authentic self so one can start to heal and actualize one's fullest potential. The formula combines that quiet, persuasive whisper, which I have termed "The God Whisper," and finding where God is showing up for you.

Let's begin.

1. Find a quiet place and enter this space with a completely sober mind. Substances drown out the God Whisper. If you need help getting sober or asking for help, reach out to me in any of the ways listed in my contact section or read the letter to the addict below. Leave the phone behind and make sure you are alone. Ideally, you want to go where you find the most peace. For some, this is sitting in the car in a parking lot, and for others, it's a natural environment far off from the noise of the world. The location doesn't matter as long as you feel safe and peaceful.

2. Take off your armor. Realize this experience is just between you and God. There is no need to perform or be anything other than exactly what you are at this moment. Visualize yourself physically removing the imagined armor and putting it next to you. Don't worry; you can pick it up and return to life later. Just be here and know you are safe without it.

3. Take your left palm and place it under your left fourth rib or just below the nipple. This is where the Apex of the heart is. The strongest beat of the heart can be felt here. Next, take your right palm and place it at the bottom of the right ribcage. This is where the most lung expansion can be felt. It's essential to use your palms. The palms are known as "Earth Gates," where you can receive energy the most. Also, a pro tip: If you are ever feeling anxious or overwhelmed, placing the Earth Gates on the Earth can help calm you. The palms and soles of the feet are considered Earth Gates. If you're out in nature for this session, feel free to start your session this way. The more grounded and calm you are, the more effective this practice will be.

4. Allow your eyes to close, and for three to five minutes, notice the heartbeat in the left palm. Stay with your natural breath and just experience the sensation of your heartbeat. Say in your inner voice to the heart: *Thank you. Thank you, dear heart, for always being here for me.* Next, do the same practice for the same amount of time with the right palm, taking notice of the lift and lower of the ribcage. Speak words of love and thanks to the lungs for keeping you alive without thought or directive.

5. Bring your awareness to both the heartbeat and lungs. Staying still and quiet with your natural breath, ask with your inner voice *What is best for me?*

   Often, a person will hear answers, yet fear slips in and convinces one it can't be done. For instance, I heard my inner voice tell me to leave my husband two years before I built the courage. Do not feel pressured to make decisions; let this be a practice of listening.

6. Next, notice where God shows up in your life. Notice the places, people, and things where you feel most at peace and safe. Notice where you can be ultimately yourself. Write them down and set a goal to do as much of this as possible. If you think you don't have the time, make the time. This is quite literally life or death if you are an addict, and this will save you.

A note to the addict,

The immediate call to action is to go to an AA or NA meeting and get a sponsor. Download the application "Meeting Guide" on any smartphone device and find a meeting near you. Group support meetings are available everywhere on the globe, daily and sometimes hourly, depending on where you are. Drop your ego and go! The beauty is participation is not required. The only requirement is the desire to be sober. In these meetings, one will see individuals raising their hands and offering sponsorship. This one action will provide you with guidance, resources, a much-needed understanding, and a supportive and loving community. Good luck on your path to sacred sobriety, and as I stated before, reach out to me anytime.

Much love and aloha, dear reader. May you find the God whisper and follow it unapologetically.

Marion Noone is a certified Life Coach/ Counselor with TheQuest 7 steps, a program created by Dr. Aurora Ariel, PH.D. to equip the masses with at-home self-counseling tools and mental health mastery.

Marion's roots are in the deep south swamps of New Orleans, Louisiana. You'll often find her making herself at home in any available kitchen, whipping up soul food soothing the hearts and bellies of all who partake in her magical meals. An embodiment of the divine mother, love radiates from her center, touching all who cross her path.

A pioneer in her field, Marion has artfully mastered a unique combination of healing techniques encompassing art therapies, inner-child play, higher divine communications, and deeper layered trauma psyche work to facilitate illumined living for her clients. If someone were to witness Marion, she would be noticed as a magical fairy holding a grounding sovereign energy.

She is a certified Reiki practitioner as well as a 200 RYT Lifepower Yoga Instructor with eight years of experience teaching a variety of yoga practices.

In 2019, Marion was hand-selected as one of the top eight yogis in the nation to celebrate the Indian/American alliance, performing on stage at NRG Stadium in Houston, Texas, for the prime minister of India and 55,000 viewers. She is a best-selling author in the genres of self-actualization and trauma work.

A living starchild of varied gifts, she enjoys singing and painting the most. A student of all things Earthly, she spends most of her time with Gaia (Earth), contemplating the human experience. She advocates for sober living and is willing to assist any of her brothers and sisters on their road to personal freedom and recovery.

Contact Marion

Instagram- http://bit.ly/MarionInsta

Facebook- https://bit.ly/MarionFacebook

Email- noone.ascending@gmail.com

CHAPTER 16

SELF-MASTERY

COURAGEOUSLY LIVE AN AUTHENTIC LIFE

Diane Marie Gallant

*Loving ourselves through the process of owning our stories
is the bravest thing we will ever do.*

~ Brené Brown

MY LOVE INITIATION

My father's harshness disabled me for the majority of my life.

Growing up in a neighborhood filled with kids was a blast. I was a happy-go-lucky girl who loved playing outside with her friends. When I heard footsteps thumping across the lawn, I'd run outside to join in the fun. I enjoyed the freedom of these years. It was a time of innocence when dogs lived off-leash, and children ran free.

When temperatures dropped, and the air got crisp, I knew school would start soon! I couldn't wait to go back to see my friends and meet new teachers. Flipping through the pages of new textbooks piqued my curiosity. I liked studying, taking exams, and playing outside during recess. Sadly, my feelings for school would be replaced with dread.

Running all the way home from the bus stop, I eagerly waited for my father to come home from work. I couldn't wait to show him my first report card. After he settles into his recliner, I demand his attention.

With pride, I show Dad my grades. He glances at my hard-earned A's and says, "Why is there a C in math?" I suddenly feel like I was punched in the stomach, and I'm consumed by shame. I want to run away and hide. "You're staying in after school from now on and working on your homework." My father's anger frightens me. Stoically, I hold back the tears.

I feel sick to my stomach. Dad thinks I'm stupid and not trying hard enough.

My relationship with my father changed that day. I was now afraid of him. I didn't want his criticism or anger. I wanted his encouragement and support. A belief began to grow inside me: *I will never be good enough no matter how hard I try.*

It was impossible to live up to Dad's high expectations. I became habitually hard on myself. Low self-esteem and self-doubt were my constant companions. I feared making a decision and constantly asked others what they thought. Trapped in self-judgment, I couldn't stop my negative thinking. Dying felt like the only solution. *I wish I was never born.*

As I got older, I consciously made decisions that went against my well-being to punish myself. Frustration and hopelessness drove me here. I couldn't hurt my father, but I could hurt myself. By the time I was sixteen, I ran with the wrong crowd and put myself in dangerous situations like reckless driving. Inside, I screamed for help. I was depressed, anxious, and insecure.

College allowed me the opportunity to escape my hometown life. I was determined to excel in my major and improve myself. I studied the dictionary, softened my local accent, and began taking care of my body by exercising and eating healthy food. Even though I was making improvements in my life, I continued to feel ashamed of who I was. I became an extrovert to hide my insecurity.

Two years after graduating from college, I married. Eventually, I left my medical sales career to stay home and raise children while my husband worked. Being a mother brought deep joy and fulfillment. My life looked great from the outside. I had everything—a husband, two great kids, a nice home, vacations. But inside, I suffered.

My input didn't seem to matter to my husband. I felt increasingly frustrated. I voiced my opinion to no avail. I reached my boiling point and knew I needed help, but I didn't know where to turn.

I saw myself as a finch in a Victorian gilded cage with a chain and shackle around one leg. I could hop outside the cage, but I wasn't allowed to fly. My cage was the comfortable lifestyle I enjoyed. The cost was my personal growth. My heart broke at this realization.

This is no way to live! I want to grow closer to my husband and grow personally, too. I want more out of life! I ignored the desperate pleas of my soul.

By the time my children left the home, I had developed persistent heart palpitations increasing in both duration and frequency. I also had debilitating migraines that put me in bed for days. I was emotionally numb, had brain fog, and was exhausted. I disconnected from myself, and the world felt unreal.

I made an appointment to see my doctor to talk about my escalating symptoms. Dr. Segil said, "Your symptoms could be the result of chronic stress. What is your number one stressor?" I hesitate, then honestly answer, "My marriage."

Listening with concern, he warns me, "If you don't get your stress under control, the consequences to your long-term health could be devastating."

Panic rises through me, and I'm instantly light-headed. The familiar prickles of stress pierce my skin.

I don't want my life shortened. I want to live a long and healthy life. I want to pursue my dreams of sacred travel and building a vibrant coaching and energy-healing practice!

My carefully constructed world comes crashing down around me. I fall apart. Fear, worry, and anxiety engulf me.

Dr. Segil writes the name of a physician friend on a piece of paper and slides it towards me, saying, "Call Susan." I ask, "Why her?" With a knowing smile, he repeats, "Just call her. You'll see."

When I met Susan for the first time, we had an instant connection. She was more than a physician and counselor to me. She was my spiritual advisor, confidant, anchor, and savior. She helped me through the most difficult time in my life. She was exactly who I needed.

It was a relief to have someone safe to talk with. For the first time in ages, I felt myself relax. The weight of the world slipped off my shoulders, and the tightness in my neck began to loosen.

I confide, "I long to talk with my husband to resolve our issues, but he turns his back on me and walks away. I get the feeling he wants me to keep my complaints to myself. I wish he would go to marriage counseling, but he says it's too expensive and won't help." Even though it feels good to talk with Susan, it doesn't remove the feeling of emptiness.

Susan takes this all in and asks me, "How do you want to spend the next twenty years of your life?" I immediately have an image of an old woman dying alone in a hospital bed, reflecting on her life thinking: *I'm not ready to die yet. I didn't follow my dreams. I want to live my life over.* I don't want this fate for my life! This is a huge wake-up call.

After a few months of intensive counseling, I came to terms with my worst fears. *My marriage is not a partnership and can't be fixed by just me alone.*

The thought of divorcing throws me into panic, and my mind starts racing. I'm gripped by fear and consumed by stress.

How will I ever get the courage to ask for a divorce? What if my kids never speak to me again? How will I take care of myself? I'm tired of having fear control me. I want this emotional turmoil to stop!

Susan's voice calls me back into my body, "You can do this. You can advocate for yourself. I will be with you every step of the way." And she was.

Breathwork was key in helping me to calm my nerves and reduce my stress. It allowed me to drop into a state of heightened awareness. From this place of inner knowing, I heard the wisdom speak within me. Practicing mindfulness helped me to see the action I needed to take if I was ever going to be happy.

I began to see how my early childhood trauma stunted my personal growth by creating sabotaging beliefs such as *I will never be good enough.* Over time, I discovered there were even more debilitating beliefs attacking me. *I can't take care of myself. If someone takes care of me, then I won't have to worry about providing for myself all on my own. Life won't be as scary.* This voice was coming from my inner child. My mature woman was nowhere to be seen.

The security of marriage offered the protection my inner child was seeking. I disempowered myself by handing my income over to my husband.

I didn't know how much it cost to live, how to budget expenses, or how to take care of the home and property. Then, this realization hit me: *I allowed this to happen. I hurt myself by not claiming power early in the relationship.*

For years, I blamed my husband and father for my unhappiness. I hadn't realized how tired the retelling of these worn-out stories was making me. When I finally owned my part of the story, I stopped my finger-pointing habit at these two men. This brought a huge sense of relief and created emotional space in my life. I felt lighter inside.

It took me a full year to gain the courage to tell my husband I was ending the marriage. When I finally told him, I learned something important: The world did not blow up, the ground did not fall out from beneath my feet, and I was still standing—tall and confident. *I stepped into my power!*

Since that day, I've learned to manage money, take care of my home, maintain my property, and keep the car running, all while caring for my aging parents. And I discovered I like taking care of myself! It's not as hard as I thought it would be!

I've thrown my stake into the ground and claimed my power.

I'm committed to reducing stress in my life as much as possible so I'll live a long and healthy life. If I need support, I know how to reach out.

Knowing how to be the director of my life, I prioritize my needs and advocate for myself as needed. I listen to my inner guidance and follow its sage advice. My goal is to live in this place of self-mastery every day. I no longer make my decisions from a place of fear. I live authentically—because I know who I am and what I want in life.

Exhilaration builds inside me as I feel my heart quicken. I am in joy, brimming with happiness of who I am—and who I'm becoming. I am expanding. And I am at peace.

My heart sings with the knowledge I'm exactly where I want to be!

THE PRACTICE

Join me in a contemplation experience to connect with your inner wisdom. This is a place of discovery. Your intuition will speak to you, guiding you toward the highest and best version of yourself.

Things you need:

- Quiet place to meditate. This can be in a favorite room or outside in nature.
- Comfortable chair or yoga mat. Gather any props you need, including a blanket and pillow if desired.
- Mirror.
- Pen.
- Journal, composition notebook (or a notepad app for recording).
- Timer (if needed).
- Glass of water.
- Twenty minutes of uninterrupted time. Set a boundary and let others know not to disturb you. This is your time to practice self-care.
- Choose a concern to contemplate or resolve.

RESET USING BREATH

Take three deep cleansing breaths to clear and reset your body.

Breathe deep into your belly and exhale all the air inside your lungs with an audible sigh. Ahhhhh. Release the tension from your body. Feel your body relax as your mind begins to slow down. Can you feel calmness filling your body? Enjoy this energetic reset.

Take a few more breaths if needed. Follow your inner guidance. Your body knows exactly what it needs.

GET COMFORTABLE

Settle into a comfortable seated or lying position. When you are ready to begin the practice, close your eyes. You may also do the practice with a soft gaze or eyes open.

Begin focusing on your breath. Only you and your breath exist at this moment in time. If your mind wanders, this is perfectly normal. Simply return your focus to the sound and natural rhythm of your breath.

Do you feel deep relaxation moving throughout your body? Enjoy these calming sensations. Allow any stress, concerns, or worries to wash away.

GO WITHIN

Ask yourself, "Is there anything that is throwing me off energetically today? Is there a concern or situation that needs my attention?"

Allow your intuition to speak to you. Simply breathe and wait. Just be. Let your awareness expand.

Zoom out from your worries or concerns so you can see a broader perspective. This will help you to move away from the emotion inside your story so you can see more clearly. Stay relaxed. Continue to breathe.

Be open to receiving messages. They may come in the form of thoughts, images, or words. Do not analyze or judge your experience. Just witness it and allow the magic of awareness to show you growth opportunities and possible solutions.

COME BACK

Slowly come back to the room. Wiggle your toes, stretch your body, and yawn. Gently open your eyes if they are closed. If you are lying down, sit in a chair.

Take a drink of water.

Offer gratitude for this experience.

FLOW WRITE

Flow writing bypasses the conscious mind and allows your inner guidance to come through. This type of writing is also known as automatic writing or spirit writing. When you write, don't pause to read or make corrections. This will interrupt your intuitive writing process. Keep writing.

Open your journal or composition notebook (or notepad app). To prepare, take three breaths and connect with your heart. Begin writing.

Let your pen move across the page, bypassing your thinking mind. Write from your heart. If your mind is blank, write anyway. Eventually, you may feel yourself shift into flow writing. Continue writing until either the flow stops or slows down. If you have a time limitation, set a timer before you begin.

Take a moment to reflect on your writing experience. Did you receive any guidance or support about the concern or situation you contemplated? If you did, allow the wisdom received to be instilled in your heart, soul, and mind.

Your flow writing is sacred because it comes from the source of your higher wisdom. It is often meant for you—only. Keep it safeguarded and close to your heart. If you do choose to share what you received, do so with great discretion. You don't want to dilute or tarnish the gift you received.

Tip: I like to write "aw" (automatic writing) on the margins of my journal when I flow write so I know the writing came from my inner wisdom.

MIRROR WORK

Look into the mirror and notice every exquisite detail of yourself. Your eye color, the shape of your nose, your hair, your complexion, everything! Look at yourself with acceptance, awe, and gratitude for the beautiful person that you are. Gaze deeply into your eyes and tell yourself, "I love you." Then give yourself a big hug.

It is now time to lovingly and mindfully go on with your day. Return to this experience throughout the day to invite in the calm and wisdom it brought.

For an audio version of this experience, go to:

https://dianemariegallant.com/contemplation-practice-session/

Your authentic, true self wants to spend time with you. It wants you to fully own every aspect of yourself and vibrantly engage with life. Living in alignment with your core essence brings you to a place of power. You know how to prioritize yourself and practice self-care while taking steps toward the life you want.

You are the central character in your life. Let yourself grow to your full potential and shine brightly!

Take my hand, and I will guide you to this powerful place. Your empowered and authentic life awaits. Self-mastery is within reach!

Diane Marie Gallant, Intuitive Life Coach, Reiki Master and Melchizedek Method Master, Death Doula, and Workshop Facilitator.

Diane lives in New Hampshire and works with individuals and groups both in-person and online. She offers intuitive life coaching with energy healing support and teaches classes and workshops.

She has been healing and empowering clients for over 15 years. She is a certified Master/Teacher in three Reiki lineages and the Melchizedek Method, and working toward certifications in Positive Intelligence® and Doulagivers Institute™. Her BS degree in Medical Technology contributes to her broad knowledge base in health and wellness. Trauma research is an area of self-study and expertise.

Diane is a highly intuitive and natural-born healer. Creating an environment of safety and trust is central to her healing work. She helps clients embody their authenticity and step into self-mastery. By uncovering sabotaging patterns that interfere with life, healing can take place. Diane's goal is to help her clients live powerfully and enjoy life!

When Diane was five years old, she had a profound experience while star gazing during a summer meteor shower. She felt her conscious mind connect with a divine and Universal knowing that supports her to this day.

Diane enjoys traveling to sacred sights, spending time in nature, swing dancing—and being with her granddaughter!

If you are ready to:

- reduce stress
- heal emotionally
- be energetically empowered
- make healthy choices to support your well-being
- take courageous steps toward living the life you want

Diane may be who you are looking for! She is committed to helping you heal and grow.

Ready to dive deep? Connect with Diane:

Website: https://www.dianemariegallant.com

Email: diane@dianemariegallant.com

Book: https://dianemariegallant.com/love-initiation-self-mastery/

Facebook: https://www.facebook.com/dianemariegallant/

Instagram: https://www.instagram.com/diane_marie_gallant

CHAPTER 17

IN THE ARMS OF THE DIVINE MOTHER, I AM HOME

FINDING FREEDOM THROUGH FORGIVENESS

Melissa Lee, RN, RM/T, IET M/I, 200hr CYT

MY LOVE INITIATION

MEXICO CITY, MEXICO FALL 2017

Standing in front of Templo Del Pocito, tears flow like a stream, releasing tension from my body, piece by piece. My shoulders fall, and my legs wobble. I steady myself on the construction barrier before me, heart pounding in my chest.

Can I do this? Am I ready? Will I forget you if I let go? I am so scared.

"I don't really understand it myself, but I know I need to go to Mexico," I declared to my family only months earlier, "I need to work through my shit and finally heal." I was ready to stop keeping silent about the trauma I experienced and let go of the pain that engulfed me ever since. Sacred travel seemed like the perfect opportunity to start healing, even though I had no idea what to expect.

Now, I stand beside Julianne, whom I've only just met. I allow her to see me as I am—broken, shamed, guilt-ridden, exhausted, ready to finally let love return to my soul.

I've borne the weight of my secret for 15 years, shielding my full truth from those around me while holding this precious little one in my heart always and everywhere. I've been called to this sacred place to heal my wounded womb.

"I loved him. I still do. I didn't want any of this. It was not my choice; none of it was," I try to explain to Julianne. I attempt to justify what happened when my entire world was upended during my sophomore year of high school.

Why am I trying to justify any of it? "Rape is not the victim's fault," one hears repeatedly. I have said it to others. Yet, it's hard for me to accept. I was dating him. But NO, I did not want THAT!

BOSTON, MASSACHUSETTS, SUMMER 2001

Please, no! Not this again, not here!

Nearly dragging me by my wrist, he leads me to the small wooded area that seems to have become home for some unfortunate being. Trash, bits of clothing, a random shoe, empty cans, and liquor bottles litter the small clearing. I've just returned from vacation with my family, which means he hasn't seen me for a few weeks. Now, it's time to pay the price for the temporary freedom I felt while away. Here I am, behind the liquor store across the street from the shopping mall, the overturned grocery cart digging into my back under his weight. I stare upward through the trees, begging the sun to blind me, separating from myself to escape reality.

When he finishes, I do as I'm told. I tremble as I dress, fumbling with buttons and zippers and brushing the dirt from my clothes. I pray someone will notice my pain as I make my way back toward the mall to wait for my ride. I can't speak about it during the drive home with my mom.

"What'd you do?" she innocently asks.

"Just hung out, walked around. Nothing really," I lie.

I want to tell the truth, but I don't know how. I'm so confused—hurt by someone who is supposed to care.

I knew in my heart the moment it happened. There was no protection. There is no need for a test when regular cycles come to a sudden halt.

I keep the pregnancy a secret. I don't know what to do and fear losing the precious baby growing in my tummy. I feel his every move as he rolls and stretches inside—my own belly flutters as he hiccups. I imagine what he might look like.

Will he have dark hair like mine or resemble the monster who did this? Will he know how much I love him despite how he was conceived?

I fear keeping him and raising him, as I, too, am just a baby. *Will I finish high school? Go to prom? Yeah, right, with whom? Who brings a teen mom to prom?* The person responsible for this has long moved on when he learns of my pregnancy—moved on to the next poor girl. *Will I be able to afford food, clothes, diapers? I don't know how any of this works!*

I silently prepare for motherhood without uttering a word.

"You did all this yourself?" my mother asks several months later. She has just returned home from work and notices the clean house, which is filled with the comforting aroma of homemade chicken and eggplant parmesan.

"Yeah, I had time after homework. I wanted to surprise you," I tell her, "you've been working all day, so I made dinner."

Cooking, cleaning, attempting to keep up with schoolwork, and plastering a false smile on my face consume each day. When I'm not trying to learn how to be a parent without any guidance, I hide in my room in oversized hoodies and the comfort of my blankets in bed.

I keep him a secret to keep him safe. As long as he's in my tummy and no one knows, he cannot be hurt. Nor can I. I learned in health class that in Massachusetts, a minor can have an abortion without parental consent at age 16. I'm a long way off, and despite how he came to be inside me, I love him. I daydream about what life will be like, just me and my baby. I don't ask my family for help. I feel too much shame and guilt, believing I put myself in a situation for this to happen.

No, it's not their fault; it's mine. I will handle it myself. Once he's here, I will be an emancipated minor, and he and I will figure out what happens next, together.

Time passes, and my midsection grows. There's nothing more I can do to hide him. I stuff my six-month swollen tummy into my black leotard and pink tights for my last ever ballet class on a cold afternoon in early February 2002.

The few weeks following class are a blur. I feel exposed and paralyzed by shame, as though I'm in a fishbowl—questions, criticisms, and disappointed faces swirling around me.

"How long has it been? When was your last period? Why didn't you speak up? Was this consensual? What were you thinking? What were you planning to do about it?"

"I don't know," is all I can utter.

My plan to raise this baby on my own now seems impossible, ridiculous even, as I witness the twisted faces of my family, who are unable to comprehend. All my strength escapes me as I reluctantly surrender to the guidance of the actual adults in my life. I'm exhausted, lonely, and terrified.

WICHITA, KANSAS, WINTER 2002

This hotel is safe for clients of the clinic here in the bible belt, according to the staff who helped make our arrangements. All the patients stay here, and there is one nurse assigned to stay within the hotel for "emergencies." My palms are sweating, and my heart racing as I wait to be ushered off using the only "safe" taxi. The ride seems routine. That is until we take the last turn.

"You'll want to have her duck down now," the driver turns to my mom, "take your jackets off and cover her."

What? Hide me? What the fuck is going on?

I glance out the windshield in time to see the protesters with their signs. "Don't worry," the driver reassures in the only way he can, "the clinic is behind walls and has a closed gate." He turns up the radio to drown out their heckles as he pulls up to the door. "Hurry! Go! Take her right in!"

As I step out of the car, I glance up—big mistake. In the corner of the parking lot, a group of protesters have climbed up behind the cinder block wall so they can see over. They hold signs that I dare not read and yell in a morbid screech, "Don't go in there! They will take your baby! Don't go in! You are a murderer! Murderer!"

I'm whisked through the clinic door and met with armed security guards. "Arms out!" They direct as they run their metal detector wands over and around me.

This clinic is one of very few that performs third-trimester abortions. It took some time to find it. And when we were referred, I was clearly informed by my doctor that the clinic would only move forward if there was something medically wrong with the mother or baby. The only way to get around the medical necessity is to state upon arrival that if I do not receive the procedure, "I will attempt to abort this baby myself."

Nothing could've been further from the truth.

Sitting across from the clinic's therapist, just moments after being called a murderer, my body writhes in agony. I hyperventilate, and the room begins to spin. I feel myself separate, just as I had during the rape. I'm not present in my body. I hardly recognize my own voice as I recite the words as instructed.

In that moment, at 27 weeks and five days pregnant, my whole world changed.

MEXICO CITY, MEXICO FALL 2017

"You were a baby yourself," Julianne exclaims, "of course you didn't have a choice; none of this is your fault." I'm seen and heard, held in a way I never have been before.

We stand together with arms locked before the temple, which is closed due to a recent earthquake. We dream into the space together. "The chairs are in a circular arrangement inside the walls of the round chapel," Julianne describes with exquisite detail, "the well is still inside, it's covered now, and there is a shrine to the divine mother..."

Julianne tells the story of Our Lady of Guadalupe, Juan Diego's vision, and how she is Mother to us all. I know in my heart that this was why I came all this way to Mexico—to climb this hill and sit in mass at the tiny temple, to witness the living tilma displayed inside the basilica once worn by Juan Diego. Lady Guadalupe's energy is alive, well, and here for us all to lean into whenever we need her love and support.

Alongside the hill where Juan saw the image of the divine mother, this small chapel was built around a well that miraculously appeared there. Water from this well is said to heal the ill and wounded.

Standing here with Julianne, she invites me to surrender my precious baby boy, my secret burden of love and pain, to the Lady of Guadalupe. As Mother to us all, she is my mother and that of my baby boy. She will love him as I do, hold him, protect him, and honor him. She will help to heal my wounds and free my soul.

I hear her voice in my heart as Divine Mother reassures me:

> *Everything has happened for a reason. You have held space in your heart for him while also being weighed down by grief and shame. You love him, and he loves you. He does not hold human emotions like judgment or anger; he sends only unconditional love. His soul was not ready for life on Earth. He belongs here with me. Together, we hold you and your human children in light. In love. We are present for you all in your hearts, your minds, and your dreams.*

She invites me to forgive myself. Gently reminding me again and again, "This was not your fault; you don't need to hide, you don't need to carry the burden of shame, guilt, or anger." My heart swells in my chest, full and aching, as it beats hard against my sternum. My breath is fast and shallow when suddenly I remember I should breathe to my toes.

I need to slow down so my heart rate can steady. I need to be present; this is why I am here. This is why she called me to her basilica.

I see myself gently wrapping this sweet bundle of innocence in the softest gauze blanket imaginable. Moving slowly, I swaddle as I recall all the people, places, and circumstances that have come together for me to realize the depth of a mother's love at such a young age.

I pause to forgive and explore gratitude individually. To myself, first and foremost. Then, to the person who did this to me. Followed by my family, friends, doctors, nurses, and even the taxi driver and hotel staff. Because of each of them, I felt the duality of deep pain and unconditional love. Because of each of them, I've been given a new lease on life, an opportunity to choose a new destiny. Because of each of them, I understand how quickly a life can be derailed and what it takes to rebuild.

Fifteen years was a long time to carry this weight. I hope I can let go of this pain, and I hope that he will still feel my love.

Just as I think this, gratitude washes over me, replacing pain, sorrow, grief, and shame. Love and acceptance fill every cell of my being.

I thank everything and everyone involved that I'm able to live the life I live today. I'm thankful I can be the mother I am to my children, the nurse I am to my patients, the healing guide and teacher I am to my clients, and the person I am today.

Lady Guadalupe extends her compassionate arms as I pass her my most precious gift.

As she accepts my bundle, I watch and he grows from baby to toddler to young boy through adolescence and now towers above me, an energetic being massive with radiant love and kindness.

Julianne's kind voice gently breaks through my internal experience, "take a deep breath, open your eyes," she invites me back to the present moment. Tears continue to stream down my face, cheeks red and stained with salted tears and streaking mascara. Surely, I am a sight for sore eyes, but I don't care. For me to be seen as I am and held there without judgment is a thing of beauty.

THE PRACTICE

While living in pain, I longed for someone, anyone, to connect with who shared an experience similar to mine—someone to confirm that I was not alone. The blanket of shame I was wrapped within was so heavy. I was not yet ready to expose my whole truth. But sharing small pieces with each of the three group leaders over the course of two days leading up to that moment allowed me to fully tell my story for the first time.

I forgave myself there, in front of that chapel. Forgiveness started within my own soul. And the more I forgive the people and pieces of my story, the lighter I become. Opening my heart and releasing the pain that bonded to my soul for so long created an abundant space of joy, happiness, and freedom. Yes, freedom! Freedom from a tangled mess of shame, guilt, and heartache has indeed been my greatest blessing during my love initiation.

Before we forgive ourselves, we must accept ourselves as we are. We are all perfectly imperfect beings learning more about ourselves every day. No one human holds all knowledge. We all have challenges that come and go constantly during our journey. Understand that this is where learning and growth are developed. When we accept ourselves as we are in the moment, we are stepping into forgiveness for ourselves and the experiences of our past.

Forgiveness is a process that takes time. Have patience with yourself as you work through this. Begin by reflecting in detail on all the parts and pieces of yourself—that which makes you who you are today, the challenges you have faced, and the lessons you've learned along the way.

Write yourself a letter of forgiveness, a love letter to your healing soul. Write a letter of love, understanding, compassion, and forgiveness as though you're writing to your best friend. Now, make a conscious decision to believe those compassionate words you wrote to yourself as you read them aloud.

Once you have written and read this letter aloud to yourself, it's time to let it go. Release the energetic hold that has kept you from forgiveness in the past and step into your own freedom.

Are you ready to be free? Take a moment, close your eyes, and envision yourself living as though you're already experiencing the freedom you seek.

Release your love letter to the universe in any way that feels right to you. One suggestion is to tear the letter up into small pieces and recycle it or to safely burn it. You may also choose to simply crumple it up and throw it away.

Forgiving the people or circumstances by which you have been affected is the next step. You've forgiven yourself. Now, forgiving all the people and circumstances surrounding your story will further free your soul.

Forgive others in the name of *your* healing. Forgiving does not mean forgetting; it simply sets you free from the energetic hold by which you have been constrained.

I encourage you to visit my website for further guidance towards freeing your soul. There, you will find step-by-step instructions for performing your own forgiveness ceremony and a recorded meditation to listen to as you work through this process.

Melissa is an Usui Reiki Master Teacher, Integrated Energy Therapy® Master Instructor, Crystal Reiki Master Teacher, 200hr Certified Yoga Teacher, Meditation leader, Psychic Medium, and Registered Nurse. She is the founder of Healing Oaks, offering heart-centered healing through a variety of the above modalities and additional healing techniques. Melissa has been practicing energy healing for over 12 years and can be found teaching and seeing clients around the Northshore of Massachusetts.

Melissa has a deep belief that scientific, energetic, and natural medicines all play a role in working together for optimal healing of the whole person. She understands that healing is most effective when the body, mind, and soul are in harmony. Melissa works with each client, tailoring the healing session to meet their individual needs. Her background in nursing provides a unique insight that blends with intuition for a comprehensive understanding of her clients' overall wellbeing. Over the last four years, Melissa has certified dozens of students in both Reiki healing and Integrated Energy Therapy. Melissa truly thrives when she is given an opportunity to share these modalities with others, and watching her students awaken to their own spirituality is a gift that never ceases to amaze.

When she is not working, you can find Melissa enjoying time with her two precious children and her beloved dog, Archie.

Website: https://www.healingoaks.net/

E-mail: Melissa.RN.RMT@gmail.com

Instagram: https://www.instagram.com/healing_oaks_yoga/

Facebook: https://www.facebook.com/profile.php?id=100063704314025

YouTube: http://bit.ly/3PX9oDI

CHAPTER 18

CONFESSIONS OF AN EVOLUTIONARY MYSTIC

FINDING SACRED EMBODIMENT IN THE KITCHEN

Margaret West, MDiv

MY LOVE INITIATION

I saw myself flying up the stairs of our cape on Shady Lane, trying to catch up to the two-year-old body my father was carrying to my crib. Details of this early trauma have never been revealed, but I was told as a child, "You jumped out of your crib and broke your crown." My mother only added to that decades later, "You cried inconsolably for three days." So, while I may not know exactly what befell me, I've come to recognize I had a form of near-death experience through which I gained access to multiple dimensions of reality. The difficulty was that at such a premature age, I didn't have any language or capacity to process it.

I can still hear my great Aunt Cris's cackling voice say, "So you're the troublemaker," when she came over to help my mom with four preschoolers one day after my return home. I remember often feeling confused, feeling too much, and crying in frustration. During one crying jag in kindergarten, my teacher grabbed me by the arms and shook me so hard I was literally stunned. I learned very young, how to dissociate to stay safe.

I've been straddling Heaven and Earth for as long as I can remember and spent my life trying to get back into and stay in my body. I've also asked age-old big questions, persistently trying to reconcile apparent dualities, of which there are many, with the bliss of unitive consciousness I've always known possible. I also believe I was tended to in those days by angels who've never left me.

This is where my Love Initiation begins.

By first grade, I joined my two older sisters in the girls' Canterbury Choir at St. Paul's Church, Mt. Lebanon. It wasn't lost on me that my twin brother was paid to sing in the Choir of Men and Boys, but such was life. We girls were just lucky to get to sing. The liturgy was sung from the 1928 BCP and 1940 Hymnal, and it moved me on every level. There were hymns for every season, festival favorites, and beautiful anthems. We chanted all the Psalms. We sang litanies of the Decalogue, praying with each commandment, "And incline our hearts to keep this law." We sang praises "with angels, archangels, and all the company of heaven." I loved church. It was a place of refuge in my turbulent world. Yet if I spoke of divine encounters or of holy longings, I was called "simple, touched, or flakey."

But I sang on, and by high school, between church and school choirs, ensembles and musical comedies, rehearsals, and performances, I was singing four to eight hours per day. This world was my second escape, with friends, laughter, and joy.

Rhythm, tone, and breath became my trinitarian formula for balance and ability to walk with grace despite my constant fear and trepidation: Stressed to live up to the standards of a highly competitive world, stressed by the unhappiness around me, especially my father's, who was a very sick man for many years before he died of lung cancer when I was 21. His alcoholic rages shook our house for years. We lived in silent shame and worry about what might happen next. Watching him decline were years of sadness and helplessness.

I walked through life with my heart on my sleeve. As a subject of frequent verbal and emotional abuse as a child, I knew the power of words to harm. I was also vulnerable to sexual and spiritual abuse later, as fundamentalism gripped my church and my own deficient needs. But my immersion in the church, in scripture, and in academic pursuits also gave me language and the power to be more than a survivor. I learned about hope, help from higher places, grace, forgiveness, and atonement. It made me a seeker of beauty, truth, goodness, kindness, patience, peace, and more. The language of soul has been a critical part of my self-understanding and development. Mudra (body and hand positions), mantra (word), and yantra (symbol) all express the language of soul that engages us on different levels. I still use my collection of dictionaries regularly.

What the heck is an evolutionary mystic? I distill it down to this: an unabashed lover of God who is changed by each encounter of the Holy. Loving God with all my heart, soul, and mind is a precondition or lens that makes accessible that which I believe is available to anyone: the unconditional love of God. I've been blessed to receive that love through visions, dreams, angels, and many, many great teachers over the past 60 years.

Some may call me crazy. Indeed, academics have called "mystics more lunatic than luminary" or "of such heavenly focus to be of no earthly value." "Direct experience is not part of scholarly pursuits," I was told. But even in that context, I moved through portals of time and place, then be present again in a lecture to find my notebook with a puddle of tears. I have kept some of my most profound experiences and knowing to myself. When is it okay to be this kind of crazy? Will I know how and when to say, "I see it different?" without being called a heretic or bomb thrower?

I had one of those time travel visions in December 1986. One minute, I was wrapping holiday gifts, and the next, I was a living witness to Jesus and his disciples.

"Do you love me?" Jesus asked.

John said, "Yes, you know that I love you."

Jesus replied, "Feed My sheep."

The dialogue repeated three times. I found it moving and even disturbing; I told no one and was haunted by this for years.

Later, with the help of local Tibetan teachers and texts, I came to discern, "Was it real? And/or is it true? Has truth been made real?"

I had another rebirth in my 30s after I quit my job with the Episcopal Church. I was home with a baby and discovered cooking as a healing art. I embraced hospitality as a time-honored ministry and focused the next 20 years on doing that.

I chewed my nails to the quick all my life. Try as I might, I couldn't shake that nervous habit. And I was embarrassed about this flaw in my beauty. Then, at age 40, I preached at the Bridgeport Rescue Mission one evening, for which the preparation and delivery were both deeply emotional. I was denied ordination, denied the 'privilege' to preach the Gospel in the church, but still called. I crossed the threshold. That night, I felt my body shake all over. It felt like the Holy Spirit moving through me. A few days later, I accidentally scratched myself, greatly surprised to see that I hadn't bitten my nails! And I never have since. My hands became a blessing in cooking, healing touch, and more.

During my early courtship with my husband, I saw a little cherub with an arrow (just like a cartoon valentine) shoot us while we watched a Sherlock Holmes mystery. It made me laugh, and it felt like a good sign. We were engaged within days. Shortly after, I also heard wedding bells. A few years later, I was anguished over the timing of having children, and a cherub visited me in my sleep, waving a chubby rear-end at me. I awoke filled with love and a deep peace that the decision was not about money. I was ready.

Some 13 years later, after launching a product line of specialty food, I had a bout of what felt like postpartum depression, but worse than any miscarriage or birth I'd been through. After spending many tens of thousands of dollars and months in the making, the packaging wasn't what was envisioned. I took to my bed in despair. This time, several little cherubs danced in front of me with banners singing, "It's a product, it's a product." I awoke feeling deeply comforted. And I got back to work.

That business failed with the financial crash of 2008. I lost my company, job, purpose, mission, identity, and all our money, and was still in debt. I was a mess and needed help. I then faced the soul-sickening disappointment in my church's incapacity to truly heal or even be present to me or my family. Our love as a family only deepened with every challenge. My children are my greatest teachers.

This begins the chapter of my deep dive into the healing arts. I was certified as a holistic health coach through The Institute of Integrative Nutrition in 2009. What followed was more classes in mind-body skills, functional medicine (nutritional supplements), energy medicine, and seeking out healers of many stripes.

I received Qigong and healing touch. I had a Sufi master, meditated with Tibetan monks, and went through Jungian analysis. I entered the 13-

moon mystery school, delving deeply into the various aspects of the Divine Feminine. I recovered parts of myself previously hidden or pathologized by patriarchy. I went to drumming circles with shamans and journeyed to commune with power animals. I felt deeply held by Bear.

Still striving for more healing, I consulted a psychic. She worked some numbers, including my birth date, and saw right through me, like she was watching a movie. "Sometimes I have to catch my breath and recover after witnessing a scene," she admitted. After pausing and without sharing details, said clearly, seriously, and without affect, "You were two. You have emotional work to do, and if you can do it, you have the capacity for ascended mastery in this lifetime." What did this even mean?

I bought a random Reiki session at a church auction and was later led back to that practitioner for detox treatments with ionic footbaths and infrared sauna. A man walked through the door, and his presence electrified me. "Who is that?" I blurted out. Sandra said, "Oh, that's John Mercede. We lead meditation on Monday evenings if you want to come."

During my first group session, John spoke of healing seven generations on either side. I was curious. He led us through intense breathing exercises and movement. He guided us on meditation journeys to other realms. I felt at home in myself again. Within weeks of this, I felt my heart break open. I received a spiritual surgery right there in meditation and was once again able to feel the deep love.

My healing touch practice seemed more effective. I was happy again. As John talked about the substance and structure of love, I was literally being restructured. I went from my highest weight back to a comfortable pre-partum size. I gained a meta-perspective. My family was supportive even if they didn't get it. Then John moved to Colorado. We stayed in contact through meditations by phone and in person when he visited.

Bad stuff doesn't stop happening just because you're on a healing path. Breakthroughs were followed by setbacks, only to discover there is more, always more to live into and through. "The brighter the light, the longer the shadow," it's been said. I confronted my rage. I pondered anew the nature of love and the fault lines of every virtue. I developed new boundaries.

John brought his beloved Julianne Santini back to Connecticut. The attraction was obvious! They announced they were planning a sacred journey to Mexico called Journey of Ascension. I had to go! It was simultaneously grounding and expansive. It was there Julianne shared with me her deep work with Bear medicine. Of the many allies we met and worked with, the spider goddess surprised me the most. She continued to weave through me my own capacities as a dreamer weaver. The journey was truly remarkable. I felt like I had found my tribe! I crossed a new threshold and was able to be on Heaven and Earth at the same time without being split.

Less than two years later, I returned to Teotihuacan for an IET training with them. I took a risk in our opening intro and ceremony and expressed my personal calling to clear the wounds of war from the earth grid (my version of healing seven generations on either side). IET training was a seriously healing experience. I recognized my connection to the angels, even as some names were new to me. The biggest thrill, however, was an add-on adventure.

Seven of us sat in a geometric formation in a cave under Quetzalcoatl, at a convergence point of the masculine and feminine ley lines of the Earth, at the apex of the universe, aligned with the Pleiades. We were asked by the lead archaeologist to reset the wheels of time. This was by far the highest level of service I have ever been called to. In that moment, my experience of the Alpha and Omega, informed by decades of study and practice, coalesced and brought me to "that of place no thing." It was beyond words. I was the word.

I was then fortunate to be invited to Peru with John and Julianne for a Journey of Divine Awakening. My tribe expanded! Our local spiritual guide, Jorge Luis Delgado, generously shared his wisdom and knowledge. I learned about Cusco, the ancient University of the Universe, in college. The words of my dear professor echoed through me. "There is nothing new under the sun," as Dr. Kenney would intone during lectures. I merged with the sun in Cusco. I climbed to the gates of the Galactic sun, high above Machu Picchu. More of my body came online with Mother Earth through the energies of those sacred lands—kissed, renewed, and sustained by the sun. "The Weavers of the Light" is the term Jorge coined to uplevel the former warrior concept. We're all weavers of light who consciously uplift our surroundings with positive thoughts, words, and actions. Ah, spider medicine again, reminding me of the interconnectedness of all things!

With each initiation, each imprinting of love, I've been changed. My awareness has changed. My behavior has changed. What flows naturally is deep devotion and a love of all creation. It's an awareness that every moment is a portal to eternity. Each moment requires humble surrender and a grateful heart.

Recently, sitting between the paws of the Sphinx in Giza was mystical, but this time on a different level. Simply breathing and remembering deeply, beyond emotions or intellect, absorbing into my every cell the memory of being held in perfect balance of the masculine and feminine. Of being a human animal, a creature that does not exist without my Creator, being made in its very image. Remembering my original blueprint, once more, to re-integrate every level of my physical through spiritual and celestial bodies as a living bridge between Heaven and Earth, continually called to reconcile dualities with unitive consciousness and divine love.

Experiencing the ancient Egyptian temples, followed by the oldest synagogue and Christian church in the world, revealed patterns that repeat and repeat and repeat. Love is eternal. Eternal life is available now. There is nothing new under the sun.

The most basic and equalizing part of being a human creature is our need for daily bread. The long biblical and theological history begins with the fallout in the Garden of Eden. To pray, "Give us this day our daily bread," and then co-create it with love makes us all divine human creatures.

THE PRACTICE

Breadmaking is "the creation of all that is," in the words of Emily Grieves, who so titled her painting of a woman baking bread. This is a favorite cooking retreat exercise because the magic of alchemy is itself exhilarating, and the rewards are delicious.

- Begin with the intention of setting a sacred space, making your kitchen feel safe and ready to co-create.
- Light a candle, say a prayer, and center yourself.
- Take a few conscious breaths. I love the mantra, "sum hom," meaning "I am that. I am" Breathe in "I am that" --- exhale, "I am."
- Whether you use a bread machine, a stand mixer with a dough hook, or mix by hand, the mindfulness is the same.

- Use quality, fresh ingredients. I use King Arthur flour, Celtic Sea salt (the sea is very old), filtered water, and yeast. Use any basic bread recipe and follow those measurements and instructions.

- When measuring the flour, honor the Earth. Our skin and bones are made of this. Earth: I am that.

- When adding the salt, remember, "You are the salt of the Earth," with a crystalline nature. Salt: I am that.

- When adding yeast, remember, "The kingdom is heaven like the woman who put a small amount of leavening in her dough." Its potency multiplies exponentially in the right conditions. Leavening: I am that.

- When adding the water, pour it in as living water. As it activates the ingredients, remember water carries more information than any other element. It makes up 70% of our physical composition. Water: I am that.

- Mix the ingredients and let rest for three to five minutes to absorb the moisture.

- Knead the dough well. In ancient times, people recited a rosary or other sets of prayers to ensure enough time had passed. Or set a timer for five to eight minutes. This is necessary to distribute the carbon dioxides created by the yeast. It also helps the gluten to develop to hold the air that makes it rise. Knead love into the bread.

- Fold it in each direction, calling in the south, west, north, and east. Shape the dough, bless it, and let it double in size. Remember that it rises with the same air we breathe, that gives us life. Air: I am that.

- Preheat the oven to 450 degrees, and after putting the bread in, turn it down to 400. With the power of this fire, the dough is transformed into bread in a matter of 20 minutes. Remember, our hearts are our physical hearth. It holds our fire, our living light. Fire: I am that.

- Let the bread cool for a few minutes before cutting.

- Say a prayer of thanks, and enjoy!

Margaret West, MDiv, CHHC, HTP, IET. After earning her Bachelor of Arts degree with distinction in Religious Studies at Bethany College, Margaret went to Yale Divinity School, where she earned a Master of Divinity degree and certificate in Anglican Studies at Berkeley. She has additional certifications in Integrative Nutrition, Healing Touch (level 4), and Integrated Energy Therapy (IET-Advanced).

Margaret has embarked on several sacred journeys and pilgrimages around the world, including the British Isles, Japan, Hong Kong, Thailand, India, Israel and the Sinai Peninsula, Mexico, Peru, and most recently, Egypt. She is dreaming into leading future sacred journeys!

Meanwhile, Margaret offers healing touch, spiritual direction, and health coaching and leads cooking retreats.

She and her husband enjoy sailing, gardening, and birding together. They have two grown children and one grandson!

CONTACT and Follow

Email: Margaretwestwellness@gmail.com

LinkedIn: https://www.linkedin.com/in/margaret-west-1328a5297/

Facebook: https://www.facebook.com/margaret.s.west.1

CHAPTER 19

I AM THE HANDS AND FEET

WALKING THROUGH THE FIRE WITH ARCHANGEL MICHAEL

Barbra Fang Babcock

MY LOVE INITIATION

I walked in from the garage into the family room, reached my arms up around his neck, and held on tightly, as was our usual greeting when we had been apart.

As I reached up to kiss him, he said, "Uh-oh!"

His eyes rolled up into his head, and his entire body stiffened like a board, and he fell straight backward onto the floor. Mouth open and gurgling, almost like speaking another language. At that moment, I realized he was having a seizure, but as usual, each one was very different.

I bent over him, yelling, "Jim, are you there? Are you there?" as I knew, sometimes hearing a familiar voice helps bring people out of a seizure.

After a minute, I could tell something was very wrong. He stopped making any noise, and he wasn't breathing. In that split second, I knew he was leaving his body.

I screamed at him as he lay there, "Don't you dare leave me!" I dropped to my knees and pounded on his chest. "Please, come back to me."

With my head lying on his chest, I couldn't hear his heartbeat or any breathing. My heart was breaking, and I was so afraid of facing a world without him.

"Please come back to me. Come back to me."

At that moment, I knew I couldn't do this by myself, so I called in my powerful guide and friend. "Please help me Michael, Archangel Michael, and all the archangels and ascended masters. Surround him; surround me. Help bring him back to me."

I felt a whirl of energy around me and asked, "What do I do now?"

Kneel next to him, put your hands on his heart and his belly, and breathe.

As I did, I felt many hands on my back, and this powerful surge of energy moved through my entire body and into him.

I kept repeating softly, "Come back to me, my love; we aren't done here yet. I need you, here in the physical; I need you."

I could feel a presence in the room, a subtle pressure. The room was filled with light, and the angels were there holding us. Tears gushed down my cheeks and dripped onto my hands, each one stinging my skin. My heart ripped wide open, and I wanted to scream, but there was a tenderness that came. A softness as I knew I was not alone; I knew no matter what happened in these next few moments, I'd be okay.

These were the longest four minutes of my life. I kept praying and asking for help, "Come back to me, my love; we aren't done here yet."

Somewhere in there, he began breathing again, and his body relaxed. As he opened his eyes, I placed my hand on his cheek and kissed him. "Are you here, my love?"

He looked confused and didn't recognize me. I helped him slide over on the carpet to the side of the room and sit up against a cabinet. There was a peacefulness surrounding us. I knew I had just witnessed a miracle.

I started to ask a string of questions: "Do you know where you are? Where do we live? Tell me your name. What's my name?"

Our nanny from years ago and her daughter visited from California the night before. "Do you remember who joined us for dinner last night?" I asked.

"Where are you going tomorrow?" He was scheduled to leave for a golf trip to Reno.

I kept asking questions for almost 45 minutes until he was fully back in his body and could answer any of my questions clearly and correctly.

In those four minutes, all the layers of protection and denial that built up over the past few years from the pain of his declining illness peeled away. This was not the first seizure, nor would it be the last, but we could no longer hide that our lives were forever altered. Those four minutes changed my world.

The denial game he had been playing was gone. He'd remember this seizure and recognized its full effects for the first time. For the past few years, he denied that his body was failing. The harder I pounded to get him to see what was happening, the more distant he became. His body ached while my heart ached.

The grief ('anticipatory grief' being the technical term) hit me like a landslide.

I saw that we could no longer function as we had and follow our grand adventure to travel and explore the world. It all came tumbling down. There was this cage around me now. I realized I was to be the hands and feet of this relationship. I tried to put the same cage around my heart because I didn't want to feel all the emotions flooding into me at once. All I could do was let the tears flow.

Soon after, doctors were hitting us with protocols and adjustments to everyday life that no person—no family—wants to make. This was happening to him (to us), and we had to make changes necessary to support both of us.

I watched our magical love and the easy life we created be torn down brick by brick. The intimacy was slowly eroding and almost gone. Every doctor's visit felt like a betrayal. It hit him hard to acknowledge the changes.

As I described what he couldn't do anymore, tears flowed down my face. I hated to acknowledge this powerful, commanding man I married was slipping away a little more each day. He once taught the secrets of spirituality and orchestrated airplane arrivals as an air traffic controller. It was difficult to admit he was barely functioning with simple tasks.

I can't go around this. I must walk directly through the fire every moment of every day.

I needed to find my path forward because I was drowning in grief and pain. I was losing my partner, and he was right here in front of me. The beloved I knew was gone.

After his first seizure, he started a continuous decline in health and personality shifts. I didn't know where to find him. I was lost, angry, and grieving. We went from having the relationship everyone wanted to one no one wanted to be near.

Here I was with all these intuitive gifts, and they didn't work. I couldn't see anything, I wasn't getting any messages, and I felt useless. I was blessed with a love so beautiful and so powerful, truly a gift, and now it was literally dissolving before my eyes.

I knew I needed to draw on my inner strength, community, and family to build a new life. I needed to show up for myself and him. I began to draw on the power of my creativity.

How can I express myself and transform our relationship and our daily lives to support us in creative and unique ways? Otherwise, I feel like I'm going to implode. How can I apply creativity to living, grieving, moving through life, and feeling good about myself?

Somehow, I know if I approach each day with creativity, optimism, and peace, I can move forward from this place where I was stuck.

First, I looked to the past. After creating a magical, loving relationship, our love was a shining example to many couples. We were filled with anticipation of what each day would bring. We went from what our friends called "full frontal intimacy," as our connection was so obvious when we looked at each other. You could feel the presence deep inside each of us come alive—a presence people wanted to be close to and feel for themselves. Our beautiful and unique experience of intimacy was now gone, snapped like a rubber band.

Yes, I grieved—the loss of our dreams of traveling the world together. The loss of this magnificent man I loved, the loss of my big dream house, financial stability, sleeping soundly, a daily consistent schedule, and the list goes on. Pop a pandemic in the mix, and life was crumbling.

Changes needed to be made. I needed to start by letting go of my clients and catering events. I quit my job as an admin at a church and let go of the idea of growing my business. My life went from riding high and smooth sailing to sinking. I didn't have the emotional bandwidth to handle any of it. I was crashing. I was also healing from Lyme disease and needed to learn how to take care of not just him but me.

The most difficult part was he was not aware that any of this was happening to him. The physical changes, yes; the personality and cognitive shifts, no. I learned it's a "real thing" in the dementia world. Who knew? I learned so much, but it's taken its toll on me.

Some days, just getting the dishes done and making dinner was a good day. Other times, it was being able to have lunch or coffee with a friend or go for a walk. Those were the "really good" days. There wasn't much energy left for extras, and yet I was still strong. I was still powerful. I wasn't declining. I needed to look at myself through a different lens.

I was blessed to be supported by a group of friends who held me up when I needed it and shook me when I was feeling sorry for myself. In the beginning, I felt like I'd wear them out by complaining and venting, but most stuck with me. I developed a close group of warriors who continued to support me. I wouldn't be here today without their presence, patience, and love. Many times, they pulled out of my rabbit hole when I got lost down there.

Each day I remind myself I love this man with all my heart and soul. I can't imagine what my life would be like without him. He changed my world by stepping into it, seeing my beauty and grace, and telling me how magnificent I am. He's still one of my cheerleaders. He is present, filled with joy, and sees the wonder of living each day. I will be here every day, whatever it takes. I have been so blessed by the love we share, and it has carried me through those tough days. The love we share is still there; it just looks different than it did before.

When we first started dating, I felt my heart burst open, and it kept opening each time I was with him. I kept waiting for it to be fully open until I finally realized it would continue to open more and more as long as I allowed the love to flow. There is no fully open heart, only one that continues to open to love. That's when I finally understood the metaphor of the lotus flower as it continues to grow. It's like becoming a parent for the first time. Your heart is so full; it's a miracle. Then, when you have another child, your heart opens more, holds more, and loves more. It keeps opening to more love.

Calling on friends and professionals, I developed a support system that holds me up and keeps me going. They listen to my frustrations and remind me that each day, our love grows deeper. It looks so very different from where we started. I learned to let go of my expectations of our relationship, of him, and most importantly, of myself.

In those four minutes, the entire trajectory of my life changed. Everything planned was wiped clean. Each moment, each day, had to be created from scratch. It was like cooking with a recipe that had no ingredients.

Several months later, I was having lunch with my daughter. Suddenly, she got very quiet and said, "Mom, I want you to know that you have shown us all a deeper way to love. Going from such a magical, loving relationship to where you are now and the tough things you face each day, you are an example of how to continue to love through it all. Thank you for showing me how to love."

I grabbed her hands, saying, "Thank you for seeing me and realizing that love is so much more than just the 'fun times.' I now know loving someone means walking through the fire together. Walking straight through. There is no walking around or looking away. There are sweet moments that fill me up and make me realize a divine relationship is magical; it just looks different every day. Please keep your heart open to love. It's worth it!"

We were both sitting there in tears after our conversation. A beautiful bond was strengthened. I felt our hearts open and intertwined as they have been for eons.

Each day I'm reminded of the miracle of love. Being present helps me see the joy we share and the love we find in the small and sweet moments. Yes, it's hard, but I find strength, peace, and wonderment in each of those moments.

When he has a seizure, or falls, or hurts himself,
or can't do something that he did before,
my heart breaks.
It breaks open a little more each time.
I know I need to keep it open,
when all I want to do is slam it shut,
not feel the pain,
not feel him slipping further and further away.

I choose to keep my heart open,
To take another step into the unknown,
To feel it all.
I cannot look away.
I can't walk away.
I have chosen to walk this path with him,
To walk through the fire,
To walk holding hands.
This is the journey of the love we share.

THE PRACTICE

I learned I can't do this journey by myself, and I won't receive help unless I continue to work at asking for help. Whether calling a friend or calling in the angels, support and help is always available. I'm never alone, even though I may feel it at times. Now, I remember to ask and feel the love that's always available. Whenever I'm in need, I use an Archangel Michael prayer to pull in the love that surrounds me.

ARCHANGEL MICHAEL HEART OPENING MEDITATION

Get comfortable and relax your body.
Take a slow deep breath in,
and blow it out.
Take another slow deep breath in,
and blow it out.
Takes a third breath in,

And slowly let it out with a sigh,
        (making a sound relaxes the body.)

Dear Archangel Michael,
I call on you for loving support.
I breathe in the golden light you bring from the angelic realm.
I breathe out all fear.
I breathe in your strength.
I breathe out all doubt.
As I breathe in your Love,
my heart opens like the wings of a butterfly.

Wrap me in your glorious, feathered wings,
Cradling me in the arms of love.
Hold me until I can,
I release all fear.
I release all pain.
Clean and clear.
I draw in your strength.
When I feel helpless,
I claim your power.
When I feel hopeless,
I ask for your guidance.
For the next step forward,
Help me to move.
When I feel paralyzed,
Reveal to me just one step.

I feel the presence of the angels that surround me,
the glow and love of each being holding my heart,
holding me, helping me when I can't help myself,
knowing I am never alone.
I am so grateful for your presence.
I am so grateful for your strength.
I and so thankful for your Love.

And so it is

Barbra Fang Babcock

Barbra feeds people; she feeds their bodies and spirits. She nourishes people with her presence and by holding them in such a loving way that the resistance and grief they carry melt away. She can touch people's souls with her unique wisdom and connects them back to themselves. While she makes food and caters special events, she loves watching people be nourished by the food, making connections to each other, and the beauty of their surroundings.

She has been guiding people on their spiritual path for over 20 years. She calls herself a creative intuitive. Her readings and sessions include accessing Divine wisdom from the Creator and spirit guides, enabling her clients to create life skills they take forward to live life fully, release grief, and embrace self-caretaking. Barbra is a curious, creative soul who is always learning something new and finding ways to teach others.

As a creative intuitive, she reads past lives, does energetic healings and clearings, and is a spiritual mentor, teacher, speaker, and writer. She is also a licensed Science of Mind and Spirit Practitioner. Her other creative pursuits over the past 40 years have been as an artist and painter, designer of wedding and evening gowns, and theatrical costume designer. She has trained as a death doula and extensively in bereavement studies after the loss of her first husband. She holds individuals and families as they move through the end-of-life experience.

Find Barbra at: https://www.BarbraFangBabcock.com

CHAPTER 20

SACRED TRAVELER

THE RECIPROCAL HEALING OF OUR INNER PLANET WITH THE WORLD

Dr. Tracey L. Ulshafer, Doctor of Ministry

MY LOVE INITIATION

My heart imploded, then heaved and erupted into a geyser of heartfelt emotions over its recognition of this foreign land.

I'm home!

A torrent of tears came for an overwhelming feeling of homecoming that was unexpectedly landing. How strange that this silly, little American girl suddenly felt more at peace, acknowledged by this place, and contented in Siem Reap, Cambodia, than in the area where I live. But this was my current realization.

"Come on, Tracey, let's get a group shot!" I heard a fellow traveler bellow out this irritating call, pulling me out of my heart.

Is she kidding me? I need a minute. I mean, I've finally made it home after, like a thousand years.

After a big sigh, I did my best to squash down the plethora of emotions that arose from my core, heart, and soul.

I wondered how I could feel stirred and completely opened the first time I stepped into this new place halfway around the world. An undeniable feeling of connection to the energy of the land fell on my heart like a block of granite. And I immediately felt happier and contented in this new place than I remembered feeling in an excruciatingly long time.

New Jersey certainly didn't elicit these emotions. Heck, not much back home elicited these types of feelings. Sure, there were happy moments, but this kind of real and true peace, the kind that takes your breath away and engulfs you in a gut-wrenching knowing that you can never not know the truth of it again—that was a special sort of high.

What do I do with this knowing?

"Tracey, come on! Let's take the group shot!" Rang the annoying cry once again.

"Oh, for the love of Buddha, I'm coming!" I yelled back.

We took the obligatory group shot in front of Ta Prohm, a Cambodian temple enveloped by overgrown trees and vines, whose roots melted like wax down the temple walls, literally crumbling it into heaps of stone. Imagining some 70,000 Buddhists, mostly monks and high priests, living here in quiet contemplation, hidden from the rest of the world by the jungle that swallowed it up, pierced my otherwise stoic heart.

Many tourists poured through the temple grounds, and my travel companions continued to press to have more of my attention. It was impossible to carve out any time to sit and be present with the feelings welling up within me and the space that felt so familiar outside of me. So, Gemini that I am, I shifted gears to match their energies as we moved through the various temples in the Siem Reap area, just like all the other tourists.

At our next stop, the red-carved sandstone Hindu temple Banteay Srei, I gave them what they wanted from me.

"Cindy, see that big block? Do crow pose, and I'll take your picture," I said.

"Okay!" She smiled, willingly jumping on a large sandstone block that had fallen off the temple. Kneeling into her arms and lifting her feet off the ground, Cindy levitated into a beautiful arm-balancing posture.

"Got it!" I said, snapping a few photos.

"Hey, let's do one with all of us," Cindy said.

Looking about, we found a section of the temple with what appeared to be a doorway and two window openings. Cindy and I each climbed into one of the windows and sported a yoga pose while our friend Ian stood in the doorway in a Warrior pose. Our other companions took several photos of us, all laughing and enjoying the moment. But that geyser still had a ton of pressure inside it, and I continued to struggle to press down those emotions, silently disgusted by my willful act of being untrue.

I have to find a way to sit and be still somewhere, or I am going to explode differently.

Our tour group moved on. Bayon Temple is known for its impressive Buddha images carved in the four directions at the temple peaks. Tourists usually take a photo lining up their faces with Buddha's.

"Tracey, stand over there. Okay, move a little to the right. Wait, let me tilt down just a bit. Okay, now pucker up."

The commands to adjust myself and pretend to kiss Buddha felt wrong. I was pleased that none of those photos worked out in the end, although I was sure to line theirs up so they'd be happy about their snapshot keepsakes.

From somewhere close, the scent of earthen incense drifted by. Instantly, my energy shifted and I began to follow the pleasing scent I'd become so familiar with in my practices. Rounding a corner inside the temple, I came upon a female monk who was attending to a Buddha statue adorned in gold and saffron silks. This area was quieter and cooler than the sticky heat outside. I felt myself soften and smile, noticing that candles and incense could be purchased and lit for blessings.

Finally! This is my chance!

I bent down and quickly found Cambodian Riel, handing it to her, then pressing my hands together and bowing. She handed me a candle and motioned for me to light it from one already lit on the altar, and then to place it into the stand. After doing as instructed, she handed me a few sticks of incense, again motioning how I should light it and where to place it. After they were placed, I looked at her, and she smiled, then pressed her hands together and bowed to me. I gladly reciprocated again, and then I took deep breaths, feeling the sacred moment. My bliss continued until my friends moved in to copy me.

As their energy bounded in, the monk smiled at me. She understood. I saw the recognition in her eyes. As my friends continued to giggle and light their toys, she held up a string and nodded her head, motioning for me to come to her. Kneeling by her side, she tied the string on my wrist with care. Once the blessing was tied, she bowed to me once again.

Ah, now this feels right.

While my companions were otherwise engaged, I moved to another quiet place around the corner and allowed myself to breathe deeply into the moment. Although I felt an overwhelming sense of peace, the emotional charge that immediately came from entering Ta Prohm was lacking.

"Group, it's time to move to Angkor Wat," said our guide, appearing out of nowhere.

He was a nice and knowledgeable man, but he didn't seem to understand his timetable was not my timetable. So, I noted to myself that I'd have to return one day when I could spend more time in each of these beautiful places.

Angkor Wat is the star of the temples in Siem Reap. The Guinness Book of World Records considers it the largest religious structure in the world, and it's said to have used the same amount of stone as Egypt's Great Pyramid.

"Wow, this place is massive! I don't think we will be able to see it all."

"Take my picture by the moat."

I can't deal with them anymore.

"I wonder if these Foo Dogs have balls underneath them?"

Oh my God, did she? She did.

"Yup, he does, look," Cindy said, showing us all the pictures she'd taken from the undercarriage of the guardian.

As the group giggled, I decided I'd be more direct about my needs as this was our final temple. How else would I understand my connections here?

When we moved into the temple grounds, I quickly found a window with spiral carved columns serving as ancient blinds. I sat inside the serene, dark space, placed my legs in a meditative posture and hands in my lap. With my eyes closed, I fell instantly into another time.

"Oh, let me get your picture," I heard from a distance that grew more vast by the second.

And then, finally, the outer world fell completely away, and I blissfully sat for what felt like ages in a deep sense of gratitude. Tears rose again. Finally, those emotions of homecoming were landing—pressure, then expansion in the heart space opened with each deep breath. Timelines dissolved, and at once, I felt myself in the present and the distant past at the same time. My being shot back to Ta Prohm, where I instantly saw myself living, caring for the temple, and loving my precious, simple life.

As what happens when timelines converge, my next memory is sitting atop the highest tower, known as Shiva's divine seat or Mount Meru. Peering out across the temple expanse, a hush fell over as I witnessed the thousands of tourists moving below like ants, infesting the temple floor. There was no intention or sacredness in their being. And the temple was not happy.

"Okay, time to go."

No!

But yes. I'd need to take the temples and the land with me in my heart for now.

This reentry home was more unusual than my previous travels.

Something shifted within me, and it also told me to dig into my past travels with a sharper lens. So I poured through photo albums and wrote down the dates and locations of my travels, revealing a pattern. Although I hadn't been consciously aware previously, I seemed to always choose very special places—sacred lands where ancient civilizations built their temples or where the land itself, the natural churches, exuded an undeniable presence.

Over the next several years, I expanded my research and travels, visiting more sacred places and experiencing greater homecomings and connections.

What is it about these planetary power places that attract humans, since our beginnings, in a magnetizing force? The energy goes by many names. Thousands of years ago, the Aboriginals sang the songlines of the planet in the Outback while the Shinto Masters rode the mighty Dragon Lines. In Chichen Itza, Mexico, the Mayans experienced the feathered serpent god, Quetzalcoatl, whose name influenced the term "plumbed" or "feathered" serpent line.

Ancient civilizations built their temples along important energy currents, and they're still calling people to them today. Why? Because they're living, breathing things, just like you and me. And you can imagine what happens when more than one of these lines intersect.

I remember the first time I made the connection to this through the Hermetic principle of "As above, so below."

Wait, so if I have chakras in my body, then the Earth must have chakras in her too!

My research into all things energy, chakras, and planetary power places continues. In my nose-dive into the rabbit hole of what this exploration is, I've moved through many of the Earth Chakra locations, and I experience uniquely different energies in each of them.

During my trip to Mt. Shasta, believed to be the world's first chakra location, I was introduced to the undeniable energy of being in the present moment. My trip to Lake Titicaca in Peru and Bolivia, the sacral chakra center of the world, was one of the most emotional roller-coaster rides of my life that ultimately shifted my entire personal understanding of what was true for me and how I could live in more joy. In Glastonbury, United Kingdom, the world's heart and possibly third-eye chakra centers, an incredible presence of divine love carried me effortlessly on my journey of seeing the holy grail within my being. During one of my many initiations in Egypt, the world's communication center, star language burst forth through my hands and ushered in a notable shift from speaking to listening.

Traveling is a passion of mine, and connecting to a land and feeling the very real and palpable energy allows me to connect more deeply to myself and the planet. In that vein, I always feel the significance of giving back to the Earth in some way when I travel. I've offered service work and healings; the specifics depend on the locations. Being with Mother Earth is such a privilege. And getting to experience an area of light and power, well, that's like pouring chocolate syrup on top of an already scrumptious dessert. So reciprocating to her is not only necessary but aligns me in a way that supports any personal work that I might do as well.

But not everyone feels the call to travel to far and remote locations, and some simply cannot make the journeys, even though they may want to. It's okay. You can cultivate a sacred power place somewhere close to home, somewhere in nature, and through the intention to experience greater healing. Remember that you can have your own beautiful, sacred traveler experience anywhere.

THE PRACTICE

CONNECTING TO YOUR POWER PLACE FOR REGULAR HEALING ACTIVATIONS

For those wanting to listen to this journey, click this link:

https://youtu.be/BdZb_tAziBU

Step 1: Go to your special place. This place is where you feel safe and content. You have a great sense of happiness and belonging here. It doesn't have to make sense to anyone else—only to you. Think of this as your sanctuary in nature. Is it a park? Your herb garden? The beach? A local mountain? Or is it in Egypt, Peru, or Bali?

Step 2: Find a quiet space for you to have uninterrupted time in your sanctuary. Turn off the cell phone, take off the smartwatch, remove your shoes, and get yourself into a comfortable position, either standing with your feet rooted in the ground, seated in a meditative posture, or lying down flat on your back, leaning into Pachamama. Your palms should be facing upward, open to receive.

Step 3: Quiet your mind with several minutes of deep, belly breathing through the nose. On the inhalations, fill the belly outward, and on the exhalations, contract the belly inward. Keep the mouth closed but soft. Allow the eyes to roll up and back. Allow yourself to disconnect from the outer world and drop into your inner world.

Step 4: Continuing to breathe deeply, ask the land there for permission to connect to her and to share in a reciprocal healing activation. With the right intention, you will know when she answers you affirmatively. Listen through your heart.

Step 5: Notice what you are feeling. What are you feeling first in your body? What sensations are coming up? Feel into the sensations. Then, when you feel ready, begin to notice what you are feeling from the land below you. What sensations are coming up from the soil, the sand, or the mud? If you are not sitting or standing directly on the Earth, then imagine a rooting system diving down through any flooring or sub-flooring and deep into the Earth. Whatever other restrictions seem to arise, find a creative solution to make the connections, and then notice what you feel there.

Step 6: With Gaia's permission, now begin to ask what her message is for you. What do you need to know at this time in your life? Do you need healing? Do you need direction? Do you need to get out of your own way? What does your highest self need to know at this moment? Wait for it. You have time because you made the space for this. It's okay to wait, open, and receive.

Each person has their way of receiving messages. Some people feel things. Others see things. Yet different people hear or smell the message. Be open, and also, don't expect that your usual way of receiving is how things will come to you. The more that you connect, the quicker the messages will come, and in different ways.

Step 7: Once you have received your message, it is time to give back to Mother Earth. Place your left hand on your heart center, palm flat, connecting to the deepest energy of love. Now, take your right hand and place it flat onto the Earth. Inhale through your nose, through your left hand, and into your heart. Filling the intention with love, send it out through your right hand and into Mother Earth.

Continue with several cycles of breath and giving back to Mother Earth, thanking her for all that she has given to you, not just today, but for being the solid bedrock below where you stand and from where you share yourself with the world. No matter what happens in life, she is always there for you. She has never failed you, and she never will. You're a part of her, and she is a part of you. And one day, you will return to her again. Allow yourself to be in the most reverent love with her as you fill her with this light of love.

Step 8: When this reciprocal healing feels complete, open your eyes, stretch, and smile. You are now ready to journal, contemplate, or act on the message that you received. And if nothing came through today, that's fine. Know that you can return to this sacred place again and perform the work on another day.

When you're ready to leave, remember to bring everything with you that you brought. Leave behind no trace.

You will notice that with regular practice, the more you return to the same spot to do these activations, some interesting things will occur. So, observe the nature around you. Witness the animals that appear to you, as they may be a part of the energy medicine. Check out the flora and fauna and the hidden meaning behind their presence. Everything is energy, and nothing is by chance.

In love,

Tracey

Dr. Tracey L. Ulshafer is the documentary filmmaker of the series *The Earth Chakras.* She visits planetary power places, discusses the energy of the locales, how they align to the chakras of the human body, and creates reciprocal healing events when visiting with intention. She welcomes others to join her in these experiences through her Earth Chakra Healing Retreats.

Tracey's tagline is "Everything is Energy," and teaches people how to heal the many dimensions of their lives by aligning to the right frequencies. As a practitioner, she is a licensed Integrative Massage Therapist and Reiki Master conducting trainings on Yoga, Thai Yoga Bodywork, and Quantum Healing. In her TV Show, *The Quantum Healer,* Tracey interviews practitioners about new technologies and ancient practices that can assist one in their body's ability to heal.

Tracey owned and operated One Yoga and Wellness Center in New Jersey for 22 years until closing its doors in 2022. Her highly praised yoga training program focused on the practice of Hatha Yoga, which allows one to create balance where it is needed within the human person—body, mind, and spirit. She became a Doctor of Ministry through the first Interfaith Seminary school in the world, The New Seminary, and is ordained to perform ceremonies and rituals that create a unique sacred experience.

When Tracey is not traveling, she enjoys her own sacred space with her husband and dogs, cuddling up to watch a good detective series. You can be sure they'll be throwing out theories as to who did it or what happened as the show progresses. And yes, she has a better track record than her husband.

Connect with Dr. T:

Website: www.TraceyUlshafer.com

YouTube: https://www.youtube.com/@TUlshafer

Facebook: https://www.facebook.com/tulshafer/

Instagram: https://www.instagram.com/tulshafer/

CHAPTER 21

LOVE ELEVATED

CHANTING MANTRA FOR CONNECTION

Kelly Connolly

MY LOVE INITIATION

Am I possessed? Permanently inhabited by an ancient soul, desperate to get out of here? 5,000-year-old dust molecules hang in the air; I breathe them in and wonder: *Am I going to be okay?*

Egypt was never a place I felt drawn to or needed to see, but there I was at 2:30 AM, standing in front of the Great Pyramid, clueless about what lay ahead.

How did I end up here?

Over the last three and a half years, I've been rebuilding my life. It all began when I was on holiday in Ireland. I spent one night in Belfast and met my future husband Brian, and within a few hours, I knew I couldn't be without him. I moved to Ireland nine months later. I hadn't considered anything when I left. I thought I would be back to visit New Hampshire soon.

How different could things possibly be? They spoke the same language, and surely things operated the same.

Perhaps I told myself these fabrications to make it less daunting, but it turns out I was completely lying to myself. Things and people in Northern Ireland were indeed very different.

I arrived in January 2020. Any previous expectations were shattered.

I was grateful to spend so much quality time with Brian during the lockdown. But outside our relationship, rebuilding my life felt impossible due to the year and a half of closures.

Slowly, the phone calls to home grew further apart with friends and family. It became difficult to talk to them and hear about them moving on without me. I couldn't be a part of their life as I once was, and it was painful.

My efforts to establish a job, a bank account, credit, or even my driving privileges were met with constant obstacles. Everything was at zero; I felt like a teenager again. I am still without so many things I used to have before I moved over, things I miss.

My new life lacked the familiarity and long-lasting connections I had with those who genuinely cared about me. The history I had with these people was missing. I was flailing, trying my best to fit in and not seem too weird. Not that my friends or family don't already know that I'm a bit strange. I only realized when I was 3,000 miles away how much I appreciated the love these people gave me. Those lifelong connections were now what I was lacking. An intrusive thought came in: *what do I have **right now**, in Belfast, that I'm not appreciating to the fullest capacity?*

It later occurred to me that the lack I felt could be transformed into space, space to fill up with new experiences and people. Never to replace, but enrich. This space would soon be filled to the brim with strength, grace, and joy. These things were always within me, but the journey to Egypt unlocked a new expression of these qualities.

Egypt called to me through a close friend, Jeffrey. We had worked together, lived together, and faced life as a team together. It was our chance to see each other three and a half years after my leaving the United States. There we were, reunited in Cairo, in balance once again. He was the reason I was here, not wanting anything but to experience Egypt together.

A gentle glow of moonlight reveals only a glimpse of the secrets it holds. I studied it in sixth grade; there are hundreds of documentaries on it, all with varying conclusions on how it got there. We stare with utter awe at this incredible structure. The Great Pyramid of Giza. We climb our way diagonally to the entryway, 60 feet above ground level. We enter in silence and soon arrive at the tunnel. Crouched, backs almost touching the ceiling, we waddle as best we can down a square passage. It's been minutes now. *Are we almost there?* I feel myself start to worry: *Is there enough air in here for all of us?* Panic sets in; there are people ahead and behind me, and no time to stop. "Don't cause a scene" is always a conscious thought in my head. We reach the Queen's Chamber. I look around at the group of 28 and wonder if I'm sweating the most out of everyone. *Focus on the breath and slow the heart rate down.*

For two weeks, we traveled around Egypt, temple after temple, each place holding something unique for each of us—a lesson, an unfolding, a healing. We endured sickness, exhaustion, and relentless calls from aggressive merchants trying to sell us their goods. It all coalesced into this moment. We are the initiates. Each person has a purpose and a role to play in our time here.

Our semicircle was formed, my back against the wall, each individual guided to the front to receive their initiation. First, my energy was cleared, then the ankh was held up to my mouth and throat, and I breathed in the eternal life it symbolized. Anointing oil was placed on my forehead, and I was guided back to my place against the wall, the teacher leading the way. Melodic voices sang, "I am the light," echoing through the chamber.

Jeff and I are the first to leave the chamber after everyone has gone to the front. Bent in half once again, we made our way back through the tunnel. I focused on reaching the large opening (grand gallery) to climb up to the King's Chamber. On the climb, we're holding Egyptian healing rods, an obsidian rod in my left hand, and one sandstone rod in Jeff's right hand. We're the balance of energies together, moon and sun. We had this same balancing task earlier in the trip in the Temple of Horus. I silently chant *Sa Sekhem Sahu*, a mantra we used in all of the temples, to awaken what is lying dormant within.

We arrive at the entrance, which is only about three feet tall, the square tunnel noticeably shorter this time before emerging into the chamber. It's larger than I imagined, with the sarcophagus situated at the far right end. It's made of granite, with a significant gouge at the top left corner, but completely solid. Jeff and I, still holding hands, circle the room three times before settling at the entrance.

As each person entered, no one looked my way, their eyes fixed on the sarcophagus. The singing resumes, now more effortless, more beautiful, and more ethereal than before. The chamber is sweltering, and the sweat trickles down from every pore. I'm perfectly still, the air inside stagnant and stale. I've never been hotter in my life. Jeff and I adjust our hands frequently to avoid the added discomfort of sweaty palms. He chants a Kundalini mantra: I don't know it; I just listen and watch.

I get an inkling to remove my sandals to feel the powerful energy emitting from the floor of the chamber. After only a short time, my feet start to feel hot. I have paranoid thoughts of ancient bacteria entering the pores of my feet and infecting me. Suddenly, I'm in the hospital, and doctors are struggling to diagnose my condition, and I don't dare tell them it's pyramid bacteria. The stabbing pain in my right hand just below the thumb brings me out of my delusion.

I better put my shoes back on so I stop thinking about this ridiculous scenario.

I put them on, and as I'm finishing, it's my turn to lay down in the sarcophagus. I step in somewhat easily. I lay down. Looking up, I see many people around me, some holding space, others working to remove unnecessary energies, and others activating the energy of the Merkaba.

I ask the universe, the omnipotent energy: *What is here for me? I am ready for my initiation, whatever that may be.*

I feel an intense energy or pressure around my entire body.

That's cool.

I no longer care if I have an energetic experience or not. This was a repeated fear of the past when trying different practices or modalities. *What if I didn't feel anything or see anything sacred, otherworldly, or significant?* This time, I'd do things differently. To let whatever was happening happen. Not to adjust it, make it more intense, or shift its direction, but watch, observe, feel, **just allow.**

I didn't have any profound visions or significant life-altering realizations, just a nice, comfortable feeling. The tingshas ring out, signaling my time has come to an end. I was helped out and led back to my place. I wait for Jeff to come back from his turn so we can continue holding hands. He places one finger in the center of my palm and gets called away to help with holding the Merkaba for people in the sarcophagus. Just then, it started to happen.

My hips began to sway in a circular motion. I'm slowly realizing I am not in control of this movement at all. It's like someone is physically holding my hips and moving them for me counterclockwise. I surrendered to the experience instead of thinking it was weird or I was losing it. No judgments from anyone in the room, *just flow.*

The swaying varied in speed and direction—circles back and forth in a figure eight. My rational brain thought: *This is insane!* But the flow continued. The more intense it gets, the more I feel my arms wildly swinging.

This is Kundalini, spiraling up the body.

The symbol of the snake wrapping around the staff we saw so many times at the temples, which we were told symbolized Kundalini: *I can feel it!*

I hear slight pops in my back as the body moves. Then the voices started, something I never experienced before. Not my thoughts but a voice other than my own. I knew I was the only one who could hear the message. The whispers were at alternating times, giving it an echo experience:

She's ready, she's ready, she's ready. Expand, expand, expand.

I listen to the words and let go. My body, my mind, my consciousness—expands. There is more space than ever before, and it's like I have lost 50 pounds. I'm slightly levitating—taller, wiser. I open my eyes and gaze around the room. I feel so much love towards these people, each one beautiful. I could truly see them for who they are. See the soul and know them. I wanted someone to look at me and experience the love I felt. I only lock eyes with two people and smile. I don't think they can tell what is happening! I'm content, regardless. I feel as though I'm someone else.

Am I possessed by a powerful spirit or goddess?

With eyes wide open, my body starts to move, circling.

I can't believe this is happening with my eyes open.

I am impressed. After about five more minutes, the movement comes to a natural stop. I'm looking out of my own eyes, yet it feels like someone else. I love how it feels—immortal, powerful, and all-loving. It was as if I was seeing the world with new eyes for the first time in ages.

As people start to leave the chamber, I look at each one with the most powerful expression of love. Jeff and I walk around the room once, symbolically closing the space. The archeologist leads us out of the chamber to join the rest of the group. I'm still feeling strange. I want to ask someone for advice. *Julianne?* I don't want to be dramatic or interrupt her experience.

I stepped out of the pyramid and felt liberation as if I'd been trapped there for centuries, now emerging into the bright lights of Cairo for the first time. Jeff took a picture of us. I feel like he can tell I'm not myself, but he doesn't say anything. I started to get worried on the bus.

Am I a stranger in my own body? Am I stuck like this now? Is this who I am? Is this a spirit that needs to stay at the pyramids that is now stuck with me? Maybe I watched too many episodes of *Ghost Adventures.*

I lean over to Jeff and ask, "Do you think I am me right now?" He gives me a curious look. "What do you mean?"

"I don't feel like I am the only one in my body right now."

He nods in understanding and asks if I'd like to be guided back. We give thanks to the four directions, upper and lower world teachers, and ask any beings to return to where they came from. I started to feel more like myself again. I'm unsure if it was something else inside me or, perhaps, as suggested by experienced friends, an expanded version of myself.

I yearn to have that feeling of expanded love and soul recognition again. I will strive endlessly to reach this expansion as I know it's the path to moving the world forward toward love and an elevated existence.

THE PRACTICE

CHANTING MANTRA FOR CONNECTION

I extend an invitation to those of you who seek a deeper connection with your higher self or a profound connection with others to explore the practice of chanting mantras. Although the word is Sanskrit in origin, the practice transcends cultural and spiritual boundaries, making it a universal tool for achieving mindfulness and inner clarity.

A mantra is a word, phrase, or sound repeated, clearing the mind of thoughts. When you chant out loud, it vibrates inside of you, soothing the nervous system and allowing you to connect more clearly to the inner self/ great beyond. In certain traditions, it's believed sound is the most direct path to divinity.

To begin your practice, find a clean, quiet space. Choose a mantra that has meaning for you (see options below) or a quality you wish to manifest in your life. Set your intention for the practice, e.g., wisdom, peace, or joy. The traditional repetition of a mantra is 108 times. You can use a mala or other counting tool to keep track. If you have time restrictions, repeat it as many times as possible; you will still achieve benefits even if it's not repeated an exact number of times.

Find a comfortable seat, spine straight, and gently close your eyes. Feel into the chest and imagine a bright light expanding outwardly from your heart. Start the mantra in a normal speaking voice. Feel the words with deep emotion as you recite them. Gradually increase the intensity of the chant. Recite the words quickly with power. Say the words as if you know they're the ultimate truth. As the cycle of the mantra comes to an end, slow down the speed and intensity of the chant into a whisper. Then repeat it in your mind only, eventually coming into silence. In this state of stillness, notice how you feel; whatever the feeling may be, don't fight it or change it; just surrender.

Suggestions to begin chanting mantra:

SO HUM—Inhale, "So." Exhale, "Hum." Meaning: I AM.

I AM LIGHT—you can replace "light" with any other quality you wish to embody.

ONG NAMO GURU DEV NAMO—I bow to the creative wisdom; I bow to the divine teacher within.

OM SHANTI OM—An invocation of peace.

OM SRI YESHU BHAGAVATE NAMAHA—Lord Jesus, I bow to you. It's becoming more common for Christians to use mantras and meditation to get closer to God.

SA SEKHEM SAHU—Sa: The breath of life/Life force. SEKHEM—The power associated with Kundalini Energy. Sekhem is the power that animates the Sahu. It is the power that leads one to spiritual consciousness. SAHU—The spiritual body. The Sahu is made conscious through spiritual practice.

This mantra was used in the temples of Egypt to activate and awaken individuals and the locations themselves. It also contributed to my personal experience inside the pyramid.

The more consistent you are with this practice, the more you'll notice the benefits. However, even if this isn't a daily practice, I still encourage you to use this tool, however sparingly it might be. Each time, you receive a gift of life perspective and peace.

 **Kelly Connolly** graduated with a B.A. in Psychology from the University of New Hampshire in 2008. She is a world explorer, spiritual adventurer, and healing arts practitioner. She is trained in three energy healing arts and possesses a deep passion for yoga, meditation, and devotional chanting.

After she received her 200-hour yoga certification in 2016, she finally found her way into the world of Shakti Flow Yoga. It was here she learned how to hold, balance, and express her body, mind, and spirit in a brand-new way. She dove into the program with all of her heart and completed her 500-hour Shakti Flow Yoga Teacher Training in 2017.

This work taught Kelly the value of engaging in an open and supportive community, the benefits of embodied emotional balance, and a wide array of practices to connect more deeply with her true self and spiritual essence.

Kelly shares her passion and expertise with her communities to support them in finding meaningful connections within themselves. Her highest hope for others in the world is that they discover personal peace, not only for themselves but to uplift humanity as a whole.

Kelly's vision for the near future is to support sacred travel journeys and eventually build her own retreat center, offering a safe haven and sacred space for others to gather for yoga, meditation, and other sacred practices.

Kelly is a certified PADI scuba diver and skydiving enthusiast. She is well described as an ultimate thrill seeker. She currently lives in Ireland with her wonderful husband, Brian.

E-mail: Kelly.Connolly888@gmail.com

CHAPTER 22

EMPOWERED TO LIVE

HELPFUL TOOLS TO SUPPORT YOUR HEALING JOURNEY

Jennifer Kreifels

MY LOVE INITIATION

I look back at periods of my life, and scattered memories are hazy and foggy. Gang rape and severe drug abuse are some of the traumatic experiences I've survived and healed. These experiences can be better understood through the events in this story. I share with you a piece of my life in this way because I only remember snapshots of my experience. I was oftentimes out of my body as I survived through it all.

It's sunrise, and I'm setting sail into the vast, open ocean with my family.

I don't know where we'll end up, but my mind is open, and I desire new experiences. After setting sail, my body begins to soften as I feel the cool ocean breeze brush against my skin. The sun rises higher in the sky. I gently close my eyes, tilt my head up, and feel the warmth of its rays soothe my face.

I slowly open my eyes to see my mom, dad, and brother breathing in the beautiful scenery.

Then BAM!

Out of nowhere, the boat shakes from side to side. I look around and see small waves turning into bigger waves around us. The gentle rocking from side to side gets stronger, and I can barely stay sitting or standing in one place.

I see the faces of my parents lose color; it's as though they have lost their voices and are frozen in a moment of time. I look around, and we're sailing into a dark, cloudy sky that appears out of nowhere.

I look back to my parents for guidance and watch them stumble around the boat as they attempt to prepare for the storm ahead. Their voices get louder, their tones feel like an electric shock to my body, and I feel myself wanting to go inward to hide.

I watch my brother hide under the bench seats. He crawls into the fetal position and seems to be talking to himself. My parents are now scooping water out of the boat and frantically searching for life vests. It feels like someone is beginning to squeeze my heart.

I become the observer. It feels as though I'm separate from this whole experience, even though I'm living it. My mind and body feel stuck in the same position, and it is hard to move. I hear a faint call of my name until I realize my parents are screaming for me to take cover.

I take a step forward towards my parents, and then, again, BAM!

A massive wave crashes over the boat and takes me with it. I flail my arms and manage to grip hold of the edge of the boat. My long, wet hair covers my face, making it hard to see anything. I hear the faint cry of my parents as they scream my name with every ounce of their being. They're crawling to the edge of the boat to pull me back on board.

They don't make it to me in time.

A bright flash of lightning strikes, and a loud, thunderous boom vibrates through the boat, the water, and my body. Another wave crashes into the boat and sucks me into the depths of the ocean.

The powerful cold water pulls me in every direction until I rise to the surface and gasp for air. After filling my lungs with as much air as possible, I desperately call out for help in the darkness. No one responds. I am alone.

My desire to fight for my life takes over. I do my best to swim with the unforgiving flow of the dark ocean. Adrenaline heightens my senses, and I'm using all my energy to stay afloat. As time goes on, I begin to think:

Will I die out here all alone?

Will I be forgotten, or will people remember me?

I don't think I am strong enough to survive this.

After what feels like days, I make it through the storm and can see clear skies off in the distance. I take a breath in and feel a sigh of relief.

I keep treading water and float on top of the ocean when possible. Soon, the hot rays of the fiery sun beam down onto me. My lips begin to dry, and it feels like the salty ocean is squeezing all the water out of my body. All I want to do is sleep. But I stay awake and keep going.

After some time, the water starts to feel warm. I lift my head and see that I'm close to land! There are exotic palm trees, white sandy beaches, and a sense of mystery in the air.

I use my last bit of energy to swim to the shore. Once I make it to the sand, my head hits the ground, and I pass out from sheer exhaustion.

After hours of sleeping, I blink myself awake. I see a bonfire off in the distance. It's nighttime. I become aware of my physical body and feel a blanket made of leaves scratching up against my dry skin. Instead of moving my whole body, I move my eyes to take in the environment around me. As I look around, I see men by the fire snorting something into their noses.

Where am I? Are these people going to hurt me?

Suddenly, I hear women screaming. It's the cry of women who are in gut-wrenching pain. Feeling like I want to throw up, I close my eyes and pretend to sleep. My senses are heightened, and I can hear every conversation and every cry of the women around me. As the night goes on, the noises subside, and the people around me fall asleep one by one.

Okay, everyone is asleep; this is my chance to get away.

I carefully sit up and move the leaf blanket off my body. As I'm standing up, I feel a heavy, calloused hand grab my right shoulder. I gasp one big breath of air and stare blankly ahead. Holding my breath, I turn my head very slowly, and my eyes meet the gaze of a man who feels like a monster. His stare is empty; his eyes are cold.

After making eye contact, this terrifying man effortlessly scoops me up. His grip is tight. There's no room for me to wiggle free. He walks slowly with a wide gait to a hut made of trees. Survival instincts kick in, and I start to look around for possible weapons and a way to escape.

What is he going to do to me? He is three times my size; what will happen if I hit him once and am not able to escape? Will he hurt me even more?

While my internal dialogue is rapidly moving, my body is hot and frozen at the same time. I'm now in this man's hut. He tosses me down onto a bed of leaves. In between my racing thoughts, I hear him say, "I will now claim you as my own."

My mind goes blank.

"No, please, no, please let me go, I will leave and never come back, please, please, please let me go."

He looks at me with an empty, dark, cold stare. As flashes of light come in from the bonfire outside, I see a nauseating smirk appear on his face. He steps closer.

"No, PLEASE! NO!" I beg and scream.

My words mean nothing. My voice means nothing.

Without pausing, he forcefully rips off my clothes and sexually assaults me until I pass out.

I wake up as he pulls the hair on the back of my head. He lifts my face up and aggressively tells me to breathe in. I breathe and feel this burning sensation in my nose. I feel more awake and see other men in the room.

He continues to play with me like I'm a ragdoll. My awareness leaves my body. It feels like I'm floating above the experience, and I watch this man and his friends abuse me in every way possible. Whenever I'm non-responsive, he puts this substance to my nose and has me breathe in.

Finally, it's over. He's done for now. My whole body aches in exhaustion. It feels like someone poked every part of me with tiny needles. It's hard to even sit up. I feel like he stole the most precious part of who I am.

My mind, heart, and body are in shock, and I feel like the person I knew myself to be is nowhere to be found.

Feeling completely separate from my body, I close my eyes and sleep.

The next morning, I wake to people talking. I move my sore muscles and slowly stand up. I feel empty; it's hard to feel anything. I see the man from the night before cooking a fish at the fire. He looks over at me.

"Come eat."

Feeling hollow, I walk over to him, sit down, and eat. The morning goes on. Midday, I see a woman come out of the trees. She waves to me. "Come," she says. Feeling nothing, I walk over to her. When our eyes meet, I know she understands the excruciating pain I feel in my chest and body.

She pulls out a pouch that is full of the powder I saw men snorting the night before.

She offers it to me, "It will make your pain go away, even if it's just for a moment." I stand here, mentally blank, and feel myself going through the motions as I breathe in this powder. I feel the familiar burn, and my mind and body go numb. There is relief.

During my time on this island, the powder becomes my ally, my escape from the pain. Over time, this powder consumes my every hour of every day. At night, I throw up blood, not knowing if I will wake up in the morning. I pray to a God I don't know. *If I am meant to wake up tomorrow, then so be it. If not, then so be it.*

Then, one morning, I visited the woman who first gave me this powder. She is the only person who feels anything like a friend to me.

As I enter her hut, she looks pale, and I see vomit on the floor. I run to her and touch her face, "Wake up! Wake up!"

She is already gone.

Sitting on my knees, I stare at her lifeless body. Again, I find myself frozen. While I sit here feeling nothing, I hear a loud voice in my head.

If you don't get off this island, you will be next. You have weathered many storms and worked really hard to be who you are today. Do you really want to throw it all away because life was cruel to you? It is time to confront your heart-wrenching pain and heal. The past is done. What will you do with your future?

Something inside of me changes. I feel a wave of heat move in the core of my belly, and I want to live. Although I don't know who I am anymore, and I feel swallowed up by pain, I want to live and remember myself for the first time in a long time.

I wait for nightfall, and while everyone is asleep, I walk back to the place where I was first found. I step into the dark ocean and begin to swim. My body feels so weak; my arms and legs are heavy. My internal desire to experience something more is strong, so I keep going.

I swim in the darkness for hours, not knowing where I am going or how long I'll be swimming for. My muscles start to give out. I lie on my back and look up at the endless darkness around me.

As I lie here, I hear voices off in the distance.

Am I hallucinating?

I hear them again.

"Hellooo?"

A bright beam of light shines on my face. I can't see anything. I panic and rapidly tread water.

Slap!

I hear an object plop into the water near me, still blinded by a powerful white light.

"You are safe now! We've been looking for you! Grab the buoy!"

Not knowing what to expect, I pause before grabbing it.

I can make it through anything; look at what I just survived.

I grab the buoy, and a group of men pull me aboard. They wrap me in a soft, warm blanket and guide me to a warm room.

"You can rest here now. No one will bother you. Come out when you're ready."

I slowly walk over to the bed. *Is this a dream? Everything feels blurry.*

I crawl into the bed and sleep. I sleep for a day and a half and wake up when the sun is high at noon.

I notice the boat is no longer moving.

Are we on shore? Have I made it back home?

With knots in my stomach, I leave the room and find my way to the upper deck. I'm greeted by a group of men and women.

"You are safe now," they say over and over, "we're so glad to have found you. You've been lost at sea for weeks, and we have no idea how you survived."

Speechless, I look around and notice we've docked on a sandy beach. My heart drops into my stomach.

"Where are we?"

Everyone smiles with soft, open eyes.

"We made it to your island. No one has ever been here before. It is all yours."

"M-my island? I've been living in deep pain for weeks. I lost my family, and now you want me to stay on this foreign island and take care of myself!"

A woman on deck approaches me.

"I can see in your eyes that you are completely lost, and I can't begin to imagine the heart-ripping pain you've endured. I want you to know that you are loved, and none of what happened to you is your fault. You are safe now. I will be here with you while you learn how to take care of yourself and discover who you are apart from the pain."

She pauses and looks at me.

"We are staying here with you. We will walk alongside you and hold a loving, safe space for you to heal. You will need to take the first step."

From my story, it's clear that people experience turbulent moments in life. Some may shake you, while others knock you off your feet and hit you hard. It's important to always accept the truth of where you're at, the truth of how you're doing. If you walk around saying, "I'm fine," all the time when you're not okay, you slowly bury your pain, lose your voice, separate yourself from the world, and deny yourself the healing you deserve. The more you deny your pain, the more you deny parts of yourself that need your love and tender care the most.

If you're feeling completely alone, lost, or separated from the world, you don't have to go through everything alone. If you were meant to handle everything by yourself, you would've come to Earth by yourself. Be open to receiving support and know that you're strong.

After I made the choice to live, I had no idea what living a meaningful life looked like. Creating new daily habits that were supportive of my healing and growth was uncomfortable, painful, and very challenging at times. With that said, meeting and learning to love myself deeply was worth the journey and commitment. Remember, the journey to healing and self-love is not linear. You may take a few steps forward and steps backward—you're still growing. One of the healing tools I used regularly was affirmations. When we look at ourselves in the mirror and speak intentional, loving words, our cells, our bodies, our hearts, and our minds begin to soften as we reprogram our internal belief system.

THE PRACTICE

With love and compassion, look at yourself in the mirror and lovingly read the following words out loud to yourself. If at any time you feel emotional, pause, breathe deeply in and out, and come back to the present moment.

"I'm asking the parts of me that are hurting or hiding, and those parts of me that I fear or judge, to be present with me now. I welcome all of me into this present moment. In this present moment, I know that I am safe, my body is safe, my mind is safe. First, I want to tell you that none of what happened to you is your fault. Not one moment, not one second, of what happened to you is your fault. It is time to stop blaming yourself. You truly did your best to survive, and I am so thankful that you did not give up. I know the endless amount of strength it's taken you to be standing here right now. I know how tiring it is to always be strong. I know all of your inner struggles and the things you tell no one about, and I love all of you. I begin to accept that the past is the past. It is done. Breathe. It is done. My body, my heart, and my mind are safe in this present moment. It is safe for me and my body to start feeling my emotions. I am learning to love myself more and more each day."

Wrap your arms around your chest and give yourself a soothing, comforting hug. Lovingly hold the parts of yourself that need to be held.

If you would like support in slowly opening your heart to new experiences, go to this link for a guided meditation. The meditation is labeled "Love Initiation Meditation." www.youtube.com/@sirius_wellness

Jennifer Kreifels is a transformational healer and teacher and owns a holistic healthcare practice. She works in the Light with people, animals, and the Earth on a multidimensional soul level and is passionate about helping others step into peace, safety, and genuine, authentic connection with themselves and others. During a session, Jennifer tunes into the physical, emotional, spiritual, and mental energies of whoever she is helping. She meets every person where they're at in the present moment and supports them in the way that they need.

She practices many different healing modalities and offers practical tools that help her clients move forward in between sessions with her. One of her favorite things to do in her practice is help people connect with their inner child and other parts of themselves they forgot or left behind.

When she's not helping others, you will find Jennifer in nature or on an adventure with a close friend. She absolutely loves trying new food and sitting next to flowing water. Well-being is her way of life, and she tunes into herself daily with spiritual practices. Jennifer also teaches spiritual workshops and loves sharing tools to help people connect more with their souls and Spirit Allies. It is a true joy and honor for her to be in service to humanity.

Website: www.siriuswellnesstransformation.com

YouTube: www.youtube.com/@sirius_wellness

CHAPTER 23

LOVE AND ACCEPTANCE

LETTING GO OF FEAR AND BECOMING YOUR AUTHENTIC SELF

Nancy Casey-Humphrey

MY LOVE INITIATION

"I have something I want to share with you," I said to Shannon, my 19-year-old daughter. "I'm gay."

We were on a road trip to California. The two of us were somewhere along the highway in Utah. I knew I needed to contain this conversation in a space we couldn't run away from. Thus, the car ride.

I gripped the steering wheel, happy to have something to hold on to. I sped down the highway, trying to escape the fear and guilt pursuing me.

How would she process this news from her mother? Why am I doing this in Utah, of all places? Her silence is so loud.

I let a moment pass and glanced over at her. She faced forward, looking out the windshield with tears streaming down her face. My heart cried. I was so afraid of losing her.

I reached for her hand. She said, "Do your friends in San Diego know?" I replied, "Yes, I dated women for four years after college. My girlfriend at the time did not want a family; she barely wanted to be monogamous. I wanted a family, and I met a fun-loving Catholic guy."

That might have been a bit too much for her to hear.

"Do you have any questions?" I asked.

"Have you told Shelby yet?" Shelby is my son.

"No, I will when we get back home." I knew telling Shelby would be different. His world wouldn't be rocked like hers.

Silence returned. Nothing else was said. We didn't talk about it again for the rest of the week-long trip. We stayed busy going hiking, going to the beach, and visiting old friends.

Neither one of my kids is homophobic. Still, the fear inside me was overwhelming. *Would this change us? My children are my world; without their love, who would I be? How do I forgive myself for living a lie for so many years?*

My daughter was mourning, mourning the mother she trusted and loved for two decades. This was an unexpected change. That mother no longer existed. That mother was doing her best to navigate rough terrain, often on the verge of losing her sanity. And now, she knew more about that tension.

A few months after our trip, I moved out of our home of 22 years.

Why did I stay for so long?

I was afraid to lose everything. I made a pact with myself to stay for my kids, hoping I raised them to be compassionate enough to understand what I did and why. The self-doubt and second-guessing consumed me. I knew I needed help.

I went to therapy and worked with an energy healer. I felt so deeply that this combination of therapies helped me learn to heal my wounds. I'm now a certified healer and teacher. I'm very grateful to my teachers, the lead writers in this book, Julianne Santini and John Mercede.

My kids and I continued to build and strengthen our relationship. After graduating from college, Shannon got engaged to her high school sweetheart. They asked me to give a toast at their wedding, and I was filled with joy! After their wedding, they moved about an hour and a half away from me, and I saw them less often. We would talk on the phone. On one of the calls, Shannon was crying, "Mom, I'm pregnant." I heard the emotion in her voice. I was the first one she called, and she needed to hear me say, "I'm so happy for you. You'll be okay. You and Matt will be wonderful parents!"

A few months later, I asked my daughter if I could be at the hospital for the baby's delivery. She said, "Actually, Mom, we were hoping you could stay at our apartment and watch Hamilton." Hamilton was their two-year-old dog.

"Of course," I said. At least I'd be close by when the baby was born.

When I got the call that the baby was on the way, I grabbed my bag and drove an hour and a half to the hospital. My son-in-law met me in the lobby with the keys to their apartment and hugged me excitedly, "I wish you could come upstairs and see Shannon, but it's against hospital policy. Only one visitor allowed." He ran back up to the maternity floor.

As I turned to leave, a woman at the administration desk said, "I overheard you talking; you can have two people in maternity. One for the mother and one for the child." I was encouraged to go up to say hi and check on my daughter. Instead, I went back to their apartment to walk and feed the dog. I got settled into the guest room that would soon be my new grandbaby's room.

I was excited, and then the old doubt and fear came back in an instant. I took a deep breath and began to hear my inner voice.

This is your only chance. You need to be there for her at one of the most important moments of her life.

I called my daughter's cell phone: "Can I come back to visit? The nurse told me two visitors are allowed." She said yes! I felt elated as I drove back to the hospital. When I arrived, she said, "You can stay; there's not much going on yet. My water broke, and they are going to induce me. They don't know why my labor isn't progressing."

Contractions started, and no matter what the midwife suggested, nothing seemed to help. As time passed, Shannon's cries became so raw I could barely breathe. The baby was in trouble, and the pain could no longer be managed.

Suddenly, everything moved very fast. The new parents had to decide to keep trying to deliver as planned or do a c-section. When they told the midwife they decided on a c-section, she looked at me. "I heard their choice," was all I'd say. I was advocating for my daughter and her family.

Every molecule in my body was broadcasting healing light and love through the empty hospital corridors.

This is why I am here. I was waiting for an invitation to this love initiation.

We sat on a little bench outside of the surgical suite. I was terrified. My son-in-law, Matt, sitting next to me, said, "What have we done?" I held him, and his whole body shook as he sobbed.

My daughter's screams were replaced with a fearful silence.

We were told the c-section would be only ten minutes, and it had already been closer to an hour. We watched as new people ran by, pulling on protective surgical garb—no time for questions. The mother and baby were both in distress.

"Thank you for being here," Matt said with tear-filled eyes.

One of the doctors finally came to talk to us, "The baby didn't have enough room to deliver and was stuck in Shannon's pelvis. Because of the anesthesia, he came into the world floppy and non-responsive. We had to insert a tube to help him to breathe. Once we get him to the NICU, we can remove it. Shannon is still in surgery and doing great. She'll be in recovery soon."

They brought baby Max out to us. I had a few moments to stand next to my grandson's tiny bassinet. I saw the tube in his mouth held in place by tape, pulling at his tiny lips. A nurse held the respirator attached to the tube and moved in unison with the tiny bed holding my heart's heart, my baby's baby.

"I love you," I said to my new grandson, and I hugged his daddy, saying, "Go be with your son. I'll wait for Shannon." They were rushed off to the NICU.

I was alone outside the operating room. I couldn't sit still and walked to the restroom. As I stood at the sink, a nurse came in, "You must be Shannon's mom. The doctor will come talk to you soon." She reached to hug me as I finally released my own sobs. With such compassion, she said, "Mothers are always so strong, and they take care of the family before themselves."

I can get lost in my emotions and cling to old patterns. By releasing my fears, I was present to support my daughter and son-in-law in those vulnerable moments. I witnessed Matt's joy and pain as he walked with his son towards the NICU, and I waited for my daughter. At this moment, we each had a child to take care of.

Shannon woke up confused, "Where is Max is he okay? Where's Matt?" I held her hand. So glad to be there so she wasn't alone. I sat next to her in the recovery room as the doctor came in to tell her about the surgery and what to expect. After a couple of hours, they moved her to her own room and promised to bring in Max and Matt. The baby can only have one visitor, and his daddy was not leaving his side. Oh, how I love my son-in-law! It was time for me to leave and return to my dog-sitting duties.

Three days later, the new family came home from the hospital. I finally got to hold my tiny grandson. He had blossomed into an adorable little newborn with a full head of black hair that shot straight up and announced, "Look at me; I am here!"

I know by holding love in my heart for my family and being a witness to my grandson's birth, I blessed my descendants with love.

My fears could've prevented me from sharing these moments of happiness with my family. By doing my work and recognizing I needed help, I started enjoying this new chapter in life. I'm setting a great example for my kids by being authentic.

I'm now happily married to my wife, Kerry. We're both excited to be new grandparents together!

Let me help you release fear and let love shine within yourself. I have practices and tools to share in the following section.

THE PRACTICE

On my healing journey, I discovered Ho'oponpono, the Hawaiian prayer of forgiveness. Let me explain how to use this prayer to bring peace into your life.

Step 1: You can use the Ho'oponopono prayer to clear accumulated negative memories. Our memories help form how we experience reality. These memories and thoughts can replay in our minds, bringing us right back to the original trauma. Using this prayer clears those memories that don't serve us.

This prayer consists of four phrases. You may use them in any order:

I am sorry.

Please forgive me.

Thank you.

I love you.

I was so intrigued by this practice that I took a course and am certified to teach others. The key to success in this healing modality is repetition.

This practice can help you release any tension. For example, if someone cuts you off on the highway, say the four phrases: "I am sorry, please forgive me, thank you, I love you." Repeat as needed. You can stop yourself from reacting. Continue driving in peace. By doing this, you stop the spread of reactive anger. The results help everyone.

Here is another example of how this prayer can help you find peace. If you can't sleep because of intrusive thoughts running through your mind, try repeating the four phrases until you begin to relax and fall back to sleep. If this happens often, I have found that it's helpful to start the prayer as soon as you realize you're awake. There is no need to identify the thoughts or attach to them. This calls in the divine and allows the prayer to do the work of clearing the thoughts for you.

I hold monthly online prayer groups where we repeat the prayer 108 times. I encourage you to join us and experience the power of this prayer. You can find a link in my bio.

Step 2: There are many tools available to practice Ho'oponopono. You can learn how to incorporate different foods and blue solar water to aid in the clearing process.

Blueberries can help you advance on your spiritual journey and can aid in connecting to angelic realms. Strawberries can be used to release negative beliefs or triggers about weight issues.

Another tool I recommend is blue solar water. You can make your own at home. Place a blue glass bottle filled with tap or filtered water in the sunlight for a minimum of one hour. Use blue solar water daily as part of your daily spiritual practice. Blue solar water aids with connecting to the Divine and changing mental patterns, helping to restore the state of perfection you were born with. I make at least one bottle daily. The process of the sun passing through the blue glass instills spiritual properties in the water that are calming. Make sure your bottle is suitable for drinking and enjoy this healing water.

Additional resources are listed in my bio, including a link to my website where you can purchase beautifully designed blue glass bottles. I will also post a link for classes.

Nancy Casey-Humphrey, healer, artist and teacher. She is an Integrated Energy Therapy and Ho'oponopono practitioner and Reiki Master. She is also the Director of Creative Services at an advertising firm in Denver, Colorado.

Nancy studied fine arts at Colorado State University. As a child, she loved to draw. Drawing was a good way to escape constant arguing at home. She lived in four different states before graduating from high school. All of this led to the ability to meet challenges and adapt to constant change. After graduating with a BFA specializing in graphic design, she started working in Denver area advertising agencies, leveraging her strengths of staying busy and meeting challenges. She is a leader in her field.

To find a balance between her corporate life and her spiritual side, Nancy has been studying energy healing for several years. Her first experience was Integrated Energy Therapy (IET). She loves connecting with the angelic realm during IET sessions. This filled a spiritual space in her life that led to a deep sense of balance and calm. She became an avid student and practitioner of energy healing modalities.

Her Reiki level three teacher taught her Reiki with a Shamanic twist. Shamanic readings and journeys are also a part of Nancy's healing toolkit. Journeying is a deep visual and spiritual method of healing. Using this practice, Nancy has connected with ascended masters and has learned to connect with her clients by doing readings.

Next, she started studying and practicing Ho'oponopono. She loves designing and creating healing tools based on the Ho'oponopono practice.

She is certified to teach both Reiki and Ho'oponopono. You can find classes on the events page of her website.

Visit her website at https://casey-creative.com

Events page: https://casey-creative.com/events

Shopping: https://caseycreativehealing.etsy.com

Email nancy.casey@casey-creative.com

CHAPTER 24

FEATHERS

LOVE REACHES OUT

Cloanne Wundrow

MY LOVE INITIATION

The words continue to ring in my ears. Three months! It's as though I'm hearing them for the first time.

Is that really what the doctor said?

The car hadn't left the parking lot. We just sat silently, side by side, trying to wrap our stunned minds around the diagnosis.

If we say nothing, will it all go away? Is it just one horrible dream?

That moment feels so present. It's hard to believe well over a quarter of a century has passed. Against all odds, my husband was graced with three more years.

His funeral was a testament to his faith. The sky was so filled with rainbows as we walked out of our parish church that day that the story made the local newspaper the following morning. I suppose that headline alone should have been a sign, my gift that all was well with Claude, but I was restless, so very restless.

When we were married, as is often poetically stated, we became one. Several years after his death, despite any number of support groups and the rallying cry from so many friends about how well I was doing, I felt like half of me was missing. I tried desperately to be there for my children, to put on my happy face, to be engaged in life, to reach out, but the truth is all I wanted to do was curl up in a little ball on the couch and hide, until that is, the gift of the feathers began.

My sister-in-law, Eunice, was a Franciscan nun. She was the oldest of his five siblings. I decided a year or so after Claude's death that a trip back to their family roots in Germany and on to Rome and Assisi would be healing for us both. At one point, midtrip, we found ourselves staying in a Franciscan convent. The nuns delighted in calling me Sr. Cloanne and made me feel 100% at home with them.

One morning, Eunice and I decided to get some fresh air and take a stroll to the local cathedral before joining the sisters for lunch. To get to the street it was necessary to cross a large vacant parking lot. As we walked, I remember telling Eunice about the story I read in a Guidepost magazine the previous night.

A young woman was away when her father died. She was crushed; she wasn't able to say goodbye. As she wandered along the ocean shore, grieving, a feather drifted down from the sky. She and her dad loved and studied seabirds, and she was certain this feather was a gift from her dad.

After retelling the story, I announced that I thought Claude should send us a feather. The expression on Eunice's face was unreadable. As she rolled her eyes, I believe it danced somewhere between, "You have got to be kidding, Cloanne. You are just setting yourself up for disappointment!" and "Could something like that really happen?"

Before I could retract my request and avoid failure, a small white feather drifted before us. It lingered a moment in the air. I put out my hand, and it settled gently on my palm. We stood in awe, in wonder. There were no words.

With that small feather came the peace I sought and an amazing initiation of love and joy. My delight in that moment could have lasted a lifetime, but Claude, in death, like he was in life, continued, and continues, to be incredibly generous. While I was trying to plan where best to keep my little feather and tell its story, more and more feathers began to appear.

Shortly after my return from Europe, a friend suggested I might enjoy a music and guided imagery (GIM) retreat. It sounded a little "out there" to me, but I signed up. It was really more about not hurting my friend's feelings than something I truly wanted to do. A week of silence did not sound that enticing.

Good grief, I live alone! How much silence does one need?

On my two-and-a-half-hour drive to the Presentation Center, my mind went into overdrive. By the time I arrived, early as always, I was absolutely sure this was not where I belonged or wanted to be. As I drove onto the property, I noticed a small lake. I made the command decision: I would take a stroll around the lake, pray for advice, and make a final decision before finally signing in.

The setting sun shimmered on the water. It was beautiful. The gentle breeze blew twinkles first this way and that on the surface.

What kind of an answer was this?

I listened. Even the birds were silent. Searching for an answer, I looked down. It was not a single feather. It was thousands of soft white duck feathers! I've never before or since seen such a fluffy bed of feathers. My question was answered. I stayed and began what has become a beautiful way of meditation and prayer in my life.

I remember the following Easter, driving to San Diego for a visit with more of Claude's family. Eunice also lived there. It was decided that after our celebration, Eunice and I would drive up the coast of California to the Bay Area where I lived. We planned on getting on the road early, but we were all having such a good time it was late in the day before we departed.

I was tired. Somewhere around six in the evening, we decided to find a motel and crash for the night. I announced, "I want a place right on the water where I can run in the sand and see the surf." Eunice laughed and said, "If I had a choice, I'd like a place with a bathtub," because there was no tub in the convent where she lived.

Now, those don't really seem like difficult requests, especially along the coast, but after an hour's effort, we found nothing. We gave up looking for beachfront places and bathtubs. We just wanted beds! Nothing, however, seemed available. I decided to forge on into the next town. As I muttered, "We could use a little help here, Claude," I missed the turn onto the freeway.

Trying to correct my error, I ended up on a short, narrow, dead-end street ending at the water. The last building was a rickety old motel. It wasn't exactly the kind of a place I would've chosen for Eunice or myself, but I decided I was exhausted. A look inside couldn't hurt. Old but clean, it was an eclectic mix of early American and God only knows what else. Doilies, hobnail lamps, and plastic flowers were everywhere.

"It will do," I thought as I eyed the beachy fish and chips dive directly across the street, beer on tap, red and white plastic tablecloths flapping in the breeze.

Eunice looked a little concerned as I led her into the lobby, but her eyes beamed with delight as we opened the door to our room. There, sitting center stage in our bathroom, was a brand new, imitation clawfoot tub, with jets no less! I left her heading for the tub as I shed my shoes and raced to the beach.

I walked in peace to the sound of the tide and the ever-present seagulls. About a mile and a half up the beach, I started having this déjà vu feeling. There ahead was a huge hotel where Claude and I stayed one night. It was one of those pockets in time I shall never forget.

We had walked on a pathway along the beach, the colors of the sunset enveloping us. We held hands and felt the love of the universe flow between us. Here, I was again surrounded by warm and wonderful memories. My feet barely touched the Earth as I headed back to our little motel.

As I crossed the dry sand from the surf's edge to our motel door, my heart singing, "Thank you, thank you," I came to a dead stop. There, sticking out of a foot-high mound of sand, were standing two very large seagull feathers. "You're welcome, you're welcome," I could almost hear Claude laughingly respond.

Feather blessings have continued on and on over the years—small spotted guinea fowl feathers, pink flamingo feathers, black crow feathers, and bright blue jay feathers. I've even been presented with an eagle feather by a Native American elder.

Sometimes, I find feathers lying at my feet along the sidewalk, and sometimes, I discover them where feathers normally do not belong. I was surprised to see a little feather atop my suitcase when I was heading off to China just a few months after 9/11, and delighted when I found a feather on the seat of my car after dropping off the first set of income tax forms, which I completed by myself.

I never know when Claude will send out his feather love and support. Sometimes, it feels like he's just saying "hi," other times, it's a hearty "chin up, carry on, I've got you covered." And sometimes, I'm certain, he's just joining in on the fun of life.

The perfect example of just pure fun came a couple of years ago on my birthday. I was traveling with one of my three daughters and her husband, who live in the Midwest. We visited Montana and took a detour to visit Mt. Rushmore on the way home. The three of us were happily traveling in my son-in-law's huge work truck.

They laughingly purchased a collapsible stool so I could climb in and out. All five feet of me felt a bit like a queen rising up to my assigned spot in the front seat where, as the miles flew by, I was given a crash course in the seasons, weather, hay baling, plants, the local flora and fauna, cloud formations, and the best way to read road conditions and navigate through traffic.

Who could possibly know so much?

As a city girl, I was totally fascinated. It was one of those fun, happy trips of a lifetime. As I slid out of the truck for dinner, our days coming soon to their end, I couldn't help thinking: *This very dirty truck would do well with a bath.* The grill alone was absolutely encrusted with mud, leaves, and every kind of dead bug known to man. We enjoyed a hearty celebration meal, and when we returned to the truck, we all stopped.

What was that? Had a bird flown into the grill?

Amid the dirty mess, something pristine and white fluttered in the breeze. As we approached, we discovered a huge, fluffy white feather wedged into all the muck. It took some doing to remove it, but we all looked at it in awe. There was no question in our minds from where it came. It not only was a birthday wish from Claude, but it was also a thank you to the family, one and all, who took such good care of me. Instead of being attached to a very dirty truck grill, that lovely white feather now sits on my desk in a black velvet shadow box, reminding me each day that life, no matter what it brings, is truly to be welcomed with love and gratitude.

Our family continues to grow, and the stories of Grandpa's feathers continue to delight. Even better yet, I'm now not the only recipient of Claude's feathers. Sometimes, I can only sit back, smile, and say, "You've done it again, Claude Wundrow. Thank you, thank you!"

Several years ago, our eldest granddaughter got married. They chose a wooded forest venue, and like most weddings, months of preparation preceded the big day. As I was packing to fly to the Midwest to add support and a little help, I noticed a bag of feathers shoved in my craft box. It had been there for a century, a leftover from some school project, or Halloween costume creation, or both.

Ah, I thought, *what a nice way to include Claude at the wedding. I will just sprinkle a few down the aisle in his memory.* And I tossed the bag in my suitcase.

And with the truism that great minds think alike, as I was packing feathers, my daughter, shopping in Hobby Lobby, picked up a small package of feathers with the exact same intent in mind. We laughed as we saw each other's feathers.

As the day of the wedding approached, life got hectic, not only with unexpected hospital stays but with a road construction project that slowed traffic to the wedding venue to a crawl. By the time the ceremony actually began, we were all exhausted yet delighted. At long last, the big moment had arrived. The wooded venue was indeed lovely with birds singing and a slight breeze blowing. My heart leaped with joy when I heard little eight-year-old Lyra's voice as she stepped into the aisle.

"Look," she gleefully announced, "Grampy's feathers."

I was so glad my daughter remembered to sprinkle the feathers. In all the commotion, I completely forgot. Little did I know that as my daughter heard Lyra's words, she was thinking: *Wow, I can't believe Mom remembered.*

She, too, was too busy. It totally slipped her mind. Claude let us know quite clearly that feathers are his domain! He's got us covered! Tears flow with gratitude as I realize I need to do nothing.

I never would've thought those many years ago that today I'd be living in this amazing abundance of love and, yes, feathers. Each little feather reminds me I am cherished. Claude and I walk, as we have always walked, together in love. I'm overwhelmed with gratitude. I need no more. I have found joy.

THE PRACTICE

I do not see clients or have a business, but if asked what one can do to enrich their life, my response would be simple.

Smile more, be kind to yourself and others, live in gratitude and add more thank yous to your day. When life seems unbalanced, stand tall and hold on to the conviction that you are cherished. Seek peace; live in joy! Choosing just one will make a difference.

Feathers are gifted to me. What has been gifted to you? Look for recurring themes in your life. Prepare to be surprised.

Cloanne Wundrow is ready to laugh, ready to help, and ready to go on her next great adventure. Her two greatest passions are family and travel.

After receiving her BA in art and religion from Holy Names College in 1961, she worked for the Red Cross and Special Services in France, Germany, and Korea. Upon her return, she jumped into her Mustang convertible and drove throughout the US, rolling out her sleeping bag each night. She married in 1968 and happily became a wife and mother of four.

Since her husband's death, she has pursued her love of adventure, traveling from the pyramids of Giza to the pyramids of Teotihuacan through China, Africa, India, Cambodia, Peru, Alaska, and beyond.

Cloanne is a dreamer who loves dreaming in many forms. She is a long-time member of a dream group and delighted in entertaining Jeremy Taylor in her home. She participated in weekends with Richard Moss and studied core Shamanism with Michael Harner.

She loves Centering Prayer promulgated by Trappist Monk Thomas Keating and considers her years with a Lectio Divina group a time of unique spiritual growth.

Well into her eighties, Cloanne still travels, whether off to see her family spread across the states or exploring the world. She will tell you quite candidly that life is truly a journey, and one of her favorite parts is the amazing people she meets along the way.

Feathers remain an integral part of her life. When asked, she will smile and say, yes, she did receive a feather on this love initiation trip to Egypt. While standing with a group waiting for a bus, someone saw a tiny feather drifting down. Cloanne put out her hand, and just like the very first feather she had received, it landed gently on her palm.

Email: cloannew@gmail.com

AFTERWORD

Christina Santini

Am I really having imposter syndrome in Egypt? I think anyone growing into who they are second-guesses it.

I had the honor of spending 13 days with individuals from all walks of life. I heard their stories. We laughed and cried together, discovering what was hidden in Ancient Egypt to find that which was hidden within ourselves. We just had to take the time to listen.

It was a once-in-a-lifetime opportunity that I experienced with my mother and grandmother. Within the group, I represented the descendants of the world and all those to come. Seems like some big shoes to fill, right? But oddly, after ruminating on the concept, it felt right. It helped me remember what not to lose sight of as I continue to grow.

At 26, I was the youngest of this group. I kept asking myself: *Why am I here among all these healers, storytellers, and entrepreneurs? Who am I, and what do I have to give these people? Have I even gone through my own initiation?*

These were the questions floating around my mind as we floated down the Nile. At times, I was fully immersed in the temples, pyramids, and experience. Other times, I was battling these questions without answers.

Now, I compare this feeling of imposter syndrome to children. They're so filled with love, laughter, and joy. They haven't yet been jaded or stuck in the ruts of routine. They get excited about the smallest of things. They feel every moment and emotion so fully. They're in contact with spirit, the unknown, the unseen, and the limitless future of what we can all become.

I'm still young, right? Although, at 26, I think I'm losing touch with that joy sometimes. I get overwhelmed with the world around me, everything I'm 'supposed to do,' and everything I'm 'supposed to be.' This trip helped me tap into my love and my power and remember the possibilities in front of me.

I asked myself: *What do I have to give these people?* I like to think the universe gave me a loving tap on the side of the head and said, *Hello? You are my daughter. You have so much to give!* I see it now! I was with this group to hold space as a reminder of who they were, who they are, who is yet to come, and what they can create. So, I gave a different gift of myself to each of the 27 other people on this trip.

Yet, still, I asked myself: *Why am I even on this trip?* Cue the second love tap. I was here to grow and find my voice, to find my strength, and to awaken my self-love. I was in Egypt to live and experience. I was here to remember.

I have a little love tap and reminder for you and for myself, too, when I forget ~

Life is full of initiations. Life is full of love.

Life is full of beginnings and ends.

Each one of us is a descendant,

and, also, an ancestor or elder.

Don't forget each of our lives started as a child,

full of love, limitless creation, ideation, and hope.

Please don't lose your inner child.

I connect with my inner child by pulling out the curliest curly fry from the bag, jumping from leaf to leaf on the sidewalk, hoping for that satisfying crunch, and feeling my heart melt and yet burst open when my boyfriend calls me his "lil chicken nuggie." I just can't help but smile! Love and happiness don't have to make sense; they just are. Don't miss these moments.

I think the world likes to limit us at times through expectations, through "shoulds," and through "what ifs." I like to look back with the ferocity of a small child, face scrunched in determination, hands bunched up at their sides, screaming, "You're wrong; I can do it!" So, I say, live your life to the fullest. Imagine everything it can be, everything you want for yourself, for your family, and even those you haven't yet met, and create it! It's possible. I'm so excited to see what beauty we can all create when we listen to how each of our souls speaks to us.

My final parting message:

- Cherish the glimmers and little moments that make you smile.
- Listen closely because your soul is always guiding you to love wherever that takes you, whomever you meet, and whomever you become.
- You are not alone.
- Don't forget to be kind to yourself.
- You are full of endless potential.
- You can do it!

Christina Santini is an innovative biomedical engineer by day and an artsy, introspective, go-with-the-flow gal by night.

Christina graduated with her BS in Biomedical Engineering from California Polytechnic State University and currently works as an R&D Engineer at Edwards Lifesciences. In her role, she designs and develops next-generation transcatheter implants to treat cardiovascular diseases and repair heart valves. She loves knowing the small projects she works on daily will have a lasting impact on the quality of life for patients worldwide.

Not only is she well-versed in engineering and the sciences, but she loves to play in nature, often seeking peace among the quiet trees and forests. Additionally, she thrives in the creative realm, jumping between a variety of projects at home, including painting, drawing, crocheting, baking, and wherever her inspiration strikes next.

This duality to Christina's character allows her to analyze her experiences and find quick and innovative solutions, and also welcome and create space for spirit. She stands as an example of how the sciences, arts, and spirituality are more intertwined than we often realize.

Christina is a lover and collector of all things small and adorable. She's always ready for adventures with her family and friends, whether it's running a Tough Mudder race with her dad and brother or sailing down the Nile with her grandmother and mother.

Email: santini.cm@gmail.com

THE JOURNEY CONTINUES

Imagine listening in on a conversation between Julianne and John relaxing on their lanai under a pink Florida sky. John picks up binoculars, setting his sights on a baby alligator while Julianne scrolls through innumerable photos. This comes on the heels of their trip to Egypt with a group of authors and a collaborative book project. They're reflecting on their journey of Spirit timing, synchronicity, and soul collaboration.

"Do you have a favorite memory from our trip?" asks Julianne.

"There are so many moments we've yet to unpack," responds John.

"What about our private moment at the Temple of Osiris in Abydos, sitting above the complex together, meditating into the Flower of Life?"

The Osirion is a unique subterranean temple dedicated to Osiris and the energies of rebirth and resurrection. On one of the huge 100-ton megalithic stones appears the image of the Flower of Life. It's burned into the rock in a way no archeologist or scientist can explain. It's as if a laser altered the atomic structure of the rock.

The Flower of Life is a geometrical design consisting of 19 interconnected circles. It evolves from the Vesica Piscis, into the Seed of Life and, ultimately, the Flower of Life. It symbolizes the building blocks of existence, the cycle of creation, and the interconnectedness of life. A deep understanding of the image is said to expand consciousness and bring peace.

"Remember the beautiful man who offered to take our picture?" asks John.

"Yes, and his sweet son who offered us bundles of wheat representing the seeds of creation. What perfect timing! We were literally holding the Seed of Life gifted to us by Ashley to connect to the Grid."

The Grid of Light Project is Ashley Woods' vision to bring light into every corner of the world. Her activated bronze Flower of Life sculptures are energy tools of transformation. Each sculpture links to a planetary grid of light connecting with every other Flower of Life sculpture around the globe. Julianne and John love delivering her sculptures to sacred sites and their gifted recipients.

"Don't we have the best jobs in the world? I can imagine someone asking me, *what do you and John do?* and responding, *oh, we're light sherpas!*"

"How synchronistic to return home from Egypt and receive the invitation for the Flower of Life installation in Mt. Shasta! What are the chances?" John queries.

"It's like we're following this score of music in the unseen realms with the Great Spirit as conductor. In some way, it makes no sense to travel now. Laura is editing our chapters, and we need to be ready to review the book.

"Nothing like handing your timetable and clock over to God."

"That reminds me of the concept of Kairos," Julianne adds, "when spirit hovers over a situation waiting for the vital moment."

"And, those moments are characterized by coincidence or serendipity."

"Have you noticed, even if you really want to, you can't push those moments forward?"

"Right," says John, "the Shasta installation was supposed to occur several years ago, or so we thought!"

"Oh, look. Ashley just sent a text message. She's inviting us to share about our experiences delivering the sculptures. How fun!"

"Julianne, do you remember the look on Jorge's face when he first saw the Flower of Life we brought to Peru? He couldn't get his hands on it fast enough. He looked like a proud papa holding a newborn baby. He was beaming from ear to ear."

Jorge Luis Delgado is a Peruvian chakaruna, author, and founder of Kontiki Tours. He's a Keeper of the knowledge of the Incas and teaches that a new consciousness is emerging.

When Julianne and John met Jorge, they realized they shared a vision to create a wave of transformation for humanity and reconnect power places on the planet. By Jorge's inspiration and urging, they deliver tektites (Peruvian cosmic stones) to sacred sites to stimulate reconnection where the energy lines are disrupted, all the while delivering energy sculptures for Ashley.

"John, you carried that heavy bronze Flower of Life all the way to the top of Machu Picchu to the Caretaker's overlook. I'm not sure how you did it."

"The energy of Machu Picchu helped! Jorge says the energy is so high everything gets amplified and brought to the surface. I thought Jorge was talking about hucha (heavy energies within), but what came to the surface was Ashley's gift. We weren't supposed to give it to Jorge until we reached Lake Titicaca, but God and the energy had something different planned!"

"Machu Picchu felt electric!" remembers Julianne. "It seemed like the energy of the Flower of Life accelerated as we pulled it out of the bag. It was like holding a generator being plugged in or synced up. And guess where the bag holding it came from? Shasta! I love the interconnections."

John interjects, "I really enjoyed having dinner with Jorge that night. He confessed when he originally talked to Ashley, he wasn't sure he wanted the Flower of Life, but something changed when it was pulled out of the bag at Machu Picchu. He was drawn to it; every part of him wanted it. He was like a moth to a flame."

"That's because he recognized it," Julianne exclaims. "He saw the circular bronze sculpture as a Solar Disc. In the Andean teachings, the Solar Disc holds a special vibration to activate the inherent powers within each of us. We're not separate from the divine. It resides in every cell of our body, and as Jorge explains, is activated by our Inner Sun."

John smiles, "It's interesting how some God moments circle back around to find us."

"What do you mean?"

"Do you remember two years beforehand? An artist contacted Jorge with a large piece of granite just perfect for a Flower of Life sculpture. Jorge declined, saying he preferred indigenous symbols, and commissioned two Andean pieces for his hotel grounds."

"What I remember is two years later, on the bus ride back to the hotel. After Jorge held the Flower of Life, he called the artist immediately to ask if the original stone was still available."

"Amazingly, it was. You can't make this stuff up!" John chuckled. "The gigantic granite Flower of Life is now at the Urubamba Hotel, while the bronze Flower of Life is in Puno, near Lake Titicaca."

"That makes sense to me!"

"Why is that?" John asks.

"Well, I notice among the many mountain ranges there are 19 Apukuna (*mountain guardians*) around Lake Titicaca, and there are 19 spheres in the Flower of Life—one Apu to guard each sphere!"

"Well, you would know, Julianne—you whose Spirit goes dancing with the Apukuna!"

Julianne chuckles. "I love being there! I so want to return. One of my favorite places to dream is floating on Lake Titicaca in a reed boat. It feels like we're being held and gently rocked by the mountains. The Apukuna guard the divine blueprint of creation while we dream a new dream together."

"Do you remember the dreaming intention we used?" John asks. "It was given to us by Shree Devi Maa—*May the unshakable power of love be active in me, and through me, and all of humanity to wake us up from this dream of separation.*"

"Beautiful. I love our life, and the life we're dreaming."

"We're more than light sherpas, Julianne. We activate the wheels of time!"

"I'd say you have a vivid imagination, but it actually tracks with our experience in Mexico."

"That's true," John adds thoughtfully. "When we bring a Flower of Life to a new destination, and it lands, I mean really lands, it magnifies, and is magnified by all the other flowers around the globe. With each delivery, there's a compounding factor."

Scrolling through more photos, Julianne asks, "Do you remember being underneath the pyramid of Quetzalcoatl in Teotihuacan? Goodness, what an installment!"

"I sure do," John replies. "We worked with the ancestors at the Place of the Elders beforehand. We even brought a tektite from Peru and connected the Seeds of Light to the sacred locations on the Earth. We carried the Flower of Life up both the Sun and Moon Pyramids, but it was the journey underneath the Quetzalcoatl Pyramid that seemed so timely. The site was just opened after 1800 years."

"It was like returning to the womb of creation!" grinned Julianne. "It was a culminating experience for me. I kept seeing the same cave in my dream for eight years but didn't know where to find it in Mexico. Each year, when I arrived in Teotihuacan, I asked Alberto Hernandez, our Dreaming House friend, to take us to another cave. Little did I know the cave I was looking for was the archeological site being excavated!"

John's smile widens, "What an honor to meet Sergio Gomez, the archeologist who discovered the site! I can only imagine finding the original sinkhole. What a discovery."

The Quetzalcoatl Pyramid looks like the head of the great feathered serpent coming up out of the Earth, its mouth wide open, creating two peaks. The 2,000-year-old tunnel was discovered in 2003 when a 54-foot-deep sinkhole appeared in the plaza in front of the pyramid.

The tunnel was excavated over an eight-year period. 250,000 pounds of rubble were removed, opening 23 gates that blocked off the main cavern under the larger peak. It's believed it was in use for only 200 years for ceremony before being walled off.

"Look what I found, John. Here's a picture of our Violet Flame Dream Team wearing hard hats. Remember climbing down several flights of stairs and a ladder to see the original sinkhole where Sergio landed?"

"I remember crouching down, and some of us even crawling, to make our way along the make-shift platforms for over 300 ft in the flickering lights. We passed the remnants of 23 walls as we carried in the 23rd Flower of Life. Can you believe the synchronicity?"

The cavernous area under the pyramid is shaped like a cross or Four-Petaled Flower. The floor depicts a mountain range complete with lakes originally filled with mercury. The ceiling was painted with cinnabar, containing pyrite, hematite, and magnetite, and once sparkled like a celestial night sky. It looked like a huge diorama. In Teotihuacan mythology, the Lower World is the world of creation. The story is depicted beautifully in the book "Teotihuacan: City of Water, City of Fire."

"Sergio's description of the chamber still fascinates me," remembers Julianne. "He called it 'The Place of the Two Wheels of Time—sacred and mundane.' When asked why he felt the tunnel was discovered at this time, he said simply, *because the wheels are broken."*

"That's when we pulled out the Flower of Life. The energy became completely still. Sergio turned off the lights, and with our ceremony in complete darkness, we explored a world of light."

Julianne runs into the house and comes back holding two large brass gears from a clock. "Remember these? One of my first meditation teachers gave them to me. When we were under the pyramid, I saw them spinning in front of me like two wheels of light connecting the images of the Flower of Life and the Four-Petaled Flower. As we entered sacred time, it felt like all the sacred flowers throughout time and space began to spin. Touched by the moment, I was in tears and reached out to hug Emily."

Emily Grieves, Alberto's daughter-in-law, made our access to the excavation site possible. She was the new recipient of the Flower of Life. She and her husband, Victor Manuel Reyes Contla, followed their dream and opened a creativity hotel and retreat center in 2019–Villa las Campanas. It's within walking distance to the archaeological sites of Teotihuacan with a view of the Sun Pyramid from the roof. It's truly a place of dreaming opportunities.

Emily's life is led by her creative muse, the Divine Mother. She is a renowned artist and teacher promoting intuitive artistic expression and making positive change in the world. She is a certified Intentional Creativity Teacher.

John muses, "I think we were the first group welcomed to Villa las Campanas. That was a day of big dreams for all of us–from intentional artwork to the Flower of Life installation. Do you remember how Emily connected with Ashley and her project?"

"McGuckin Hardware!" responds Julianne immediately.

"What?"

"It's one of those synchronistic stories," Julianne laughs. "Retreat leaders Rita and Ed Fox were at McGuckin Hardware at the same time as Ashley. They met in the art aisle, and after talking about projects and sacred sites, Ashley found herself invited to tea. That tea led to a discussion about Teotihuacan, Alberto Hernandez and the Dreaming House, and its then-current manager, Emily Grieves.

"Several days later, Ashley shared with us about this magical meeting. That alone would have been amazing enough. Then, we told her we were leaving for Mexico in just a few days, and *guess who we were staying with*– Emily and her family! She just stopped talking. The dramatic pause in the conversation was priceless."

John smiles, "I think Spirit was just showing off that day! The interconnection of soul family never ceases to amaze me. Remember how our paths crossed with Patrick Zeigler several months before our Love Initiation trip to Egypt?"

Patrick Zeigler is the founder of Sekhem All Love. He brought awareness of this energy stream and how to work with it to the US 40 years ago. After spending an evening alone in the Great Pyramid, he experienced a spontaneous initiation in the sarcophagus of the King's Chamber. He became aware of a remarkable healing energy opening his heart and touching his soul, which ultimately inspired him to create a healing system to share with others.

"I so enjoyed our dinner conversation with Patrick."

"And our discussion about Sekhem," adds Julianne.

"We know Sekhem as the 'power of powers.' We experience it as spiritual oneness and the energy beyond form." Looking upward, John continues, "Some might call it heaven, or in Egypt, the place where the gods were born."

"Patrick referred to Sekhem as masculine. He explained that by adding the letters ET to SKHM, you have Sekhmet, the feminine form of the energy. Interesting."

"Do you remember another teaching we received about Sekhmet and the Flower of Life from Sai Maa?" asks Julianne.

"I heard her saying Sekhmet carries a Flower of Life on her chest."

"Yes, I remember seeing it as an energetic tattoo and envisioning it as an easy way for Sekhmet to bless the grid, the world, and all of life. She can simply touch her heart and give blessings of peace, love, harmony, and unity.

"That's exactly what we were doing at the Osirion Complex!" John replies. "Gracing the Grid."

"It's such a simple practice, John. Let's do it now."

Gracing the Grid: Place your hands on your heart over an energetic imprint of the Flower of Life. Imagine you're connected to all flowers in the Grid of Light and the sacred wheels of time. Experience yourself in the subtle energies of peace and love—in harmony with yourself, and unity with all others. Now, experience yourself adding your light, and blessing the grid, the world, and all of life."

As Julianne and John connected to the Flower of Life, several people mentioned in this chapter reached out via text, telegram, and phone. All in divine timing!

John says, "All these calls are yet another amazing synchronicity. Each moment we play the part needed. No part is greater than another; each ultimately supports the whole."

"Do you remember when Lauren Rainbow *(a fellow practitioner and friend)* facilitated a retreat with us down in Teotihuacan?" Julianne asks. "That trip magically led to us working together in Egypt, where we met our favorite Egyptologist, Emil Shaker, and travel expert, Ihab Rashad!"

"And when we traveled to Peru and worked with Jorge, we became his connection to Egypt and Emil, let alone Ashley and the Flower of Life."

"The circle continues," Julianne chimes in, "with our mutual connection with Emily and Alberto, Stephanie Jones and Jeremy Pajer invited us to become authors in *Shaman Heart*. Soon afterward, they led a trip to Peru working with Jorge."

"And to complete the circle," John adds, "in a few weeks, Jorge travels to meet Stephanie and Jeremy in Egypt with Emil, followed shortly by Lauren. We all keep passing the light forward however it's needed. The connection of souls and divine timing is fascinating."

Julianne smiles, "I love how Emil says, *'Time is my religion.'*" I understand this. God's timing feels like our religion as well. We grew up Christian, were raised Roman Catholic, and studied with shamans, Native Americans, Buddhists, Hindus, and others. Through it all, we were moved by God, the formless nature of the divine beyond any tradition—the energy of all love.

"Can you imagine at this point in our lives not believing in God, the whisper of soul, and the movement of Spirit?"

John answers, "That would be a whole different life!"

John heads into the bedroom and pulls down the suitcases in preparation for the trip to Shasta. Julianne follows behind and opens a drawer to begin packing. Something catches her eye. She notices the first gift her son Marco ever bought for her on his own. She remembers dropping him off at Macy's to do his Christmas shopping. Marco chose a piece of jewelry for her—an ornate flower of life. *How did he know? Even way back then?* Julianne keeps this piece ready for special occasions. It's going to Shasta!

SOULFUL COLLABORATION

When following Spirit and the prompting of the soul, magic happens! The opportunity for soulful collaboration occurs. This is one of Julianne and John's greatest joys, just like it is for all the authors of this book.

The authors are waiting in the wings to serve you. What story taps you on the shoulder? Who inspires you to reach out? Listen to your soul. Don't miss this opportunity. Remember, when you see through the eyes of love, anything is possible. You are ready!

MEET OUR FRIENDS AROUND THE WORLD:

Grid of Light Project - Light Design Art by Ashley Woods
https://lightdesign.love/about-the-grid-of-light

Kontiki Tours – Jorge Luis Delgado
https://www.kontikiperu.com/en/

The Dreaming House - Alberto Hernandez
http://www.thedreaminghousemx.com/

Villa Las Companas – Sacred Art Journeys by Emily Grieves
https://www.villalascampanasmexico.com

Rita Rivera Fox and Ed Fox
https://ritariverafox.com

Vidalineada and Centro Sai Maa - Shree Devi Maa
https://awakenedlife.love/shree-devi-maa/

Sekhem All Love – Patrick Zeigler
Instagram: @sekhemalllove

Simply Spiritual LLC - Lauren Rainbow
https://www.laurenrainbow.com

Freedom Folk & Soul - Stephanie Jones and Jeremy Pajer
https://www.freedomfolkandsoul.org

Luxury Nile Lily Cruises - Emil Shaker
https://luxurynilelilycruises.com/

Executive Travel - Ihab Rashad
https://www.facebook.com/ihabrashad

Julianne and John holding the Seed of Life at the Osirion
Temple in Abydos, Egypt.

Jorge Luis Delgado receiving the Flower of Life at
Machu Picchu, Peru.

The Violet Flame Team underground with **Emily Grieves** in the Quetzalcoatl Pyramid in Teotihuacan, Mexico.

John and Julianne with **Ashley Woods,** grand dreamer of the Grid of Light Project in Colorado, USA.

MORE ABOUT THE AUTHORS

WELCOME TO PROFOUND LIFE WELLNESS!

OUR MISSION—PERSONAL AND GLOBAL AWAKENING

Julianne Santini and John Mercede are the co-founders of Profound Life Wellness. Starting in 2000, they each traveled around the world to study with teachers, elders, shamans, chakarunas, enlightened masters, and gurus. It's their joy to continually create a new synthesis of living light and share their mastery in the world through individual healing sessions, group classes, training, and sacred travel journeys.

Whether you are looking to enhance your relationships, break through limiting beliefs, or walk the path of self-discovery, they offer a wide range of services. These are professional energy healers, coaches, and spiritual mentors, well-equipped to guide you on life's journey. Their offerings include:

- Individual energy healing sessions
- In-person energy healing certification courses
- On-line and in-person shamanic training
- Self-healing and meditation resources
- Sacred travel

Profound Life Wellness organizes sacred travel journeys to take people to some of the most breathtaking and meaningful sites around the world. Julianne and John team up with local experts to create the itineraries for an unforgettable experience.

ARE YOU INTERESTED IN JOINING THEM FOR THE TRIP OF A LIFETIME?

Join the sacred travel mailing list here:
https://www.profoundlifewellness.com/travel

ARE YOU READY TO TAKE THE NEXT STEP ON YOUR PATH TO SELF-DISCOVERY?

Julianne and John work with people all over the world via phone or video conference. They make sure clients feel welcome, comfortable, cared for, and heard. You're in great hands!

For more details about sessions and training visit:

https://www.profoundlifewellness.com/services

REVIEWS

"Love Initiation is a heartfelt tribute, highlighting the resilience and strength inherent in each contributing writer. Through vivid narratives, the authors share moments where they triumphed over significant challenges through an initiation of love. The inspiring stories prompt a deep appreciation for life's transformative journey, guiding us toward evolutionary growth and empowering us to radiate our light in the world."

⁓ **Carley Mattimore,** Co-Author of *Sacred Messengers of Shamanic Africa: Land of Zep Tepi*

"This inspiring collaborative book, curated by healers Julianne and John, weaves a common thread of commitment to uncovering profound soul truths that guide us through life's challenges. Authors share diverse experiences, from navigating trauma to addressing emotional blocks, offering unique remedies as practical guidance. Each presented practice is a valuable tool to connect with the heart and discover love as the ultimate truth. A beacon of hope, this book serves as a soothing balm for the seeking soul, promising a brighter future."

⁓ **Emily K. Grieves,** Visionary Artist, Best-Selling Author, and Healer

"Love Initiation reminds us that love holds a profound power in energy healing, acting as a transformative force that nurtures both the mind and body. Scientifically, positive emotions associated with love release healing neurotransmitters and the emotional support derived from love can reduce stress and strengthen the immune system. In essence, love acts as a catalyst for healing, by harnessing the inherent connection between emotional states and physical health."

⁓ **Patrick Zeigler,** International Teacher, and Founder of Sekhem All Love

"When *Love Initiation* raises your frequency, it signifies your readiness to authentically share your light, unrestricted and without measurement. My heartfelt gratitude to all the authors for presenting this beautiful bouquet of blossoming flowers."

~ **Jorge Luis Delgado,** Best-Selling Author, Peruvian Mystic, and Shaman

"True medicine for the ages. An illuminating collection of inspiring and enlightening psycho-spiritual stories that walk us between the worlds of science and spirituality, guiding our hearts to a heightened understanding and respect for our intuition and sacred longing. This book reminds us that our soul always knows the way home to wholeness. Each chapter is an invitation into your own journey and sacred initiation of love."

~ **Stephanie Urbina Jones,** Best-Selling Author of the *Shaman Heart* book series, Singer-Songwriter, Co-Founder of Freedom Folk and Soul

"In *Love Initiation,* embrace a constellation of inspiring tales where love illuminates even the darkest paths. The authors, like bright stars, shine light on their unique journeys, surrendering to love amidst challenges and offering a beacon of inspiration for your path. Let their stories guide you towards thriving in the embrace of love!"

~ **Lauren Rainbow,** Hay House Best-Selling Co-Author, Medium, Spiritual Teacher

"*Love Initiation* masterfully illustrates how love serves as the fundamental bond uniting us, the healing balm for all wounds, and the key to unlocking our fullest potential. Each chapter stirs a unique, soul-level awakening to our true essence as human beings—we are the tangible embodiment of Love, manifest in our actions, emotions, and connections. I recommend this book wholeheartedly! It's a life-changer!"

~ **Dr. Ahriana Platten,** Best-Selling Author of *Rites and Rituals: Harnessing the Power of Sacred Ceremony*

Love Makes the Ride Worthwhile

~Julianne and John

Made in United States
Orlando, FL
22 January 2024

42801274R10148